PREVENTION'S PRACTICAL ENCYCLOPEDIA OF

WALKING
FOR HEALTH

PREVENTION's PRACTICAL ENCYCLOPEDIA OF

WALKING
FOR HEALTH

From Age-Reversal to Weight Loss, the Most Complete Guide Ever Written

BY **MARK BRICKLIN,** Editor,
and **MAGGIE SPILNER,** Walking Editor,
PREVENTION Magazine

Rodale Press, Emmaus, Pennsylvania

NOTICE: This book is intended as a reference volume only, not as a medical guide or manual for self-treatment. Before beginning any exercise program, check with your doctor. Your physician can help you design an exercise program to meet your personal health needs.

Managing Editor: Alice Feinstein
Production Editor: Jane Sherman
Copy Editor: Lisa D. Andruscavage
Office Manager: Roberta Mulliner
Office Staff: Eve Buchay, Karen Earl-Braymer, Julie Kehs, Mary Lou Stephen
Cover and Interior Design: Darlene Schneck
Cover Photography: John Hamel
Illustrations: Leslie Flis
Walker's World logo: Bob Shema

Contributing Writers

Mark Bricklin
Maggie Spilner

Melanie Chadwick-Steven
Karen Feridun
Bill Gale
Susanne Garland
Steve Lally
Gale Maleskey
Eileen Nechas
Charles Norelli, M.D.
Tom Shealey
Porter Shimer
Susan Zarrow

If you have any questions or comments concerning this book, please write:
Rodale Press
Book Readers' Service
33 East Minor Street
Emmaus, PA 18098

Library of Congress Cataloging-in-Publication Data

Bricklin, Mark.
Prevention's practical encyclopedia of walking for health : from age reversal to weight loss, the most complete guide ever written / by Mark Bricklin and Maggie Spilner.
    p.   cm.
Includes index.
ISBN 0-87596-110-X   hardcover
1. Walking—Health aspects.
I. Spilner, Maggie. II. Prevention (Emmaus, Pa.) III. Title. IV. Title: Practical encyclopedia of walking for health. V. Title: Walking for Health.
RA781.65.B75   1992
613.7'176—dc20   91-47878
                                    CIP

Distributed in the book trade by St. Martin's Press

2 4 6 8 10 9 7 5 3 1   hardcover

Contents

Introduction / viii

WALKING FOR HEALTH

Aging   *Stepping Out to Slow the Process* / 3

Allergies   *Don't Let Pollens Ground You* / 5

Arthritis   *Keep It Moving* / 8

Back Pain   *A Case for Relief* / 11

Blisters   *Prevention and Treatment* / 14

Body Sculpting   *Looking Your Best* / 16

Brain Power   *Getting Your Head in Shape* / 18

Cancer   *Staying One Step Ahead* / 20

Children   *Giving the Gift of Walking* / 25

Clubs   *How to Start One* / 30

Coffee Breaks and Snack Attacks
  Break the Break Habit / 31

Cold Weather   *Staying Comfortable* / 33

Depression   *Chase Away the Blues* / 36

Diabetes   *Control through Exercise* / 38

Dogs   *Making Your Pet Your Partner* / 41

Evolution   *Why Lovers Love Walking* / 46

Famous Walkers   *You're in Good Company* / 48

Foot Care   *So They Can Take Care of You* / 53

Good Samaritan Walking   *It's in the Bag* / 66

Gremlins   *Chasing Away Minor Distractions
  and Inconveniences* / 70

Headaches   *A Prescription for Relief* / 76

Heart Health   *Improve Your Odds* / **78**

High Blood Pressure   *Coaxing It Down* / **82**

Hiking   *Heading for the Hills* / **87**

Hill Striding   *Getting Fit Faster* / **89**

Injury and Overuse   *Avoiding the Down Side* / **91**

Intermittent Claudication   *Check Yourself* / **95**

Journal Keeping   *Provide Your Own Inspiration* / **96**

Love   *That Special Walking Partner* / **98**

Mallwalking   *Undercover Work* / **101**

Mini-Walking Vacations   *A Fast Getaway* / **104**

Moonwalking   *A Lightweight Fantasy* / **106**

Music   *Tunes That Move* / **107**

Nutrition   *Boosting the Benefits of Walking* / **110**

Orienteering   *Fast Thinking on Your Feet* / **114**

Ozone Alert   *Protect Yourself* / **120**

Partners   *Two-Stepping for Better Performance* / **121**

Pedometers   *Counting Your Steps* / **125**

Personal Safety   *Protecting Yourself* / **127**

Photography   *Taking Pictures on the Hoof* / **131**

Posture   *Benefits of Walking Tall* / **134**

Presidential Walking Awards   *Go for the Red, White, and Blue* / **138**

The *Prevention* Walking Club   *We'll Coach You and Encourage You* / **143**

Racewalking   *Fast and Challenging* / **145**

Rainy-Day Walking   *Go On, You Won't Melt!* / **151**

Shoes   *The Fit and the Foot* / **154**

Socks   *Keeping Feet Sweet* / **161**

Spirit   *Healing for Body and Mind* / **166**

Stress   *Learning to Step Away* / **168**

Stretching   *Flexibility Feels Fabulous* / **173**

Summer *Beating the Dog Days of August* / **179**

Terrain Therapy *Healing through Challenge* / **182**

Treadmills *Stationary Striding* / **187**

Vacations *Walking Away from It All* / **189**

Volksmarching *The People's Sport* / **194**

Walkathons *Fitness with an Altruistic Twist* / **197**

Walking Sticks *Support Yourself in Style* / **201**

Waterfall Walks *Refresh Your Spirit* / **204**

Weight Loss *Shed Unwanted Pounds, Permanently!* / **207**

Weights *The Pros and Cons* / **214**

Words for Walking *A Universal Language* / **217**

Zoo Walks *A Walk on the Wild Side* / **220**

MARK BRICKLIN'S 1-YEAR WALKING PROGRAM

From Beginner to Fitness Walker, Step-by-Step / **225**

Index / **269**

Introduction

About ten years ago, I was traveling with Bob Rodale, the late and wonderful editor of *Prevention* magazine and chairman of Rodale Press. We were heading south, where we were going to talk with some forward-thinking doctors at a university. But now we were stuck in an airport, waiting to change planes, and Bob said, "Want to walk around the airport?"

Now, I thought he meant do you want to walk down to the newsstand, drop by the bar, that sort of thing. So I said, "Sure!"

But then I noticed he was heading in the opposite direction—walking out of the lounge area to the outside. I scurried to catch up with him, and as we walked along the tarmac, past the parked airplanes, it suddenly dawned on me that he didn't mean "walk around the airport" but "walk *around* the airport."

I thought he was flipping out.

But we did—we walked past the hangars, past the cargo facilities, past the rental car areas, then all around the entire airport back to the lounge, just in time to board our plane.

And I thought, that was great! Just what I needed to get the stiffness out, from all the sitting on planes and in lounges. I was relaxed—even refreshed.

If I were smarter, I would have realized then that Bob was on to something and perhaps would have done something on walking in *Prevention,* of which I was executive editor. But the point went right by me.

On another distant occasion, I found myself in Santa Barbara—my first trip to that sunny and pleasant city. Only I wasn't feeling very pleasant. The long flight from the East Coast and a night in a strange, uncomfortable bed had put a killer kink in my back. I couldn't walk at all—all I could do was shuffle along, bent over like an orangutan. But I was determined to see the city, so I decided to go for a walk anyway—no matter how slowly I had to go.

An hour or two later, I passed a big display window and caught sight of my reflection. I was astonished to see myself standing perfectly upright. Only then did I realize my pain was gone—completely. Somehow, the long, rhythmic walk and the California sunshine had performed a magic healing act. Fascinating, I thought. But that's all I thought.

It wasn't until half a dozen years ago that I finally put it all together and decided that millions of people could feel better if they walked. So we began writing about walking every month in *Prevention* magazine and simultaneously launched the *Prevention* Walking Club. We expected that perhaps 10,000 people would join. But in short order, we were flabbergasted to get membership applications from over 100,000 people. There were so many new members we had to scramble for months to get our act together, all the while feeding tranquilizers to the small computer used to keep track of our eager walkers. Since then, some half a million people have joined the *Prevention* Walking Club, and walking has emerged as the most popular form of physical recreation in America.

While we were discovering the benefits of walking, so were doctors and physiologists. Scores of research studies began to appear, showing that walking could indeed perform "magic" healing acts.

Until then, it was the general consensus that exercise, to be really beneficial, had to be strenuous. Your heartbeat had to be well over 100 per minute. If you weren't drenched with sweat, you wouldn't receive the blessing of cardiovascular improvement.

But the new research gave us an entirely different outlook. Brisk walking—*not* racing, not huffing and puffing—was found to have essentially all the benefits of running without the all-too-common body bash that can come with it—knee pain, hamstring tenderness, and a sore back.

Regular walking, the scientists discovered:

- Burns away excess weight
- Lowers blood pressure
- Improves the cholesterol profile
- Improves blood sugar and insulin dynamics
- Helps prevent bone-thinning osteoporosis
- Helps alleviate chronic low back pain
- Improves immune function
- Improves mood and mental performance

Perhaps you will read all those benefits and think I'm painting a picture of walking as some kind of panacea—a cure-all.

Well, that's our point.

Nothing, of course, is a cure-all. But walking has a special place in the world of preventive health because it is the most natural of all human physical activities.

Yes, we can swim like fish. We can run like wolves. We can even hop like kangaroos. But our anatomy says we were *made to walk*—the stable foot, straight leg, broad pelvis, and generous buttocks are all indications of the natural walker.

When we accept a lifestyle that omits any prolonged periods of walking, is it any wonder we develop all sorts of problems?

Many of us get virtually no exercise at all these days. Between cars with power-steering, TVs with remote controls, computers that need to be stared at for hours on end—where is there the opportunity to exercise—let alone the need?

Just in the last few years, the Centers for Disease Control have performed two large studies that both pinpoint exercise as the number one deficiency of Americans. One study concluded that lack of exercise is roughly equivalent to smoking a pack of cigarettes a day; another that not getting exercise was the single most dangerous risk factor for heart disease—worse than high blood pressure, worse than high cholesterol, even worse than smoking.

What's more, there is now a widespread belief among health researchers that walking is the best answer to this critical challenge. Why? Simply because it's easier, safer, cheaper, and more convenient than any other kind of exercise going.

This book will spell out the benefits of walking and how to achieve them in unprecedented detail. It sums up everything we have learned from talking with doctors; meeting thousands of walkers at rallies all over the United States; hiking in cities, mountains, and deserts; being coached by expert racewalkers and practicing our form day after day; and, perhaps most important of all, reading the thousands of letters we've received from beginning and experienced walkers, telling us of their problems, their accomplishments, their joys.

Walker's World Editor Maggie Spilner and I have recently broadened our walking horizons and are now ardent advocates of making our world more walkable. We are working in concert with U.S. government officials to create more safe walkways, so that people everywhere, regardless of age, can enjoy the benefits of walking throughout their communities, and throughout the country.

Our hope is that this book will inspire and guide you to join us and millions of others who are discovering and sharing the great joys of walking.

Mark Bricklin

WALKING
FOR HEALTH

Aging

Stepping Out to Slow the Process

If you think aging means wrinkles and graying hair, then this chapter is not going to mean much to you. Walk all you want and you will not reverse these natural trends. But if you're laboring under the mistaken notion that aging means less mobility, less capacity to do what you want to do, and poorer mental and physical agility, then read on. We may have news for you.

You've Got to Keep on Moving

More and more research is showing that what we once mistook for the inevitable decline of the body due to the aging process is really simply a matter of using it or losing it. Mostly because of cultural influences and habits, we tend to become less active as we age. We have less muscle mass, hence we burn fewer calories at a slower rate. We put on weight. The weight slows us down even more. We get out of shape and we do even less. It's a vicious circle, but it can be broken. How? Keep moving!

Here are some examples of research that supports the idea that aging is as much in your lifestyle as in your genes.

Two groups of 15 middle-aged men have been engaged in a study that began 23 years ago. One group exercised regularly for 23 years, the other exercised for about 5 years and then stopped for 18 years.

When researchers at the Department of Physical Education at San Diego State University tested these men after 23 years, this is what they found: The nonexercisers lost 41 percent of their maximal aerobic power. Loss of aerobic power has long been considered a natural effect of aging. The exercisers lost only 13 percent.

Sixty percent of the nonexercisers developed high blood pressure. While two of the exercisers had high blood pressure initially, no others developed this problem. In fact, on average, the exercisers had blood pressures 25 percent below the average for men their age—the same blood pressure profile of young men.

The nonexercisers also gained weight and increased their body fat.

Stay Fast, Stay Sharp

In another extensive study conducted at Brown University, it was found that people who remain physically active throughout their later years can gain as much as a 25-year advantage in performance over those who retire to their easy chairs! Some 4,500 people between the ages of 40 and 85 were studied. According to Vincent Mor, Ph.D., physically active 70-year-olds could perform physical tasks as well as 50-year-olds who were inactive. And moderate activity, such as walking, was all that was needed to keep these people agile.

Or how about mental ability? A lifelong habit of walking may help keep you on your toes mentally, too, according to a study at Scripps College in Claremont, California.

In a series of tests, researchers there compared 62 highly active people aged 55 to 91 with an equal number of nonexercisers of the same age. The purpose was to see if being physically active has positive effects on cognitive (thinking) skills as we grow older. The high-exercise group included older athletes of all shapes and stripes—serious walkers, weight lifters, and marathon runners among them. The 1½-hour sessions of tests assessed reasoning, reaction time, and memory. The researchers found the high-exercise group performed significantly better in all reasoning tests, in all reaction-time tests, and in two of the three memory tests.

"I think this study strongly suggests that exercise is important in preserving our mental abilities as we grow older," says Louise Clarkson-Smith, Ph.D., who conducted the research with Alan A. Hartley, Ph.D.

Some researchers speculate that the decline of mental and physical energy as we age may be linked to a decline in our central nervous system's efficiency, which may be affected by circulation to the brain. So physical exercise, which is known to improve efficiency of circulation in older people, might help keep the cognitive skills fresh.

Lengthening Life Span

While you may feel that living a long life is less important than living a happy, active one, the two may go hand in hand. If there is one thing you can do to prolong your life expectancy, it's walking.

An ongoing study has tracked the health and lifestyles of 16,936 Harvard alumni. The researchers found lower death rates in all age groups as physical activity increased. Those men who burned 2,000 or more calories a week in exercise had a 28 percent lower death rate than men who exercised less or not at all.

Walking regularly and often is like putting money in a lifetime health account, where the time you put in pays off interest in time added to your life. In fact, says Ralph Paffenberger, Jr., M.D., Ph.D., one of the authors of this study, "For every hour you walk, you can add an hour to your life."

Allergies

Don't Let Pollens Ground You

Can you keep your hay-fever symptoms from getting the best of your walking program? Yes! If you take the right precautions at the right time.

In general, people who have seasonal allergy (hay fever) can expect to experience the most discomfort between August and October. That's when the big pollen offenders—ragweed, pigweed, and lamb's-quarters—will be scattering their unwelcome bounty over most of the country. In August, mold allergies also can be especially troublesome, since mold-spore levels will be high and their growth spurred by summer rains.

If you have allergies, a pleasant outdoor stroll can turn into a nose-blowing, sniffling, red-eyed ordeal. What can you do besides give up walking till after the first frost?

Identify Your Personal Allergens

An allergist can perform skin tests to determine exactly which substances are triggering your symptoms. Knowing the specific offenders can help you plan your walking program so that you avoid them.

If you're allergic to weed pollen, for example, you'll be more comfortable taking your walk late in the day, because weeds typically release pollen early in the morning.

If you're allergic to molds, you'll do better by walking immediately after a rain. You'll have a few hours lag between the time the rain wets everything and the time molds start producing spores like crazy.

Premedicate: Proper Use of Antihistamines

Over-the-counter antihistamines may be sufficient to help you keep walking through the allergy season. Your pharmacist or doctor can help you choose the one that's right for you. Antihistamines are preventive medications. So for maximum effectiveness, you can schedule your walk ½ hour after taking your medication.

Some antihistamines can cause drowsiness or a jittery feeling. These side effects can sometimes be lessened by starting with one-quarter to one-half of the recommended dosage and increasing your intake daily, working up to a full dose over a period of three or four days. If over-the-counter antihistamines fail to provide relief, ask your doctor about prescription antihistamines. Several forms are available, including pills, eyedrops that relieve itching, and nasal sprays that prevent allergy-caused stuffiness.

Injecting Some Prevention

Allergy shots must be taken all year long in order for them to be effective during the allergy season. If medication doesn't bring you relief, talk to an allergist about this option for next year.

Walkers' Anti-allergy Strategy

There are a number of other steps you can take to prevent allergies from interfering with your walking program.

Shower and wash your hair right after you walk. You can rinse away most of the pollen you picked up. If you can't fit a shower into your schedule, try washing your hands and face and rinsing your eyes to remove any pollen.

Don a surgical mask. If your symptoms are really annoying, you may not mind looking like Dr. Kildare. A mask offers some protection by filtering pollen. Look for those designed to protect industrial workers and home renovators. They're available in hardware stores and home centers.

Stretch indoors. If you like to do stretching exercises before you walk, do them indoors rather than outside, so your exposure

---

Sneeze-Free Walking Trips

If you're planning a walking vacation and you have allergies, be sure to take your schnozzola into consideration. To find out if your particular allergy culprits will be in bloom when you arrive at your destination, call the Asthma and Allergy Foundation of America's allergy hotline at 1-800-7-ASTHMA. Tell them where and when you plan to travel, and they'll tell you what allergens are particular hazards at that location and time of year. For more extensive information on seasonal allergies throughout the country, send a self-addressed, stamped envelope to the foundation at 1717 Massachusetts Avenue NW, Suite 305, Washington, DC 20036.

to allergens is less. Your body reacts cumulatively, so the less exposure to pollen or mold, the less severe your reaction.

Steer clear of vacant lots. Offending weeds tend to proliferate in vacant lots or any area that is not mowed regularly. To avoid them, you may have to find another route.

Check the pollen count. Daily readings on pollen and mold levels are often included in newspaper, radio, or television weather forecasts. If it's going to be a very bad day (on windy days, for example, pollen is really flying), consider an indoor treadmill workout or head for a mall, where you can walk in climate-controlled, pollen-free comfort (see the treadmill chapter, beginning on page 187, and the mallwalking chapter, beginning on page 101).

Arthritis

Keep It Moving

PATIENT: Hey, Doc, it hurts when I do this.
DOCTOR: Then don't do it.

Most of us are probably all too familiar with that old Henny Youngman joke. But for people with arthritis, it's no joke. They respond to achy joints just that way, not realizing that lack of movement can compound the problem. Once properly diagnosed and treated (with appropriate medication, if needed, and physical therapy), most people with arthritis can benefit from a regular exercise program, says rheumatologist Sam Schatten, M.D., of Atlanta, Georgia. And recent research suggests that walking may be the best exercise for them.

Walking helps to strengthen the muscles, may prevent joint injury and disfigurement, and seems to relieve some of the pain that may occur when bones rub against bones. The natural tranquilizing effect of walking also helps to ease arthritis pain. And its mood-elevating effect offers an added benefit.

Feeling Better about Yourself

Walking can greatly improve a person's attitude and fight the vicious circle of depression and pain, says Dr. Schatten.

Gale Snyder knows this all too well. A schoolteacher and mother of two who's had rheumatoid arthritis for four years, she finds that walking eases her pain and depression like nothing else. "I feel terrible when I'm sitting and feeling stiff. That hurts more than moving," says Gale. "Plus, walking is a great stress reliever for me. I can cope with my fears so much better after a good walk. And I found that when I listen to music on a walk, I get a rush of good feeling, of feeling strong and powerful." In fact, Gale shared her enthusiasm for walking to music by creating the first aerobic walking tape, called "Walktime," distributed by Columbia Records.

Building Stronger Bones

Kate Lorig, D.P.H., of the Stanford University Arthritis Center and coauthor of *The Arthritis Help-Book*, endorses walking for arthritis management. "In addition to increasing muscle and joint strength and alleviating depression, walking helps bone maintain calcium," she says.

At the Stanford Center, Dr. Lorig encourages patients to use their common sense to develop a personalized walking regimen. "I tell people to start slowly, walking as far as they can without feeling more pain than before they started. If that means walking across the room, fine. One block or two blocks? That's a good start," she says. It's very important for people who have arthritis to listen to their bodies. "Pain is a valuable indicator of misuse," Dr. Lorig adds. Although people who have arthritis may experience some pain with any movement, if the pain worsens when they begin to walk, they may be damaging their joints.

Strengthening or stretching exercises or perhaps some medication may be needed. It's very important to work with your physician. "Some people fear that their pain might flare up on a long walk, leaving them stranded. I remind them that they can walk 5 miles and never be more than a half-block from home if they walk up and down the street."

Water Works Wonders

You may never be able to walk on water, but how about walking *in* water? For some people with arthritis, even the gentlest exercise can cause discomfort. If that sounds like you, consider this soothing alternative: aquatic exercise.

It's not water ballet but an excellent way to improve and maintain joint flexibility and increase muscle strength. The water displaces body weight, putting less stress on the joints. There is also a kind of external massagelike effect, and the water offers enough resistance to strengthen the muscles. And because exercising in the water is less painful, people are more likely to do it on a regular basis.

The Arthritis Foundation and the YMCA co-sponsor water exercise programs around the country. Classes led by a qualified instructor meet at least once a week.

People find the social atmosphere of a water workout to be supportive and encouraging. At the YMCA in Bethlehem, Pennsylvania, for example, a group of about 30 men and women meet three days a week for range-of-motion exercises and walking in the pool. For some, this is their only form of exercise. For others, this is part of a fitness program that also includes regular walks on land.

"The social atmosphere of the classes really helps," says Doris Transue of Hellertown, Pennsylvania. "And because of the classes, I don't have to work out on a resistance machine anymore."

For more information on an aquatics program near you, contact your local Arthritis Foundation, YMCA, or YWCA.

Once a person has established the distance he or she can comfortably walk, Dr. Lorig suggests getting into a routine. "Walk three or four times a week, increasing your distance by no more than 10 percent every two weeks," she says. "Keep in mind, too, that your walking program has to remain flexible. If pain or inflammation flares up, trim your schedule, even put your fitness program on hold for a few days. This isn't a setback," says Dr. Lorig. "Consider it an integral part of your overall plan for pain management."

Back Pain

A Case for Relief

For many Americans, back pain is an all-too-familiar source of agony, aggravation, and days missed from work. Sometimes it even leads to feelings of hopelessness and depression. Walking, fortunately, is a wonderful preventive *and* curative of the most common kinds of muscular backache. Even some cases of back pain where a disk problem has been identified will respond well to regular, rhythmic walking—three to six days a week, for 30 to 60 minutes per session.

Walking is no cure-all—*nothing* is, not even surgery. You'll need to check with your doctor to see if it may help you. But be optimistic: The complete abolition of low back pain, or at least great relief, is perhaps the most common, clearly perceived health benefit reported by walkers. If you *do* need medical treatment, be sure to ask about walking afterward, to help ensure that your problem doesn't return.

Here's a story from one of our *Prevention* walkers about how walking relieved her nagging backache.

Polly McNabb Tells Her Story

"At work I was constantly rubbing my shoulders and neck, trying to get relief from the burning and aching sensations that could hang on for hours. It was not unusual for me to dash home from work, throw off my coat, and flop down flat on my back on the living room floor, waiting for the gnawing back pain to subside before I fixed dinner.

"I couldn't sleep at night because of the aching numbness in my hands. After waking up half a dozen times to rub my hands back to life, the rest of my body would also be wide awake.

"I had to give up one of my favorite pastimes, playing the piano, because after 5 minutes of playing, my back would burn like fire. I'd taken up piano late in life (never mind how late) and had plans of becoming a great pianist. The back pain forced me to give up my plans for a debut at Carnegie Hall."

Inaction from Traction

"My doctor called the source of this distress a 'pinched nerve' and said it was very common among office workers. He prescribed a traction apparatus to be used for 15 minutes twice a day.

"Not being the meditative type, I found sitting still for 15 minutes twice a day a real chore—not to mention the discomfort of the traction device. I had to sit in a doorway in order to string the device through a hook in the door frame. A brace fit under my chin while a brick weight suspended from the door frame attempted to stretch me out of my pain. I couldn't watch TV because I couldn't look down through my bifocals. And reading was even worse. Soon my chin would feel so tired that I'd pick up the brick and put it in my lap, which would relieve my chin, but, of course, did nothing for my back.

"Besides the physical discomfort, the device smashed my hairdo. It just about killed me (figuratively speaking) to see all that shampoo-and-set money go down the drain. A smashed hairdo lowered my morale, and then I suffered not only from an aching back but depression as well. Needless to say, I'm not known for my patience, so traction was out."

Getting Started

"To top this off, I started having a 'clothes-shrinkage problem.' Yep, right after the holidays, all my clothes had suddenly shrunk.

"I heard from a friend that walking might be an effective way of dealing with my clothes-shrinkage problem. So I started. I walked nearly a mile to work, home for lunch, back to work, and home again at night, for a total of about 3.2 miles. I was practically crawling by the time I got home that first day. I ached all over, including my back, but the pie sure tasted good at dinner.

"Looking forward to pie, I did it again the next day, and the next. By the fourth day, I couldn't believe how good my back felt when I got home from work. I even worked around the house and never had to stop and lie down to rest. Fact is, I really didn't give my back a thought all evening."

The Spinal Payoff

"The next day, I was sitting at my desk and it suddenly occurred to me that my back was not hurting. For the first time in *years,* my neck and back didn't seem tired, even though I was bending over my desk and doing all the same things I'd always done.

"Why, after all these years of pain, had my back suddenly stopped hurting? Surely in that short span of time it couldn't be the walking! Or could it?

"I had to be sure. So I began an experiment. The next day, I walked only 1½ miles. That night my hands didn't fall asleep, but my back did hurt. Eventually I found it takes about 3½ miles a day to keep my hands from going to sleep and my back free of pain.

"On long automobile trips, the pain comes back. But I have learned that it doesn't take long now to walk the pain away, and I stick to a regular walking schedule."

Doctors' Stamp of Approval

Polly McNabb is not alone in finding that walking can bring natural relief from back pain. In an informal poll of 492 people with a variety of back problems, published in 1985, 98 percent of those who made walking a part of their regular routine found it helpful.

The American Medical Association (AMA) in its *Guide to Back Care* cites the merits of walking. Since walking puts less stress on the lower spine than sitting without a backrest, says the AMA, many people with back problems realize that they are "better off walking than sitting."

Walking affects the spine in positive ways, agrees E. C. Frederick, Ph.D., of the Pennsylvania State University Center for Locomotion Studies. "It strengthens muscles in the pelvis and lower back, which may help some people with back problems."

Be sure to check with your doctor to make certain your particular back problem will not be aggravated by exercise. If you get clearance, remember that good posture is critical to walking without pain. If you lean forward at the waist, jut your chin out, or hunch your shoulders while you walk, you may be aggravating, if not creating, your back pain. Have a friend watch you while you walk to make sure that you're standing tall and balancing your head over your shoulders and your torso over your hips. You don't need to be stiff, just straight!

Blisters

Prevention and Treatment

Blisters get a bad rap, but they're just your body's way of protecting itself from too much friction.

In the life of a walker, blisters should be only an occasional occurrence brought on by either a longer-than-usual walk, a walking vacation, new shoes, or damp weather conditions.

Most people just take the occasional blister as a fact of life. But if you're on a walking vacation, you can be hobbled for part of the trip if you're not prepared. We can give you several tips on how to avoid blisters in the first place. And if you do happen to get one, we can tell you the dos and don'ts of treating them.

Antiblister Measures

First and foremost, wear a walking shoe that fits. There should be plenty of room for all of your toes to move around up front, even after your foot has swelled. The heel should fit snugly without slippage but not be so snug that it rubs at any point. Lacing your shoes carefully and fully also can help to keep them fitting well, even after they stretch and wear a bit. (See the shoe chapter, beginning on page 154.)

Wearing two pairs of socks is another way to prevent friction. Wear an inner sock made of a fabric that wicks perspiration away from your feet—wool or polypropylene is better than cotton—and add an outer sock. Some manufacturers are now creating socks that are made with two layers.

Making sure your feet are dry and powdered will help, too. Moisture makes the skin soft and more sensitive to abrasive action.

For a Blister-Free Vacation

If you're planning a walking vacation, prepare your feet for the experience. You'll have a lot more fun if you're not wincing at every step.

Here's some advice from Gary Yanker, author of several books on walking, for enjoying a blister-free walking vacation.

"A few weeks before your trip, try to begin toughening your feet by walking barefoot on some slightly rough surface. A beach is ideal if you happen to live close to one. Cement or macadam is fine, but go slowly. If you can't walk barefoot, try wearing your shoes without socks. That will have somewhat of a toughening effect.

"On vacation, make sure you take plenty of extra socks and change them several times a day. This will take care of any moisture problem. Don't ignore hot spots. Take your shoes off, air them, powder them, and put on dry socks. You can really head off blisters if you act in time.

"If you know you are going to be getting your feet wet, try to have appropriate waterproof shoes or hiking boots. You can't depend on your average shoe to get you through rainy weather or dewy pastures.

"When you take a break, elevate your feet to take the pressure off them and decrease the blood flow. Some people also rub petroleum jelly on their feet, creating almost a second skin that helps protect them from friction and moisture." says Yanker.

When Blisters Strike

Once blisters form, try to keep them from tearing. The best treatment is to protect them and let the fluid be reabsorbed. James C. Puffer, M.D., head physician of the Summer Olympic Team in 1988, suggests using precut doughnut-shaped bandages (available at drugstores) to surround the blistered area with a cushioned surface.

If the blister is likely to break, drain it yourself, says Dr. Puffer. First, clean it thoroughly with soap and water. Then, using a needle that you've sterilized in a flame, puncture the blister's edge. Press it gently and cover it with a sterile pad. Check frequently for signs of infection (like bright redness or pus), and see a doctor promptly if you find any.

Prepare a Blister Kit

Don't go on a long walk, hike, or walking vacation without an emergency blister kit. You'll need moleskin and scissors or precut bandages, a needle, some antibiotic ointment, a few sterile pads, moist towelettes to cleanse the area, and a pack of matches. If you feel a hot spot, sometimes you can ward off an oncoming blister by creating a moleskin bandage that cushions the area without touching the actual hot spot. Your pharmacist may have a complete blister prevention kit, ready to travel.

Body Sculpting
Looking Your Best

Carve a little off those thighs. Whittle a bit from the waist. Add a bit of modeling to the calves. For those of us who want to look as good on the outside as we feel on the inside, walking offers superb body sculpting benefits.

To begin with, walking is your best low-impact exercise for weight loss. "Mile for mile, jogging burns only about 20 percent more calories than brisk walking," says James M. Rippe, M.D., associate professor of medicine at the University of Massachusetts Medical Center in Worcester. Plus, walking off your calories carries less chance of joint injury than jogging.

Lose Where It Counts

Best of all, through walking, you'll lose weight in all the right places—not just on the legs, but also on the abdomen, hips, upper arms—wherever you have too much fat. Surprised? Don't be. Walking is an aerobic activity, which means it burns off body fat. And usually the areas of highest fat concentration melt away first. In men, that usually means the gut; in women, the hips and thighs. The good news is that you can burn off much of that fat!

"It won't all go away overnight. And some people won't take off as much as they'd like to in certain areas," explains Charles Eichenberg, Ph.D., director of the New Start Health Center in St. Petersburg, Florida. "But for most of us, regular walking will make visible changes."

Toward a Tonier Look

The sculpting effect isn't all due to fat loss. Walking tones up muscles, too—and again, the legs aren't the only beneficiaries. "Walking is a carefully designed balancing act. The muscles of the abdomen and lower back can get a moderate workout just keeping your trunk in line with your legs during a brisk walk. That's how you keep moving forward without falling flat on your face," says Randall L. Braddom, M.D., director of physical medicine and rehabilitation at Providence Hospital in Cincinnati.

Your arms and upper torso get a mild to moderate workout when you walk, because you naturally swing your arms. You can increase that workout by deliberately pumping your arms. That also helps you pick up the pace. And if you really want to strengthen your upper body as you walk, you can use hand-held weights (2 pounds per hand is sufficient). Properly used, the weights won't cause injury, and they can increase the aerobic value of your workout while toning your arms.

Slow and Steady

Walking can work wonders for your health and body image, but you have to stick with it. Regular workouts are the key. And you have to keep your expectations in pace with your workouts.

"If it took you 40 years to get the body shape you have today, you can't expect to reverse the process in 40 days," says James Stray-Gundersen, M.D., assistant professor of surgery and physiology at the University of Texas Southwestern Medical Center. "Nature does things best gradually."

Brain Power
Getting Your Head in Shape

Regular walking workouts can fine-tune your brain. Keeping active, research strongly suggests, helps keep our emotions balanced, our moods uplifted, and our creativity bubbling.

Okay, so we all know that a bracing walk makes us feel good. But over recent years, scientists have found that the active lifestyle does as much for the brain—in fact, the whole nervous system—as it does for the circulatory system. And that's saying a lot.

A powerhouse review of research on exercise and psychology from Canada, analyzing no less than 81 different studies, found that in 70 percent of the studies, significant improvement in mental state was associated with fitness. Looking at only those studies that were rigorously scientific, 13 of 26 revealed significant improvement in mental state and 5 reported partial improvement. In 8 cases, depression was significantly relieved. In 3, stress was relieved.

Drive Away Depression

A doctoral thesis that reviewed 77 studies concluded that depression exits the body along with sweat. "In fact," wrote Thomas Christian North, Ph.D., "exercise appears to be a better antidepressant than psychological treatment." The best results of all, though, come when psychology and exercise are combined.

Most of us who walk regularly know that it helps us keep stress under control. But that control may be more powerful than we suspect.

When put in front of a screen and instructed to get a high score on a video game, just about anyone will have an increase in heart rate and blood pressure. But now it has been found that such a reaction is much less pronounced in people who are physically fit than in those who aren't fit. Evidently, the protection exercise offers extends well beyond physically stressful challenges to encompass mental stress as well.

Lighten Up

These same fit people were found to report being less anxious and less angry than the unfit, according to research by Susan M. Czajkowski, Ph.D., of the Behavioral Medicine Branch, National Heart, Lung, and Blood Institute, and her colleagues.

A related study carried out with men who were judged to be type A in character (chronically impatient and hostile) had similar results. It's widely believed that type-A behavior constitutes a risk factor for heart disease, especially among otherwise healthy middle-aged men (which all the men in this study were).

The researchers put all the men on a 12-week exercise program. Half did aerobic walking or jogging; the other half did strength and flexibility exercises. At the end of the period, both groups of men were acting less like hard-core type As. But the walkers and joggers fared the best.

Both before and after the exercise program, all the men were given a tough math problem to solve (or try to solve) while equipment monitored their internal responses to stress. After the exercise regimen, the aerobic group showed much less rise in heart rate, in blood pressure level (both systolic and diastolic blood pressure), and in oxygen consumption by the heart muscle than nonaerobic exercisers.

"These results," say James A. Blumenthal, Ph.D., and his colleagues from Duke University Medical Center in Durham, North Carolina, "support the use of aerobic exercise as a method of reducing cardiovascular risk among healthy type-A men."

Boost Mental Performance

All this is just a taste of what a regular walking program can do for the most important organ in your body—your brain— *regardless of age!* At Scripps College in Claremont, California, researchers found that highly active people aged 55 to 91 performed better in reasoning tests, reaction-time tests, and memory tests than people of the same age who got little exercise. At the Veterans Administration Medical Center in Salt Lake City, 55- to 70-year-olds who practiced what we call speedwalking improved their memory, reaction time, and creativity as well. Two other research centers have shown that senior-age exercisers have a better sense of balance, while at Johns Hopkins University, researchers report that older men who are fit even have a much better sense of taste!

It seems the entire nervous system, from the taste buds right up to a taste for intellectual pleasures, does better when we walk. That's something to think about.

Cancer

Staying One Step Ahead

Could being physically fit help prevent cancer? Nobody knows for sure, but recent studies suggest an intriguing association between levels of activity and some kinds of cancer. While these studies do not deal with walkers per se, they do suggest that any regular exercise may help to protect you. And unless your lifestyle or job requires some type of day-to-day activity, walking may be the safest, simplest way to incorporate the protective effect of exercise into your daily routine.

Walk Away from Breast Cancer

Researchers at Harvard University found that women who had been active in basketball, swimming, tennis, track, gymnastics, volleyball, or other sports in college later developed significantly less breast cancer than their inactive peers. Their sedentary classmates had twice the risk for breast cancer as well as two to four times more cancer of the uterus, ovaries, cervix, and vagina.

Sidestep Colon Cancer

Colon cancer has also been associated with an inactive lifestyle. Three separate, large population studies have found that men with physically active jobs, such as carpenters, plumbers, gardeners, and mail carriers (all-day walkers!), have an advantage. They are much less likely to develop colon cancer than accountants, lawyers, bookkeepers, and other workers who tend to sit still most of the day.

Walking Makes Protective Sense

Of course, researchers say these studies don't prove that exercise such as walking helps prevent cancer. They do say, though, that the few studies done so far have all reached the same conclusion: that physically active people get less of certain types of cancer. That evidence has been enough to convince the American Cancer Society to recommend exercise as one possible way to reduce the risk of this killer disease.

In some ways, animal studies can demonstrate a clearer association between exercise and cancer than human population studies. "With animals, we can control most of the variables that could confound population studies," says Leonard Cohen, Ph.D., head of the Section of Nutrition and Endocrinology at the American Health Foundation in Valhalla, New York.

Researchers know mice aren't going to smoke cigarettes or stay up all night drinking and playing cards—complicating variables that can skew the results in human studies.

In a study done by Dr. Cohen, laboratory animals were given a chemical that induces breast cancer. Then, half the rats were put in cages that allowed them free access to an exercise wheel. These animals could run anytime they wished, and they did so frequently.

"It's important to stress here that the *only* difference between the two groups was the exercise wheel," Dr. Cohen says. "The rats with access to the wheel developed one-third fewer cases of cancer than the inactive rats. And the tumors appeared much later in the active animals."

What does this all mean? "There seems to be some good evidence that exercise reduces your chance of getting breast cancer, and possibly other cancers, by means that we don't yet understand," Dr. Cohen says. "More questions need to be answered before we can confirm the cancer/exercise link." In fact, studies to get a better handle on the exercise connection are under way at this moment.

The Body Fat Link

Researchers think one reason exercise may protect against cancer is that it whittles away body fat. They've noted that overweight women get more cancer of the uterine lining. Overweight women who are past menopause tend to do less well once they have breast cancer.

How does body fat relate to cancer? Fat seems to have a direct effect on a woman's hormones. "The fatter you are, the more you convert androgen (a male hormone) to estrogen (a female hormone). Also, more of the estrogen is metabolized to a more potent form. This may explain why excessive fatness is a risk factor for breast and reproductive cancers," says Rose Frisch, Ph.D., of Harvard, who conducted the study of women who were former college athletes. "Estrogen stimulates cells to divide in the breast and reproductive system, particularly the uterine lining. So excess or too much potent estrogen could be implicated for cancerous growth." Lean women also produce less of a hormone called prolactin, which stimulates cell growth in the breasts' milk ducts, a very common cancer site.

Researchers are less sure what role body fat plays in colon cancer. But they think it might involve the body's manufacture of prostaglandins. These potent biochemicals are made from fats. Some cause an inflammatory response, which might be linked with cancer development.

Constipation, too, has been linked with colon cancer, and there's evidence that inactive people are more likely to be constipated. Exercise stimulates the peristaltic action of the intestines that results in regular and more frequent bowel movements, which may shorten the time that cancer-promoting materials remain in contact with the intestinal lining.

Exercise can easily cause a temporary negative energy balance. It can force the body to dip into its energy reserves, converting stored protein into usable glucose. Some researchers think that the hormones used to initiate this process, glucocorticoids, provide the body with cancer protection.

"In experiments with rodents, treatment with glucocorticoids retarded the development of a number of cancers, including mammary and skin cancer," says Michael Pariza, Ph.D., of the University of Wisconsin. "And we know that glucocorticoid levels can go up during exercise.

"But there are still many questions about what type of exercise is best and the extent to which exercise can really help people."

Researchers have also noted that, in a number of animal studies, food restriction leads to reduced rates of cancer, while free access to food leads to increases. They think glucocorticoids are involved. "It's thought that exercise may reinforce the favorable hormonal changes that occur during modest food restriction," adds Dr. Pariza.

Walking for Immunity?

Several studies have indicated that exercise stimulates the body's cancer-fighting immune system. In some of the studies, exercise increased numbers of potential cancer-fighting white blood cells called lymphocytes. In others, it boosted levels of lymphokines, chemical messengers that rally lymphocytes to action.

Studies done in the United States and England found that bicycling, running, and stair climbing increased the numbers of lymphocytes circulating in the blood. Certain lymphocytes, known as natural killer cells, are one of the body's first defenses against cancer. They can kill certain tumor- and virus-infected cells.

In an Italian study, blood levels of interferon, a virus-fighting substance, more than doubled in men who rode bicycles for an hour at a moderately intense pace.

And in a study from Tufts University School of Medicine, levels of interleukin-1, a biochemical that stimulates proliferation of lymphocytes, increased in men after an hour of moderate bicycle riding.

Just how does exercise work in these cases? No one really knows. It may cause an inflammatory reaction in the muscles, to which the body responds by sending in lymphocytes. Exercise also breaks down a small number of red blood cells, which means that lymphocytes could be sent into the bloodstream to clean up the pieces.

Endorphins, the body's naturally occurring "feel-good" bio-chemicals reportedly responsible for the euphoria that runners feel, may also play a role. Endorphins might create chemical changes in the body that may have a cancer-inhibiting effect, Dr. Cohen says.

The big question—whether exercise boosts immunity enough to ward off cancer—is not yet answered. There is still no real proof that it can prevent cancer or that it's useful in treating cancer. But the studies certainly *hint* at these possibilities. And considering how many *other* health benefits come from regular exercise such as walking, there's every reason to lace up those shoes and head for the door.

Walk, Don't Run

Before researchers can recommend how hard or how much you should exercise, more studies need to be done. In animal studies so far, moderate activity seems to work better than extremely intense exercise. Animals forced to exercise at a relatively high intensity actually have increased cancer rates.

"The animals in my study are walking fast. But they are not panting," Dr. Cohen says. "They are very relaxed and docile, having a good time. They stop when they want, and they go when they want."

One of the biggest pluses for exercise might actually be its ability to relieve stress, Dr. Cohen and other researchers agree. "I'd tell people to find a physical activity that leaves them relaxed and happy."

Sounds like a walking prescription to us! So, the next time you go out to walk, you can add one more item to your list of "Reasons I Feel Good about Walking." You may be protecting yourself from cancer.

Children
Giving the Gift of Walking

Imagine that you could bequeath to your children a unique gift they would value all their lives. Suppose it was a gift that could bestow fantastic health benefits, such as weight control, lowered stress, healthy blood pressure, lowered cholesterol; a gift that would protect them against osteoporosis and cancer, defend them from backaches while strengthening their hearts, and at the same time offer pleasure and diversion. Who wouldn't want to do that for their kids?

Well, that is exactly the gift you'll be giving if you introduce your children to the pleasure of fitness walking. It's a pastime they'll be able to afford even if they don't become president of General Motors. And if they do, it's an activity that will help them cope with the aggravation. Walking is a sport they'll never have to give up because of age or agility or "not fitting in."

"So let me at 'em," you say. "Let's get started!" You're all enthusiasm. But when you bound into the darkened TV room on Saturday morning, bubbling with energy, and ask your kids if they wouldn't "just love" to go for a walk with you, they wouldn't. Walking is just about on the bottom of their list of fun things to do, right above washing the dishes or cleaning out the car.

"Walking," claim Aaron Sussman and Ruth Goode in *The Magic of Walking*, "is an adult and sophisticated taste, like a taste

for oysters, caviar, or wine. Children prefer hamburgers and Coke."
So what's a parent to do?

Well, you can start your own walking program and leave the
kids out of it, hoping that someday, before they're fat and 40, they'll
notice you. Being a positive role model is the best way to influence
kids. In addition, if you're willing to scout around, you may find
some local programs that make walking fun, that offer kid-type
incentives, or that the whole family can participate in at the same
time. Here are some places to start.

Scouting Gets Them Moving

There are actually merit badges for walking. In the Girl Scouts
it's called the Foot Traveler Proficiency Badge. To earn it, scouts
must complete a required number of walks, prepare and pack a
snack, walk with a group and alone, dress correctly for the weather,
and learn to read street and road maps.

To earn the Boy Scout Hiking Merit Badge, scouts must plan
a 10-mile hike, take five hikes (on five different days) of 10 miles
each, take a continuous 20-mile hike in one day, and write about
their experiences. Check with your pack leaders for additional information on any walking-related activities.

Turn On to Orienteering

Walking becomes utterly painless when kids are hunting for
clues in the woods. Most orienteering clubs around the country
hold weekend meets and elite orienteers run courses alongside
families who are out for a stroll. Given a map and compass, orienteers search for "controls"—orange and white markers that have
special punches attached. Each punch leaves a specific mark on
your control card to show that you found that control. Courses are
set up for all levels of participants, and some meets have what are
called line courses, equipped with ropes that children hold in order
to make their way from control to control. (See also the orienteering
chapter, beginning on page 114.)

Some permanent courses, called Trim courses, are now being
set up in parks across the country, with maps so that families can
practice anytime. (Boy Scouts can also earn a badge for orienteer-

ing.) To locate the orienteering club nearest you, write to the U.S. Orienteering Federation, P.O. Box 1444, Forest Park, GA 30051.

The Y's Way

The YMCA and YWCA are becoming very interested in promoting walking for physical fitness to adults. And branching out from adults, some Ys are trying to get the whole family on the march.

Walt Price, director of the Health Maintenance Programs of the YMCA in Syracuse, New York, would like to see his successful program of *Folksmarches* instituted in Ys across the country. Folksmarches are 5- or 10-kilometer walks sponsored by the Y once a month. Participants register at the event, walk the distance, and receive colorful, commemorative pins as rewards. Thousands of people have turned out for these walks, and Price says they are a big hit with families, even those with babies in backpacks or strollers. Folksmarches are supplemented by additional walking programs at the Y. The Y gives rewards for accumulated miles—your Folksmarch miles can be counted toward your totals. For more information about this program and how you might get one started at your own Y, contact Walt Price at the Syracuse YMCA, 340 Montgomery Street, Syracuse, NY 13202.

Volksmarching Marches On

Undoubtedly, Price's Folksmarches are modeled after the German import, *Volksmarches* (see page 194). Volksmarches represent yet another family-oriented walking organization to provide your children with something to work up to, to look forward to, and to enjoy with their friends.

Professional Advice

Don't overlook your family doctor when looking for walking encouragement, especially if your child has a weight problem. Your doctor may know of walks sponsored by health organizations in the area.

Some doctors have come up with creative ideas to get kids to walk for weight loss. Frances Lankford, M.D., and Nell Robinson, Ph.D., at the Children's Medical Center in Arlington, Texas, have created a program to help youngsters lose weight. Called TWIGS, (Team Watchers in Growth Standards), the group meets weekly for special fun walks, in addition to diet education and other fitness activities. Dr. Lankford agrees that walking is an excellent weight-loss activity for children (or anyone) but also finds that kids need a little coddling to warm up to it. She plans treasure hunts with written clues that send children scrambling through the woods.

Another favorite is the bunny walk, in which a child dressed in a rabbit costume is given a bag of dried corn and a 15-minute head start. She drops corn, á la Hansel and Gretel; the kids follow the trail until they find her—and the birds clean up the corn. That's an act plenty of parents and kids could follow on their own. Just beware of those funky gingerbread houses!

A Walking Curriculum

In 1984, a man named Rob Sweetgall walked through all 50 states to promote cardiovascular health. After four heart-related deaths in his family, he quit his job as a chemical engineer with DuPont and headed out on foot to try to convince Americans that walking has the power to reverse the risk of heart disease.

On the way, Sweetgall visited schools, spoke at assemblies, and ran workshops for teachers. During the solitude of those 11,208 miles, he developed the concept for a total walking-wellness curriculum. With walking as the mainstay of the program, Sweetgall included health and physical education, reading, writing, math, science, and lifestyle planning. He created a workbook to teach kids how to walk briskly, how to pace themselves, and how to measure their target heart rate. It teaches the math of calorie burn and the science of nutrition and healthy eating habits. Also included are homework assignments to encourage parent participation.

The program can be taught by the classroom teacher, demands no equipment, and can be carried on anywhere. Best of all, it's a fitness program in which all kids succeed and no one is left on the

Shoe Sense

No child will ever enjoy walking if the shoes she's wearing are uncomfortable. According to professional shoe fitter Charles Smith, it's best to wear something that ties across the instep to keep the shoe securely on the foot—such as sneakers or oxfords. Choose a shoe that breathes. Those made out of plastic or vinyl may become soaked with sweat, causing all kinds of problems, not to mention odors.

Sizing is crucial. There's nothing like a too-small shoe to cramp anyone's walking style. Children's shoes should be checked regularly for fit. The shoes they walk and play in should allow plenty of room for a thick pair of socks to help absorb moisture and prevent blisters. Smith makes this suggestion about trying on a shoe in the store: "Don't ask a child if a shoe hurts, but *where* it hurts. Ask her to point to the spot. If she can't, then it's probably just a 'new shoe' feeling." The new pair just may not feel as comfortable as the old, worn-out pair. If she points across the front of the shoes, she may be unused to the stiffness inherent in a sturdy shoe. If she points to the toes, it may mean a size adjustment is necessary.

bench. The benefits of walking as a *lifetime* fitness activity are stressed and the kids come away knowing they can help themselves to better health through a simple, pleasurable activity.

Said Emma Guttler, a fifth-grader from the Fort River Elementary School in Amherst, Massachusetts, one of the first schools to adopt the program: "I always liked to walk, but since I started this special walking program, I realized that walking is more than just a way to stay warm."

If you'd be interested in seeing this walking curriculum instituted in your school, talk to your principal, PTA president, and school physical education teacher, and write to Robert Sweetgall, Creative Walking, P.O. Box 50296, Clayton, MO 63105.

Clubs

How to Start One

So many people have written to us at the *Prevention* Walking Club to ask how to start a local walking group that we decided to give it a try ourselves. This is not the only way to start or run a club. It's just one way. Here's how we did it.

We knew there was local interest in walking because two years ago, more than 300 would-be walkers showed up at a nearby mall in response to a notice in the paper. But six months later the club had dwindled to 6 people, and they had never even gotten together for a walk. We decided we didn't want meetings; we wanted to walk. We didn't want officers or dues or anything to get in the way of walking.

First, we contacted our city's recreation department officials and asked for their support in starting a club. There were already city-supported hiking, canoeing, bicycling, and running clubs. They said they'd be happy to sponsor us, and that took care of any insurance problems we might have encountered as an independent organization.

We selected a meeting place. Our city has a park with a 1.2-mile circular paved course. With permission from the parks department, we marked off the course with pink spray-paint arrows (the parks department provided the paint) to show tenths of a mile. We decided that our club would be pacing oriented rather than destination oriented. We would help people learn to pace their walks for fun and fitness.

We planned to meet in the park every Sunday morning at 9:00, rain or shine. Our local newspaper has a calendar section, so we placed our club on the roster of events for Sundays. We spread the word at work, told our friends, and showed up on Sunday, stopwatches in hand. More than 50 people signed up the first day.

The club has been meeting for over two years at the writing of this book and more than 100 people have participated. Attendance varies according to the weather. We do two or three laps with people divided into groups according to specific paces. We pay attention to posture and breathing, and we try to walk the same pace all the way around the track. When we practice without our watches, we're amazed at how well we do!

We had a club picnic and ran a pacewalking event in which everyone got a ribbon according to how fast (or slow) he walked. We encourage people to walk during the week on their own and to use Sundays as a special boost to their regular program. The next step—our own T-shirts!

This is a simple and fun way to run a walking club, and nobody is stuck with paperwork or committee meetings. After all, most of us have too many commitments as it is. There's no need to make a walking club a chore for anybody.

Coffee Breaks and Snack Attacks

Break the Break Habit

It's a ritual of American life—the 10-minute coffee break. Whether you're a coffee drinker or not, everybody needs to take a break, and let's face it, most of us head for food and beverages to give ourselves a boost.

What do we expect from a coffee break or a snack attack? Renewed energy, a little personal pampering, a lift in spirits? If those are the things you're looking for, let us make a suggestion. The next time your co-workers head for the vending machines, do an about-face and try a brisk walk, whether it's around the halls or out around the company parking lot. A short brisk walk will pep you up faster and keep you feeling energetic longer than eating something sweet. And low energy (and habit) is probably what sent you after sugar in the first place.

During a study conducted at California State University, Long Beach, 18 volunteers rated their energy levels before and after walking and snacking. After 12 days, results showed participants experienced a brief spurt of energy after eating a sugary snack, but within an hour they began to feel even more tense and tired than before they snacked. After taking a brisk, 10-minute walk, participants felt calmly energized for up to 2 hours.

Kind of makes you wonder, doesn't it, why snacking is the more familiar solution to boosting your energy, if it's less likely to do the job. Robert Thayer, Ph.D., who conducted the study at CSU, theorizes that people get hooked on sugary snacking because of the immediate energy boost that it provides. Later, they can't connect their tension with a candy bar they ate an hour earlier.

The thought of a quick trek around the block when you're already tired may seem like an aggravation, not a solution. But, comments Dr. Thayer, many participants in his study changed their snacking habits considerably once they became aware of the tension-producing effects of sugar snacking versus the calming, energizing effects of walking.

Coffee Lover's Walk Break

Switching from coffee breaks to walking breaks may seem like taking things a step too far. Sure, you may get the same energy boost without the caffeine or sugar, but what's going to soothe those taste buds? Try this neat trick the next time you feel the need for a pick-me-up cup of coffee but want to avoid caffeine nerves. Fix a cup of coffee the way you normally would. Warm your hands on that steamy cup, then sit back and breathe in the sweet coffee smell. Close your eyes and inhale deeply so that you can almost taste the coffee itself. Mmmmm! Then put down that cup and go for a walk instead!

Cold Weather
Staying Comfortable

When the temperature starts to drop, don't give in to the temptation to hibernate in the family den and give up walking till the spring thaw. Instead, work with winter. After all, there's nothing more invigorating than a brisk walk in the crisp, cold air. It's all a matter of how you prepare yourself.

Bundle up. But be prepared to shed a layer or two of clothes as body heat builds. The key is to stay comfortable—not too cold, not too hot. Of course, protect vulnerable areas like your toes, nose, and earlobes from the cold.

Be Prepared

Morning walkers, make the "Will I or won't I?" decision the night before. It's too easy to talk yourself out of a walk when you awaken to a cold and dark morning. Make sure you lay out all your walking clothes before you go to bed.

Time your walk so you will step out of the door and into a beautiful sunrise.

Turn on your favorite walking tape as soon as you open your eyes.

Have a bowl of warm cereal before heading out.

Try to schedule your walks over lunch hour, when the sun is high in the sky. You can really appreciate the warmth and the extra vitamin D of those rays, instead of hiding from them. (Get out the sunscreen and the sunglasses, all the same.)

Be aware of the temperature and the windchill factor when you're going out for a walk. If the temperature is below 20°F and feels like 40 below or lower, it's probably best to take a day off. Also, don't risk a slip on icy sidewalks and trails. On frigid days, take your walking program indoors to a local mall.

Walking in brisk weather delivers a fat-burning bonus. Research has shown that exercising in cold temperatures may shift the body's metabolism into high gear, burning fat and calories to generate heat.

Of course, if you have a heart condition, diabetes, or other health concern, check with your doctor before battling the elements.

Tips from Cold-Weather Veterans

The authors of this book live in an area where the four seasons are moderate. Pennsylvania winters are cold, but not unbearably so. But many of the *Prevention* Walking Club members live in frigid zones—like the shores of Lake Michigan, or Alaska. We've gotten some great tips from them and others on how to stick it out through 30-below weather. We'd like to share their strategies with you.

From Irene Deprey, Creston, British Columbia: "I like to eat a warm meal 1 hour before I go for a walk. Then I'll drink a warm beverage right before I go out. This seems to help keep my body warm.

"My insulated, waterproof boots with a good grip on the bottom are what makes winter a pleasure for me!

"Dress for the winter conditions like Mom always wanted you to do. This means a jacket, turtleneck, long johns, and gloves.

"If you use a Walkman, take an insulated pouch to keep your batteries from freezing up.

"On my long winter walks I carry a Thermos of herb tea, hot cider, or hot grain coffee and some nuts and dried fruit."

From Mary LaBrecque, White River Junction, Vermont: "Use a ski pole for a walking stick when there's snow or ice on the ground."

From Del Mello, Danielson, Connecticut: "To prepare my body for the cold, I do stretching exercises indoors first. By the time I hit that cold air, I'm already warmed up."

From E. Burnell, Strathclair, Manitoba: "If the wind is blowing, walk against it at the beginning of your walk. At the end, walk with the wind and you'll be exerting less energy when you're tired."

From Liz Wolbach, Emmaus, Pennsylvania: "I never wear finger gloves. I always wear mittens."

The Ice Shoe Cometh

Not snow, no, nor rain, nor heat, nor night keeps them from accomplishing their appointed courses with all speed.
—Herodotus (485–425 B.C.)

Wintry weather presents many obstacles to walkers, but the one question that seems to surface again and again is, "What am I going to wear on my feet?" Most walking shoes do not seem to offer enough protection from snow, slush, or ice.

A good choice for really messy, cold weather is a lightweight hiking boot, lined with Gore-Tex for protection from moisture. Don't feel you have to get something insulated. Then it will be impractical for warmer weather. Instead, wear your boots with wool socks and polypropylene liner socks to wick away sweat. When your feet sweat, that moisture freezes in cold weather, and that is often what makes your feet feel cold.

A hiking boot will give you better traction than regular walking shoes on snowy or icy roads, and their high tops will protect you from twisting an ankle should you slip and slide. The boot will also protect your feet from snow should you ramble off the beaten track for a while.

Sporting goods stores are a good place to try on a wide variety of hiking boots. Try to find a store that has knowledgeable salespeople to fit you. Let them know you plan to use this boot for your exercise walking, and they'll help you select the most appropriate style. Make sure you spend time walking around the store with the boots on, and don't leave with a pair unless you're satisfied they fit well. You shouldn't feel any uncomfortable rubbing spots, even when you have thick socks on.

From Helen Moritz, Richfield, Minnesota: "My favorite pair of walking boots is fur-lined. When I wear them with a pair of wool socks, I can go anywhere!"

From Bambi Girafalco, Downingtown, Pennsylvania: "I wear layers. A pair of long, cotton underwear, a sweat suit, and a vest.

Everything is cotton. On really cold days, I prefer to wear something 40 percent wool and 60 percent cotton."

From Bert Welton, Cumberland, Rhode Island: "When it's really cold, I wear a thermal vest. It makes my whole body feel warm."

From E. E. Dallin, Prince Albert, Saskatchewan: "A great way to keep warm is to wear flannel-lined blue jeans over synthetic long johns. Also, I always wear a lightweight, close-fitting knit cap that covers most of my face."

From F. E. Sosnowski, Chicago, Ilinois: "I wear a heavy night cream on my face to protect my skin from the cold and wind."

Depression

Chase Away the Blues

Thanks to science, a lot of people are discovering that a potent new antidote to depression doesn't come in pill form, can't be injected, and has no bad side effects. It's exercise, regular exercise like walking every day.

We've accepted for years that our minds affect our bodies, but we're just beginning to realize how much our bodies affect our minds. While nobody is really sure just what it is about exercise that seems to lift some people out of the doldrums, research over the last ten years seems to support the body/mind connection. Studies suggest that people who are depressed feel better when they exercise on a regular basis. Why? Some researchers speculate that exercising gives people a sense of gaining control, of mastering their bodies and making them feel better about themselves. That feeling then may spread from exercise to other areas of their lives.

Other studies have shown that a moderate increase in aerobic capacity (maximum oxygen uptake), such as that produced during a brisk walk, generates a significant antidepressant effect. And some research suggests that exercise can reduce anxiety as effectively as a mild tranquilizer. The cause of such positive mood changes, some scientists think, is the exercise-induced release of endorphins, brain chemicals that seem to produce a feeling of well-being. Granted, there's a lot about depression that's controversial. And we're not suggesting self-prescribing a brisk walk for serious or prolonged depression. But if you suffer occasional mild depression, then experts suggest that a positive step you can take is into your walking shoes and out the door—every day.

Walking to Lift Your Mood

Here are some tips gathered from researchers and mental health professionals to help you walk to the lighter side of life.

Think ahead. To get motivated, it may help to think about how much better you'll feel by the time you get back from a good walk.

Take some deep, slow breaths. Do this before you start out, to begin relaxing body and mind. Once you get moving, your breathing will deepen naturally. Walk briskly, but don't push too hard. You don't want to complicate matters by injuring yourself or becoming overly sore or stiff.

Act upbeat. Smile, lift your head, straighten your back, and imagine how you walk when you're feeling most lively and confident. Behavioral therapists say that sometimes, as simplistic as it may sound, acting happy can make you feel happy.

Plan a specific route and stick to it. If you're feeling confused and depressed, wandering aimlessly may add to your anxiety.

Walk to the music. If you have a cassette player, pop in a favorite tape. We've all experienced the mood-altering potential of music.

Make noise. Lots of times we're depressed because we're harboring unexpressed anger. Walking can help dissipate some of that stored-up emotion. And you can help it along by what psychologists call venting. Allow yourself a little growl or groan as you walk. Or a sigh, if you're feeling more sad than mad.

Banish tension. Be aware of your shoulders as you walk. When we're tense or anxious, many of us hold our shoulders high and create tension in our upper backs. Let your arms swing, but don't force them.

Share the load. Find a compassionate walking partner. Sometimes we just need somebody to talk to, someone who knows how to listen without judging or giving advice. We need to speak out about what's bothering us, instead of letting it rattle around in our heads.

Diabetes

Control through Exercise

Here's some sweet news for people with diabetes—regular exercise, including walking, can help protect the body from the degenerative effects of this disease. In fact, some people who have Type I (insulin-dependent) diabetes find that they can reduce the amount of insulin they need when they keep up a walking program.

People with Type II (non-insulin-dependent) diabetes have particular incentive to hit the pavement on a regular basis—they can often reverse the course of the disease through diet, exercise, and weight loss. Finally, aerobic exercise, which promotes heart and lung health, is especially important for people with both forms of the disease because the condition places them at increased risk for coronary heart disease.

"Brisk walking is an excellent exercise for diabetics in good shape," says Henry Dolger, M.D., former chief of the Diabetes Department at Mount Sinai Medical Center in New York City.

Not only does walking deliver all of these fitness benefits, but it's easy on the body and there is very little risk of serious injury.

Of course, if you have diabetes, you must check with your doctor before you begin your walking program. Not everyone with this disease will benefit from exercise, and in some cases, working out may be dangerous. After you get your doctor's approval, keep him or her informed of your fitness progress. As you exercise more and perhaps lose weight, your medication needs may change. But only your physician can make that determination.

Aim for High Frequency

People who have diabetes should try to walk at least three times a week. That's the frequency that doctors usually recommend to maintain a healthy heart. It seems that the positive effect exercise has on blood sugar regulation is quickly lost once exercise is discontinued. So map out your walking log and make every effort to stick with your program. If you do skip a workout or two, don't try to make it up by walking faster or twice as far. Vigorous exercise can cause a rise in blood sugar, especially in people who have insulin deficiency.

Non-insulin-dependent diabetics, 90 percent of whom are overweight, may do well to walk five to seven times a week. This may improve the rate of weight loss.

A Question of Time

Whether you use insulin or not, be sure to check with your physician regarding how long you should walk at each workout.

Exercising at the same time each day—whether early in the morning, over the lunch hour, or after work—helps everyone develop a habit of regularity. For people with diabetes, the timing of exercise can also help control blood sugar levels, says Dr. Dolger. Non-insulin-dependent diabetics may benefit from exercising before meals. Premeal walks help regulate appetite and promote weight loss. On the other hand, insulin-dependent diabetics are ill-advised to exercise on an empty stomach when blood sugar is low. They should plan their walks for an hour or so *after* a meal, Dr. Dolger explains, when blood sugar levels are reaching their peak.

Exercise can sometimes send blood sugar levels into a tailspin. And if you use insulin, you're more likely to experience this hypoglycemic (too-low blood sugar) reaction. So eat up *before* you walk and always carry along a snack for emergency purposes. Talk with your doctor about how much exercise you can tolerate before you need to replenish your store of carbohydrates.

Pamper Your Feet

For diabetics, comfortable walking shoes and socks are not just important, they're essential, says Marc A. Brenner, D.P.M. (doctor of podiatric medicine), director of the Institute of Diabetic Foot Research. A small blister or callus may be insignificant to most people. But such irritation may be life- or limb-threatening to a person with diabetes. To complicate the matter, people with this condition often have difficulty feeling irritations on their feet. They are also more prone to infections. A slight irritation, if it goes undetected, can generate major complications.

If you are a walker with diabetes, seek out a professional shoe fitter when selecting walking shoes, suggests Dr. Brenner. As daily precautions, powder your feet to keep them dry and check your shoes and socks for any foreign particles and rough spots. If, despite these precautions, you develop a blister or other type of irritation, consult a physician or a podiatrist immediately—certainly no later than the next day.

Keep Your Cool

Walkers who have diabetes should avoid temperature extremes, says Dr. Brenner. If the weather outside is too hot (over 80°F with humidity above 70 percent) or too cold (below freezing, taking into account the windchill factor), head for the nearest shopping mall. Many doctors recommend that their diabetic patients walk in these temperature-controlled environments. And many malls now welcome walkers and have special walking programs. (See the mallwalking chapter, beginning on page 101.)

Name That Walker

Always carry identification. Your ID should include your name, address, and phone number as well as your physician's phone number and information on your medical condition and the medications you take. If your walking pants don't have pockets to hold your ID, consider a fanny pack, wrist wallet, or small pouch that attaches to the instep of your walking shoe.

If there's a silver lining here, it's this: Often, a health problem like diabetes can motivate a person to embrace a more healthful lifestyle, one that includes regular walks. The result is not only improved health but increased enjoyment of life.

Dogs

Making Your Pet Your Partner

With 105 million dogs in the United States, walkers might expect to trip over leashes on every street corner. But William Winter, D.V.M., of Minneapolis, Minnesota, estimates that only about a third of those pooches pound the sidewalks with their owners. The rest stay cooped up in backyards, houses, and apartments, getting out only to "do their duty" and shuffling back inside for some more rest.

"Healthy people, though, have healthy, exercised dogs," says Dr. Winter. "They recognize the benefits of exercise for themselves and their animals."

Since there are only so many hours in a day, it's only practical that you and your pet get your exercise together. Dogs make wonderful walking partners. They can help to remind you that it's time for your daily workout, be a source of companionship, and offer you a certain amount of protection. And once you get them used to your routine, they'll be a pleasure to take along.

Check Out Your Pet

If you have not been exercising your pet regularly, chances are he may have turned into a couch potato with four legs. He needs to be treated with the same care and concern as any human partner. Although he may be more receptive to the idea of going for a walk than your spouse, he still needs to be checked out and readied for his new lifestyle.

Dr. Winter suggests taking your pet for a checkup, just as you'd have yourself checked if you were out of shape and beginning an exercise program. "A little preventive medicine is well worth the money you may put out. Your vet can spot problems that may be invisible to you," says Dr. Winter.

Ask your vet about your pet's diet while you're there, and explain to her that you plan to start exercising with your pet. She may have specific suggestions for you based on your dog's breed or any health problems your pup may have.

Train Yourself

If walks with your dog are going to be pleasurable and invigorating, your dog may need some training. Actually, that means *you* need to be trained in the laws of dog obedience. Look in your phone book for a listing of the American Kennel Club. It often offers obedience training classes that last for about ten weeks and help you learn the rudiments of training. (Your dog learns a little, too, but it all goes away if you don't keep practicing.) There are also many good books available on dog training. Check out your local library. Basically, you want to train your dog to heel, which means to trot comfortably at your side, stopping when you stop, starting when you start, and not crossing all over your path, tripping you and whoever happens to come your way. Actually, a well-trained dog is a rarity and a pleasure to see. Most of us are satisfied with our dogs if they stay reasonably close to us and don't pull constantly on the leash.

Rules of the Leash

Dr. Winter walks his dog, Daisy, every day. He offers these suggestions for walking with your pet.

"Start slowly to condition your dog. Two shorter walks in one day would be better than one long one. Eventually, you could be walking your dog 3 to 5 miles a day.

Maggie Spilner's Personal Tip for Exercise Walkers

I have a small, terrier-type dog that I like to take for long walks on the weekends. (He likes it, too!) Although I took him to obedience classes, I never had the time or patience to get him to heel so well that I could walk him on a thread, like Dr. William Winter of Minneapolis. Sometimes walking him could be kind of a drag . . . him dragging me down the street, that is. I had to hold on tight, with my arm fully extended. Not a great way to get a balanced walking workout.

About a year ago, I purchased a special leash, made in West Germany, called Flexi-Leash. They're sold at most pet stores or groomers. The leash allows you to control the length of the lead, which usually extends from 3 to 16 feet; some go as far as 26 feet. You can lock the length in place, or you can allow it to extend and recoil itself, picking up the slack as your dog changes distance from you. I bought it so that I could keep my dog tightly reined in on the sidewalk, but give him room to play when we got to the park.

One Saturday I took Petey out for a long walk. I was kind of drifting mentally and I accidentally unlocked the leash, allowing it to extend and recoil as I walked. When I came back to earth, I realized I'd been using my regular fitness walking style, arms swinging back and forth, because the leash allowed me to pull my arm backward without knocking the dog off his feet. When my arms swung forward, the leash neatly recoiled. This way we managed to fall into step together. Even though he was pulling ahead, I was walking fast enough so that he was never at the end of his tether. Now I use it all the time when I want to fitness walk and exercise the dog at the same time. It's great! Beware, though, that you unlock the leash only when your dog is safe from traffic or bicycles.

"When you first go out to walk, let your animal sniff around and take care of business. Let him be playful for a few minutes to get the excitement of being outside with you out of his system.

Then, when you're ready to really start walking, let him know you're serious. No sniffing, no pulling, no investigating, just straight-ahead walking. Most dogs are able to learn this mode of behavior and stay with you. Get a choker collar and make short, sharp tugs on his leash whenever he strays. Be sure the chain around his neck releases after you tug. As he comes back to your side, praise him sincerely with a cheerful voice. No food treats please! Your appreciation is all he really wants.

"I could walk my dog, Daisy, with a thread," comments Dr. Winter. "It's not the leash that keeps her near me. That is what makes walking with her a total joy. When I stop, she stops and sits down."

Although hard surfaces do the essential task of trimming your dog's toenails, try to walk your dog on grass at least part of the time. "When a dog comes clickety-clacking into my office, I know right away that he hasn't been exercising. People wonder how I know!" laughs Dr. Winter.

Watch for sore pads on your dog's feet to make sure you aren't overdoing it before your pet is ready.

"Two miles shouldn't be too far, unless your dog has been carried around on a pillow for several years," says Dr. Winter. But ask your vet about your dog. Some dogs simply were not bred for walking or strenuous activity. Others can't stand heat or cold. Be sure to know your pet's special needs and adapt to them.

If you're thinking of acquiring a dog and you want him to be able to accompany you on your walks, Dr. Winter suggests mutts, standard poodles, female Dobermans, setters, bird dogs, terriers, shelties, and collies. Avoid dogs with smashed-in faces or stubby legs. You want a dog who is a good breather and has good muscles.

Volunteer Dogs

If you've ever considered getting a dog for a walking partner but realized that your lifestyle just wouldn't allow it or you can't have pets in your apartment, maybe you and your local humane society have something to offer each other. They have dogs and you have dog-walking time!

At the Humane Society of New York, Sarah C. Haywood oversees a volunteer cadre of dog walkers. Encouraged by a sign in the

Walking and Dogs Go Hand in Leash

When the *Prevention* Walking Club offered a special award to members who walked with their dogs during the month of April, hundreds participated to capture a patch for their pooch. These two letters were the best. There is no doubt that people learn to rely on their pets for companionship and protection. These two ladies display an obvious affection for their charges as well as a healthy sense of humor.

Pumpkin the Pug

"I am a 12-year old pug. When I saw my owner clean up my leash, I nearly had a nervous breakdown. I pretended to be asleep when walking was suggested. I had to start out very slowly, but I did it! I walked for 20 hours during the month of April!

"Let me tell you, I now have a lot more energy! I beg to walk and I get real excited whenever I see my leash. I stay awake and happy most of the day now. When I went to the doctor, he was amazed at how well my heart is doing. I was so proud!

"I sure hope I get my patch to display to my other dog friends."

Pumpkin Troxell
Greensboro, North Carolina

A Woman's Best Friend

"I am 44 years old and single. When I got divorced, I found myself the mother of a great Dane/Labrador puppy. She weighs 100 pounds, and I weigh 125. Her name is Stoner and we go for a walk every day (whether I need to or not).

"Stoner has dragged me out of the dark bed of depression and she has dragged me out on nights not fit for a beast. (Winter is harsh in the Ozarks.) But when we come back, we feel better and we wave to our neighbors. I can walk anytime of the day or night and we are fine. I don't have any problem reaching aerobic levels.

"Me and Stoner, we walk. We have found a certain peace.

"By the way, she ate my club patch. How do I get another?"

Amber Bernard
(No address given)

window, "Volunteer—Walk a Dog!" people with some time, energy, and compassion for animals sign out pooches and perambulate around the city.

Before they let a dog out for a walk, humane society personnel interview the volunteers and observe them with the dog. And volunteers must sign a release form. Sometimes a kennel person will go with them and give them some tips. Walkers also must be willing to clean up after the animal. Fines in most cities can be hundreds of dollars if you don't stoop to scoop.

"Some people come on their lunch hours. Others walk only on the weekends. Some call when they can come by rather than keeping a regular schedule. Some take the dogs for a half hour, others for 2 hours. We're flexible," says Haywood.

"We're really grateful for the enthusiasm, and our regulars are really quite dedicated. We can learn a lot about an animal from the walkers, and that can help us to get the dog adopted."

Interested in a part-time pooch arrangement? Call your local humane society to find out if they have a volunteer dog-walking program. A walker can be a dog's best friend. And that leash in your hand can lead you to a healthier lifestyle.

Evolution

Why Lovers Love Walking

We were born to walk. Literally. The very shape of the human birth canal was determined millions of years ago by our ancestors' newly developed talent for walking around on two legs, with the body held erect, says anthropologist Helen Fisher, Ph.D. Other members of our primate family—chimps, for instance—have longer birth canals and rounder hips, good for bearing young but not good at all for walking on two feet.

The human ability to walk erect, with hands free to gather and carry food over long distances and to use tools, was so advantageous to survival, Dr. Fisher says, that our body went through a whole series of dramatic evolutionary changes to make us not just so-so walkers, but great walkers. The feet of our early ancestors, says the anthropologist at the American Museum of Natural History, became flatter and the ankles stronger to provide a firm platform for long, steady walking. The knees rotated inward, the legs straightened. And the pelvic area became flatter from front to back and wider from side to side so we could walk quickly and efficiently without waddling.

There is more to the story, though, than a mere anatomical makeover. In time, walking also gave us an emotional makeover.

When our hips changed and the birth canal narrowed as a result, Dr. Fisher believes, it became markedly more difficult for women to bear children. Adding to the problem was another evolutionary trend that occurred somewhat later: The early human (prehuman, actually) brain was increasing in size, and so was the head. Some predicament—bigger heads coming through narrower birth canals!

Meandering into Monogamy

That evolutionary crisis—which could have aborted the whole human race—was solved, says Dr. Fisher, by another development: the bearing of human young in a relatively premature state, before the head could grow too large. But the completely dependent condition of a new human child, compared with that of a chimp or gorilla, created still another problem. How was a mother supposed to feed, protect, and take care of herself in the prehistoric wild while also caring for an infant so helpless it couldn't even hold onto its mother's hairy chest or back (like chimps do) when she went to gather food?

The answer was simple, says Dr. Fisher. Get a husband.

And in fact, humans are the only ground-dwelling primates who are monogamous, forming male/female bonds that typically last for years. Chimps are promiscuous, while male gorillas maintain harems. Nurturing the young is largely left to Mama. But human beings fall in love. We become filled with an overwhelming desire to latch on to another person, stay by his or her side, share food, and help raise a family. Why? Because, says Dr. Fisher, we wouldn't be here if we didn't. Our tender, helpless infants wouldn't have survived those early precivilization days unless their parents had a powerful bonding urge—a yen to walk down the aisle, even if that aisle zigzagged through the underbrush of 2,000,000 B.C.

The Grand Design

Now, part of this account is fact and part is still only theory. But if much of it is true, it has some interesting implications.

One is that our human anatomy is designed in large measure to support the practice of walking. That being the case, it follows that we should thrive on generous doses of it—an idea supported by ever-increasing medical evidence.

It also suggests that our human ability to fall in love and the high value we attach to intense, long-lasting, mutually supportive relationships are the indirect result of being born to walk.

Which is, perhaps, why we love to walk. And why we especially love to walk with the one we love.

Famous Walkers

You're in Good Company

Screen legends Greta Garbo and Katharine Hepburn are famous walkers. So is Minta Beach.

Minta Beach? you ask. Yes. In 1912, this wealthy 35-year-old matron walked—trailed by her chauffeured limousine—from her home in New York City to Chicago, a distance of 1,071 miles. Averaging 25 miles a day, she made it there in 42½ days—4 days ahead of schedule.

Every major daily newspaper in the country chronicled her

progress—what she wore, what she ate, and especially what she said to the crowds gathered along her route. She reveled in the rain, for instance, and urged those watching her from beneath their umbrellas to join her for at least a couple of miles.

"If you think the world is against you, that nothing will ever go right again," she said, smiling encouragement from under her rubber hat, "come splash along the road with me. I'll guarantee that all your troubles will be over before you've walked a mile."

Famous walkers come in two categories: Famous people who are passionate walkers and passionate walkers whose long-distance exploits make them famous.

Celebrity Walkers

Famous walkers abound in history. Hippocrates, the ancient Greek physician known as the Father of Medicine, was positively evangelical when it came to extolling the benefits of man's first exercise. As part of his recommended treatments for a wide variety of illnesses, he prescribed early-morning walks, after-dinner walks, and night walks.

Almost all famous philosophers, men of letters, and statesmen have been passionate walkers. Aristotle, perhaps the most famous of the Greek philosophers, heads a list of walkers that includes Marcel Proust, Charles Dickens, William Wordsworth, Jane Austen, Walt Whitman, and Robert Louis Stevenson (whose classic *Travels with a Donkey in the Cévennes* describes a 120-mile walk in southern France he completed in 12 days, with his donkey carrying his gear).

Ambling into the twentieth century, we find Albert Einstein striding about the campus of Princeton University.

Bertrand Russell, the brilliant mathematician and social philosopher who was vigorous and creative until his death in 1970 at the age of 98, once said, "Unhappy businessmen, I am convinced, would increase their happiness more by walking 6 miles every day than by any conceivable change in philosophy."

Harry S. Truman was known as "our walkingest president" to the reporters who tried to keep up with him during his brisk prebreakfast walks. "I believe walking will make me live longer," he told them.

More modern political figures have also discovered the pleasure and benefits of walking. Senator William Proxmire regularly walked the 5 miles from his office to his home every day Congress was in session. And Supreme Court Justice William O. Douglas said that when he had a knotty legal case to consider, he always went for a walk.

Walking Their Way to Fame

But it's the long-distance walkers of the other sort who make the front pages of newspapers—and sometimes the *Guinness Book of World Records*. These are the people whose walking exploits put them in the spotlight of public attention.

A Young Man with a Purpose

Edward Payson Weston first made headlines in 1861. It seems that at the age of 22, Weston made a wager with a friend that if Abe Lincoln was elected president, he would walk from his native Boston to Washington, D.C. (a distance of 478 miles) within ten consecutive days. The nation's press adored this "snappy little kid." He arrived in the capitol after ten days, 4 hours, and 20 minutes and attended the Inaugural Ball that same day. He met the new president and, politely declining Lincoln's kind offer to pay his train fare back to Boston, opted instead to *walk* the return trip.

Six years later, Weston, then 28, walked from Portland, Maine, to Chicago—a distance of 1,326 miles—in 26 days. *Harper's Weekly*, a leading magazine of the day, observed: "This walk makes Weston's name a household word."

During the next year Weston walked 200 miles in St. Louis (2 miles of it *backward*), and the press started referring to the small, wiry Weston as "a walking machine."

He enjoyed giving interviews to the press. "Nature," he told reporters, "has provided us with precisely the equipment that furnishes to *everyone* the possibility of having the right kind of exercise—the *daily* use of the great external muscular system of the body, particularly of the lower extremities—in other words, *walking*." It was, he said, the only proper exercise for a lifetime, and he fully intended to live to be 100.

Weston spent the period from 1876 to 1884 abroad and became a true international celebrity when he walked through England at the rate of 50 miles per day for 100 days. Back home, the now-graying walkaholic set out, riding crop in hand, on what he called his "ocean-to-ocean" tramp from New York to San Francisco, and the next year, from Los Angeles to New York. The *New York Times* dubbed him the best-known pedestrian in the world.

Interest in walking had never been so high, thanks to the example set by Weston. An uncommonly large number of people were now walking "the Weston way," and the *New York Times* received countless letters from readers wondering why America had no walking clubs like those in England and Germany.

A septuagenarian in 1913, still sleek and bursting with energy, Weston was ready for yet another long-distance walk, this time the 1,000 miles from New York to Minneapolis in 60 days. The press considered it "the crowning achievement of his pedestrian career" and marveled that, at 75, "he has the same buoyant step, the alert eye, and quick nervous muscularity that he has possessed for a generation." Weston told reporters that he took on this, his final challenge, to prove "that the individual who walks, eats moderately, and leads a simple life can accomplish a greater task in his 75th year than the ordinary man at 50 years can do." In 1922, at 84, he walked a distance of 500 miles in 30 days, matching the pace he kept at 75.

Weston passed away in 1929, just two weeks before his 91st birthday, still a daily walker and still maintaining that walking is the one perfect exercise.

A Living Monument to Determination

The chauffeured limousine that accompanied Beach on her walk from New York to Chicago in 1912 carried not only her personal maid and luggage but also a reporter. As she left New York that first day, he noted that the streets were "black with people, the police clearing the way for her up Broadway as she walked between two mounted police, talking to the crowd as she passed."

On the 18th day, when a woman she passed asked, "In your heart, do you actually have any hopes of getting there?" Beach replied, "Nothing in the world can prevent me from reaching Chicago. I know I can do it, because I love to walk, and since I know the right foods to eat and how to live, I can do almost anything I set my mind upon."

Arriving in Chicago, she set out for City Hall where the mayor was waiting for her. Again the crowds were so dense that police had to clear a path for her.

Later, writing *My Walk from New York to Chicago,* a book detailing her experiences, Beach admonished her readers: "Don't plead that you haven't time to walk. Take time. You have time to sleep and eat, haven't you? Exercise is just as important as sleeping and eating, and the person who realizes this grows stronger and brighter each year instead of more feeble and helpless.

"If you live in a city, make a beeline for the nearest park. If in the country, take the most secluded road, if you don't mind the unevenness of the path. Get out and see what nature can do for you. You'll never regret it."

A Proper Bostonian

Eleanora Sears, a proper, middle-aged Boston socialite, began her long-distance walking in 1912, with a 109-mile walk through New England. Beach had completed her New York–Chicago walk only months before, and the public was once again titillated by the spectacle of a wealthy woman choosing to walk such a distance.

In 1925, she really hit her stride when she walked from Providence, Rhode Island, to Boston in just 10½ hours. The following year, she did it again, this time shaving 43 minutes from her previous time and celebrated with a dinner dance in her Back Bay mansion that evening.

An Emissary from England

Dr. Barbara Moore, a middle-aged, Russian-born Englishwoman credited with starting the long-distance walking craze in England after walking the length of Britain in 23 days, arrived on these shores in 1960, determined to walk across America "to prove we women can do all that men can do." A strict vegetarian, Dr. Moore was said to eat grass and, as she put it, "quite a lot of air, too, especially air in the mountains." She promptly flew to San Francisco, and from there she started the 3,387-mile walk to New York City.

Dr. Moore arrived at Times Square 85 days later, having averaged some 40 miles a day despite a series of mishaps. In Utah, she twisted her ankle. In Indiana, she was sideswiped by a car. She had survived a couple of dust storms as well as a tornado. The press lionized this petite woman with "the constitution of Atlas, the stubbornness of Noah, and a handshake like Jack Dempsey's." But later that year, she departed this country in a huff when U.S. customs officials confiscated her fruits and vegetables.

A Walk through the U.S.A.

In 1978, Peter Jenkins set out with Cooper, his dog, to discover his country. Young, idealistic, inquisitive, and upbeat, he came home "turned on by America and its people in a thousand fantastic ways." He wrote a best-seller, *A Walk across America*, based on his experiences.

How could he possibly top that? He did when he married a young woman he'd met on his walk. Together they set out on another walk westward. That, too, evolved into a best-seller. Today, they and their three children live on a farm in Tennessee, and Jenkins, not yet 40, recently completed a walk across China to the vast northern grasslands of Inner Mongolia.

Jenkins bids fair to becoming the Edward Payson Weston of the twenty-first century.

Foot Care
So They Can Take Care of You

Along with "Hello," "Good-bye," "How are you?" and "I didn't do it," one of the most often-repeated phrases in any language has to be, "My feet are killing me."

No wonder. The human foot is a complex mechanism, with more bones than a $10 bucket of fried chicken and such an intricate

This chapter was prepared in cooperation with the American Podiatric Medical Association.

network of muscles, ligaments, nerves, and blood vessels that most of us have little understanding of what makes our feet work, much less how to prevent problems. Add to this the fact that you may be walking your way to better health but neglecting your feet until something goes wrong, and it's easy to see why foot ailments are among the most common health problems in the country.

"If people gave half as much thought to foot health as they did to foot fashion, we could prevent a lot of problems," says Norman Klombers, D.P.M., executive director of the American Podiatric Medical Association. "You spend up to 80 percent of your waking hours on your feet. They affect the alignment of your entire skeletal system, and most people don't realize that foot problems can be the reason for aches and pains elsewhere."

Feet also act as a barometer for the general state of the body. Anemia; arthritis; diabetes; heart, circulation, and kidney disorders; and other conditions may be detected first in the feet.

Practically all of us are born with healthy feet, but 70 percent develop foot problems by adulthood. Among the most common causes are: heredity, improper foot care (including wearing shoes, socks, or stockings that don't fit properly), injury, and the loss of

---

Meet the Podiatrist

Because foot disorders are so widespread, more people are turning to the 8,500-plus members of the American Podiatric Medical Association (APMA). APMA members graduate from one of seven podiatric colleges in the United States. They must meet the same entrance requirements as do traditional medical students. The first two years of podiatric medical training are similar to the medical school training that an M.D. receives. The final two years focus on courses that specialize in the feet. Internships and residency training in hospitals and clinics may also be part of the podiatrist's educational process. A graduating podiatrist receives the degree of Doctor of Podiatric Medicine (D.P.M.). APMA headquarters are in Washington, D.C.

muscle and ligament tone that comes with aging. Women suffer four times as many foot ailments as men, with high-heeled shoes often to blame.

Your feet carry a heavy load and need all the consideration they can get. If you're like most people, you walk several miles daily, not including your exercise walking program, usually on hard, unyielding surfaces, and about 115,000 miles in a lifetime—more than four times around the earth. The feet of most active people absorb the impact of up to five million pounds a day.

Winning the Skin Game

Feet are also dermatological wonders. The skin on your soles is up to ten times thicker than elsewhere on your body, for protection and padding. Unfortunately, the rest of your feet are covered with ordinary, easily damaged skin, which is why skin-related problems are the main reason people visit podiatrists.

Controlling Corns

Corns, for instance, those small, circular, hard areas of skin cells typically found on top of a toe, above a joint, or on the sole of the foot, are one of the most common foot afflictions. They are also preventable.

Because corns are usually caused by shoe friction against a contracted toe, the easiest way to avoid them is to wear only properly fitting footwear. Proper fit is especially important in your walking shoes! If your shoes don't rub against your toes, it's doubtful you'll ever develop a corn. Soft corns can develop between toes if shoes are too narrow.

If you have a corn, don't try to cut it off with a razor blade because bathroom surgery can lead to infections, says Marc A. Brenner, D.P.M., past president of the American Society of Podiatric Dermatology. "A doctor using sterilized instruments can do this safely and with little pain, but it's dangerous for anyone to try it at home."

He also advises against the home remedy of soaking your feet and then using sandpaper or a callus file to grind away the corn. "You can cause a more serious problem, such as an infection, and not correct the cause of the corn. Even if it works, the corn will probably reappear in three to five weeks," he says.

Over-the-counter corn-removal medications should be avoided because they contain an acid that penetrates the hard skin surface but can burn the surrounding soft, healthy skin. Podiatrists often treat skin ulcers caused by these products.

If you wear wide-toed shoes but still suffer from corns, the cause may be a biomechanical fault, such as a hammertoe, in which the knuckle of the toe rises above its normal position and rubs the top of the shoe because of the poor mechanics of the foot. Another cause can be an underlying bone spur, a bony growth created when local inflammation is present over an extended period of time. x-rays may be needed to determine the problem. Treatment is necessary if the cause is biomechanical.

Counting Out Calluses

If you develop a callus, a common podiatric problem that usually appears on the heel or ball of the foot, the treatment is the same as for a corn. The hard, thick-skinned callus, however, is more difficult to prevent because it's caused not by your shoes but by your foot structure and the way you walk.

"Insoles are often prescribed to reduce the friction that causes calluses," says Dr. Brenner. Orthoses, or custom shoe inserts, are designed to accommodate your calluses if the cause is an out-of-line bone that hits the ground harder than other foot bones. Orthoses also help restore foot balance. With chronic calluses, surgery may be necessary to correct an underlying structural problem.

Forgoing Fungus

The area between your toes is just as prone to skin problems, and the most common is a fungal infection known as athlete's foot. It's contagious and loves to live in a warm, moist, dark environment, such as your shoes. The best way to keep the fungi out of your walking shoes is to create an inhospitable environment by wearing shoes made of natural materials, such as leather and canvas, that let moisture escape and feet breathe. Dust inside the shoes with cornstarch before and after wearing to absorb moisture. Keep your shoes dry and try not to wear them on consecutive days, because it takes a day or two for them to dry completely.

Bathe your feet at least once a day using soap and water, and be sure to dry thoroughly between your toes. It helps to change your socks twice a day, and if your feet sweat excessively, wear socks made of some "wicking" fiber, because they keep feet cooler and drier. (Check out the sock chapter, beginning on page 161, before you go shopping.)

Another way to prevent the flaking, cracking, itching, burning skin caused by fungal infections is to apply an over-the-counter medicated powder to your shoes each day, especially your walking shoes, because that's where your feet sweat the most. If the problem persists, a podiatrist can prescribe a stronger medication.

It also helps to wear thongs or other protective footwear wherever a fungus may be lurking, such as around the community pool or in the showers at the local health club.

Warding Off Warts

The same precautionary footwear can shield your feet against the virus that causes plantar warts, painful skin growths that occur on the soles of the feet. They are caused by a highly contagious virus that can be contracted by stepping on a wet, abrasive, virus-infected surface. Abrasion helps rub the virus into the skin on the bottom of your foot, which explains why these warts generally occur on weight-bearing areas.

The virus thrives in the same warm, moist conditions that help foster the athlete's foot fungus, so preventive measures are the same for both.

A wart should never be treated with an over-the-counter medication. "Check with a podiatrist to make sure you have a wart, and not a callus, corn, or skin cancer," says Dr. Brenner. A podiatrist has a wide array of treatment alternatives that may include dry ice, vitamin A injections, acid treatments, surgically scooping out the wart, or vaporizing it with a laser. But be aware that regardless of the method used, there is a 5 to 15 percent recurrence rate.

Plantar warts are slow growing. If you spot a suspicious growth on your foot, have it checked immediately, because a wart is easier to treat when small. More important, warts can spread to other parts of your foot or to your hands and even other areas of skin if not checked.

Allaying Allergies

If you notice that the skin on your feet is irritated, itchy, red, and painful, and there are small blisters, you may conclude that you have athlete's foot. But it could be contact dermatitis, an allergic skin reaction to some substance, perhaps nail polish, soap, foot powder, spray, or shoe material. Contact dermatitis is often mistaken for a fungal or bacterial infection.

To both treat and prevent the condition, find out what you're allergic to and avoid it. If the problem can't be traced to a medication, food, or cosmetic product, special hypo-allergenic shoes may be needed. Avoid using strong soaps and detergents, and instead use gentle, hypo-allergenic products to cleanse the skin. Over-the-counter preparations containing cortisone may help, but see a podiatrist if your condition fails to respond to the medication.

Banishing Blisters

One common foot ailment that's not often misdiagnosed is a blister, an annoying sore that all shoe wearers have experienced at least once. Excessive friction and pressure on the skin are a main cause. To prevent blisters, moleskin padding can be applied to areas that, because of the shape of your foot, may rub against every pair of shoes you buy, constantly causing the sores.

Skin that is too dry or too sweaty is also prone to blisters. Apply a thin coat of petroleum jelly to dry skin before activity. If your feet sweat a lot, sprinkling cornstarch in shoes and socks helps.

"For a small blister, you only need to cover it with a sterile dressing," says Dr. Klombers. "For a larger blister, a little home first-aid isn't out of order."

Sterilize a sewing needle with 70 percent isopropyl alcohol. Clean the blistered skin with an antiseptic and make small holes to release the fluid. Blot the fluid with a piece of sterile gauze. You can also apply an antibiotic cream and cover the area with a protective pad.

"Knowing when to deal with a blister yourself is a tricky decision," says Dr. Klombers. "Generally, if you can get to it easily and it's not too severe, you can handle it yourself. If there are signs of blood inside the blister, or if it becomes infected, see your podiatrist."

Inherited Foot Problems

A few common foot ailments have little to do with lack of consideration for your feet and are instead the result of inborn problems. Bunions, for instance, are usually hereditary and aren't caused by improperly fitted shoes, although pointed shoes aggravate and accelerate bunion formation.

Beating Out Bunions

A bunion starts as a small enlargement on the side of the big toe and grows over the years. Because it's the result of faulty foot structure and function, there are no self-care measures or ways to prevent the condition. "Surgery is the only way to correct the bone problem," says John McCrea, D.P.M., of Beloit, Wisconsin, "and then orthoses may be necessary to control any abnormal motion. If we can spot potential bunion problems in young patients, we can design orthoses that may help prevent future problems."

Supporting Flat Feet

An inborn structural or functional defect is also often the cause of flat feet. Totally flat, archless feet are rare, however, and most people who think they have the condition actually have normally low arches. Low or flat arches won't keep you out of the Army anymore, but they can cause a strain that may lead to discomfort in the foot, knee, hip, or lower back.

"Collapsed arches are quite common in people in their fifties and sixties. When the arch starts to give way, orthoses can be used for support. This should prevent the strained ligaments that lead to other problems," Dr. McCrea says.

High arches can also cause discomfort because the ball of the foot and heel absorb the total impact while walking. Shoes with good shock-absorbing qualities are crucial, and orthoses may be needed for extra support.

Getting Treatment for Gout

Yet another inborn condition that can lead to foot problems concerns how your body deals with uric acid. The inner workings of some people either produce too much uric acid or can't remove what's created. The result is a metabolic disease called gout, in which crystals of the uric acid accumulate in body joints, often the joint of the big toe.

Gout attacks are sudden and very painful, and even the weight of a bed sheet on a swollen, gouty toe can be agonizing. The condition, a form of arthritis, is most prevalent in middle-aged men and often runs in families.

In some susceptible people, foods such as sardines, shellfish, anchovies, liver, sweetbreads, and the like, which are high in substances known as purines, can trigger a uric acid increase and a gout attack, as can alcohol and some medications.

Besides suggesting dietary changes, a doctor may prescribe an anti-inflammatory medication or one that controls uric acid levels. In rare cases, repeated attacks can leave a toe stiff, and surgery or orthoses may be required.

Nails You Shouldn't Pound

Your toenails are protective devices that occasionally cause discomfort if not properly cared for. Ingrown toenails are the most common and painful nail condition, occurring when the side of the nail digs into the skin. Improper nail cutting is generally the cause, although a toe injury or fungal infection can also trigger problems.

Ingrown toenails can be easily avoided by using good, clean clippers designed to cut the nail straight across—not rounded to match the shape of the toe and not too short. Many ingrown nails result from picking or ripping the nails, which usually leaves a small piece, known as a spicule, to easily grow into the skin. Cutting into the corners of your nails can also lead to spicule formation.

To help relieve some of the discomfort until you can get to a podiatrist, soak your foot in lukewarm water to soften the nail, then tuck a small wisp of cotton between the offending nail edge and the skin. "This provides temporary relief but does nothing to cure the problem," says Dr. Brenner. "It also doesn't do any good to cut a V in the center of the nail. The nail won't grow toward the center and away from the ingrown edge, as some people believe. All nails grow from back to front only."

Over-the-counter remedies that contain tannic acid may help

toughen the skin on the side of the nail and resist ingrowing in some cases. Avoid remedies that contain other kinds of acids, because they often are too harsh.

Injured toenails are just as common because so many people drop things on their feet. The nails turn black and blue, and the pressure from blood collecting under the nail is quite painful. While there are several home remedies that have been around for years, consult a podiatrist, who will use an electronic needle or drill to safely relieve the pressure.

Your toenails can also turn black and blue if they stub against your shoe during activity, in which case either the nails are too long, or more likely, your shoes don't fit. (For tips on good fit see the shoe chapter, beginning on page 154.)

Special Care for Vulnerable Feet

While foot self-care is important to all, the elderly and people with diabetes have special concerns.

After decades of use and abuse, older people's feet are highly vulnerable to problems like injury and infections. Half of all podiatrists' patients are senior citizens.

Perhaps the most common foot malady affecting the elderly is osteoarthritis, which results from chronic wear of bones and joints. It's often felt in the joints in the ball of the foot. A bunion is a more dramatic form of osteoarthritis.

While your podiatrist or physician may prescribe an anti-inflammatory drug, ordinary aspirin is still one of the safest, most effective means of relief. Soaking your feet in warm water and Epsom salts or a whirlpool helps loosen joints. Afterward, dry your feet and take a short walk. Walking forces the joints of the feet to stay more active, which is crucial to any arthritis prevention and treatment program. Try to walk each day, with the range depending on the severity of your condition.

It's also wise to avoid overexertion and standing for long periods of time, since overstressed muscles can lead to severe cramps in the arch area of the foot. Occasional cramps are common in older feet and legs, but if they are a chronic problem, it could be a symptom of poor circulation and a signal to visit the doctor.

"If you know the cramp is from plain old stress, working it out by kneading the muscle is fine," says Dr. McCrea. But if you're not sure, check with your doctor to make sure it's not poor circulation or phlebitis.

Stretching exercises can prevent the cramps that many older people experience in their feet and legs after going to bed. Dr. McCrea suggests you stand at arm's length from a wall, with your hands on the wall at shoulder height, then lean into the wall, keeping your feet flat on the floor for a count of ten.

Similarly, swollen ankles could be a sign of congestive heart problems. Feet insensitive to pain or temperature extremes may be signaling diabetes or other conditions that affect the neurovascular system. Consistently cold feet might be the result of a circulatory disease or hardening of the arteries.

"Almost all systemic diseases may show signs on the feet first," Dr. Klombers says. "The early signs of the cancer associated with AIDS are also found on the lower extremities."

Diabetes Alert

"People with diabetes often suffer from premature hardening of the arteries, which causes poor circulation and nerve insensitivity in their feet," says Dr. Brenner, who also specializes in diabetic foot care. "There's little or no feeling, and as a result, infection is a constant and serious danger."

Anything that restricts circulation should be avoided, which means wear roomy socks and shoes and avoid garters and rolled hose. Walking is an excellent way to improve circulation, which in turn helps prevent the cold feet that often come with poor circulation. Exercise also helps lower blood sugar, says Dr. Brenner. "I can't emphasize enough the importance of exercise."

Keeping feet warm and dry also aids circulation, and for cold nights, he recommends bed socks instead of electric blankets or heating pads that could burn insensitive feet. Avoid over-the-counter corn or callus treatments, because the chemicals are too harsh for a diabetic's sensitive skin.

"If you're a diabetic, you should never cut corns or calluses, because the risk of injury and infection is too great," he adds. "In general, avoid any kind of foot self-care and let a doctor tend to your needs."

Let someone inspect your feet daily for injuries, to make sure no potential problems are overlooked. Moisturizing lotion should be routinely applied to prevent skin cracking.

Most important of all, treat your diabetes, follow your diet, and take your medication, when prescribed.

An Open-and-Closed Case for Surgery

If you go to a podiatrist and find that surgery is in order, you'll also find that there are two distinct techniques currently being used.

One is conventional foot surgery, in which the surgeon makes an incision that opens up the area. It's usually performed in hospitals but may be performed in an office or ambulatory care setting and is used to correct major foot deformities, such as replacing joints or remodeling bone structure.

The other is an approach known as minimal-incision surgery, which is often performed in a doctor's office. A small incision is made and a tiny dental-type drill is used to grind off bone. Unlike conventional "open" surgery, where the surgeon can see the area in question, the minimal procedure is considered "closed" because the surgeon can't view the bone. Closed surgery is reserved for less complex procedures, such as removing bone spurs on toes. The patient saves time and money, there's no overnight stay in a hospital, and the recovery time may be shorter.

"The technique performed on your foot depends on several factors, including your age and health status, the severity of the problem, and whether you have any condition that could increase the risk of complications," says Dr. Klombers.

If you do have surgery on your feet, there are several things to keep in mind.

■ Most foot surgery is elective. Agree to an operation only after more conservative therapies have been exhausted.

■ Avoid having surgery on the same day a problem is diagnosed. Go home and think about it, and get a second opinion if you prefer. The only type of surgical procedure that should be performed during an initial visit is one to resolve an acute condition, such as removal of an ingrown toenail.

■ Consider surgery primarily for pain relief or to correct deformities to help you walk better.

Checkups Just for Feet

You'd probably consult a podiatrist if any foot ailment becomes severe, persists, or recurs. But a regular foot checkup isn't something usually found at the top of most people's health-care lists.

"The public's not tuned in to general foot care or to having a routine foot exam," says Dr. Klombers. "And most M.D.s have you strip for an examination, but not take your shoes off. It's as if your body stops just above the ankles. If more people had their feet checked regularly, we'd be able to prevent a lot of serious problems."

Cancer can show early symptoms as foot sores. The signs to watch for are the same as for cancers elsewhere on the body: changes in skin color, tone, or temperature; change in size of any sore; bleeding of a sore for no obvious reason; a sore that spreads in size or number; and a sore that does not seem to heal.

Walk Your Way to Stronger Feet

How do your feet shape up? The stronger your feet, the better your chances of warding off problems.

Any good foot self-care program should include walking, one of the best ways to strengthen and keep feet in shape. "Walking is great for the feet and the total person," says Gary Gordon, D.P.M., of Glenside, Pennsylvania, whose specialty is sports and feet.

If you're starting a fitness regimen that includes walking, Dr. Gordon advises that you begin slowly. "If you have no history of medical problems, walk for 30 to 60 minutes four times a week. After three months, if you're ready, increase your workout time."

In general, take brisk walks with long strides. Wear good walking shoes that support and cushion your heel. Use soft, thick socks and allow your shoes to dry thoroughly between walks.

Try walking barefoot occasionally on sand or grass, but be careful of sharp objects.

Footbaths to Delight Your Feet

Want to have an *aprés* walking party that's sure to delight your favorite walking partners? Set up some aromatic footbaths that will soothe their feet while providing a psychological lift.

As far as easing tired feet goes, plain old warm water will do the trick. But to increase the sensuous quality of the experience, try adding aromatic herbs to the water.

The simplest way to add aroma is to purchase small bottles of essential oils. Add a few drops of the oil to warm water and plunge those tootsies in. Since we're not talking medicinal value, whatever appeals to your sense of smell is the right choice. These essential oils are strong—a drop or two per footbath is plenty. A ¼-ounce bottle will last a long time.

If you'd like to brew your own bath essence, take a muslin bag or an old sock, toss in your selection of dried herbs or flowers, and steep it in a quart of hot water. Then add the water to your footbath. Use lavender, rose petals, lemon peel, sandalwood, verbena, virtually anything you like. You can even raid the kitchen spice rack and use cinnamon, cloves, thyme, or rosemary.

Ask each friend to bring along a plastic dishpan to soak in. Have a variety of oils on hand so your walking partners can have the fun of making their own selection. Have some money-hungry teens around? Hire them to serve as warm-water bearers. Dress 'em up in togas or in tuxedos for a really fancy affair. They can keep the water warm while your party is walking, and have some tempting beverages to pass out when you get back, too.

If your feet tire easily, exercise them daily and try these routines: Point your toes outward for a few seconds, then flex them inward; alternate standing on tiptoe for a few seconds with normal standing. Repeat each exercise ten times, if possible.

Other exercises for maintaining healthy feet:

■ Strengthen your calf and heel muscles by sitting on the floor with your legs straight ahead, then bend your feet toward you as far as possible.

■ To relieve strain on the arches, rest your weight on the outer borders of your feet, then roll them inward.

■ To ease tightness in your ankles and arches, stand flat on your feet, rise to your toes, and repeat several times.

■ Strengthen your toes and the muscles on top of the foot by sitting in a relaxed position with your bare feet on the floor. Try to pick up a towel, pencil, or marbles with your toes.

Good Samaritan Walking

It's in the Bag

Sometimes invitations to do good works can sound heavy-handed. You admire the concept, but that little kid part of you wants to stick out your chin and say "What's in it for me?" Or maybe just plain "No! I don't want to!" That's why we loved it when Karen Feridun, a former *Prevention* senior researcher, came up with this tongue-in-cheek way to tell the story of Yale professor Lowell Levin, a former *Prevention* adviser who loved to clean up the city while he walked. This approach appeals to the kid in you. Read it and enjoy the story. And hey, don't blame us if you suddenly take to carrying plastic garbage bags occasionally on your neighborhood walks. And remember, somewhere a parrot is probably watching you, too!

The Case of the Walking Pickup Artist

I had just tied up the loose ends of a forgery case in the city and was heading up to Connecticut for a little R&R.

Suddenly, it hit me. I knew there was something wrong. Where were all the beer cans? The plastic cups? The fast-food wrappers? The mufflers? It was all too perfect. Then I saw my answer. A guy with a dog, picking up garbage. As I got closer, I slowed down. He was a classy-looking guy. No con on work release. I could see that something fishy was going on here. My vacation would have to wait. That's the life of a private eye.

I decided to look up an old friend they call the Parrot. I don't know where he got the name. Maybe because, if the price is right, that bird would talk.

"Parrot, what can you tell me about a guy across town who picks up litter from sidewalks?"

"Who wants to know?" He had seen too many movies. So I slipped him a new addition to his collection of greenbacks.

"Yeah, I know the guy you mean. Works with a dog. He's a professor over at the university."

"So how much does he get for moonlighting as a garbage man?"

"No, man, you got it all wrong. He doesn't do it for cash; he does it because it makes him feel good."

Now John Q. Public might buy that story hook, line, and sinker, but a flatfoot like me can spot a con game a mile away. I told the Parrot to come clean with me. He told me to get it from the horse's mouth if I didn't believe him.

His name was Lowell Levin, professor of public health at Yale University—the big time! When I called, I got right to the point.

"Where were you at precisely 8:02 this morning?"

"Walking. I walk every morning around that time."

"What if I were to tell you that I saw you picking up garbage this morning?" I had him now.

"That's true." I didn't expect him to break so easily.

"Nice guy with a nice job cleaning the streets? What gives?"

"Well, I started picking up garbage about 12 years ago. I was already walking my dog, so I thought I'd make my walking a more conscious effort. You know, walk for fitness, but that only satisfies me. It does nothing for the community. So I realized, 'Here I am, fitness walking through a garbage dump!' I found I felt better walking while doing something for the community. Not just for me."

I could tell he was sincere. I'd have to apologize to the Parrot.

He was a part-time philosopher, too. "I think you can't distinguish outdoors from indoors. I wouldn't throw junk on my living room floor. What kind of people open their car windows and throw out their garbage? It's where they live. It's not like it's another world or like the stuff will go away. But it does go away because I follow them and pick it up. My worst offenders must wonder where all that junk is they threw out the day before."

I was feeling pretty guilty about the coffee cup I'd tossed out my window that morning.

"I find all sorts of things—lots of food wrappers, plastic jugs, car parts, shoes, diapers, baby bottles, baby clothing, rattles. Enough stuff to open a baby boutique. Love letters. I read one that was so juicy that, before I realized it, I had walked 10 feet beyond my driveway!

"Lots of what I find is seasonal. I don't need to look at a calendar to tell what part of the year it is: I just look at the garbage."

"Well, I guess I owe you an apology for thinking you were up to something suspicious," I said.

"Don't worry about it. Many times eyes follow me across the street as I carry 25 pounds worth of tailpipes, tires, and other assorted garbage. I'll carry anything I can, especially if it could be hazardous if left on the ground.

"I had some trouble with City Hall. When I called to ask them to put a garbage can at the end of my walk route, they thought I was pulling some sort of prank. They finally believed me and obliged."

"You're an all-right guy. By the way, you think I could find anything valuable if I gave it a go?" I asked.

"It's not for someone who's looking for excitement and treasure. The real reward is in knowing that people never have to see how bad it was before you cleaned up. That makes me feel good. And that's not a bad thing."

Clues Lead to New Suspects

I was hooked. I had to find out if there were more Lowell Levins out there. I started digging and didn't come up empty-handed.

Roberta Westbrook, a *Prevention* Walking Club member in Livermore, California, is another person who gives new meaning to the words "pickup artist." "I've been walking with a friend for years," she says. "At first, we did it to lose weight; now we do it just to feel good. Then we started picking up cans for a friend's grandson to recycle. We net 30 or 40 cans per day. Now I kind of consider myself the Livermore bag lady."

"Do you ever find anything, say, valuable in your travels?" I had still not completely abandoned the idea of a second career.

"I think the most valuable things I find are the birds, trees, and beautiful flowers I get to look at."

June Mills, of Olalla, Washington, another *Prevention* Walking Club member (is this a cult?), told me about her "combo walk." "I've been walking and collecting cans for about 12 years now. 'Combo' is short for combination, the variety of benefits I get from a walk. It benefits my health, plus I get financial rewards when I turn in the cans at a recycling center, and the countryside has its face improved."

You might say the trail of cans led me to yet another club member, Nancy Clay, of Sierra Vista, Arizona.

"I'm retired and I walk between 2½ and 3 miles a day. I started collecting cans by putting a cardboard box next to the soda machine at work. I still pick them up as I walk. Whatever I find, I give to the 'Golden Agers,' a local senior citizens' group. They use the recycling money they get for monthly outings.

"I'm getting pretty good at spotting cans. My daughter says I've got radar, I can spot 'em so far away!"

I was all mixed up. These folks were swell in my book. But they made me nervous. They all seemed to have the kind of eagle eyes you have to have in the detective business. Competition was the last thing I needed.

I decided to think it all out over a cup of java. I was on my way to a favorite hole-in-the-wall when I spied a milk carton on the sidewalk. Just getting it out of my sight and into a trash can made me feel like a million bucks. And Levin was right. That's not a bad thing.

Gremlins

Chasing Away Minor Distractions and Inconveniences

Walking is a pretty care-free exercise. The kinds of things that distract you often don't seem bothersome enough to send you questing for a solution. But why let a few unpleasant details or minor fears spoil your enjoyment of a summer walk?

We asked walkers at Rodale Press for a list of their personal "walking gremlins," the little things that disturb their enjoyment of taking a summer stroll or a speedwalk around the park. Then we called the experts to find out: Should we worry about this? Can we do anything to prevent it? Or should we just say "Oh yeah, that again!" and keep walking?

Here are ten of the most worrisome problems Rodale walkers had. We hope our suggestions help to banish some of your walking gremlins!

Swollen Hands

You step out for a brisk walk and after 15 minutes or so, your hands feel like balloons. They're red, puffy and—if you're wearing any rings—choking! Many walkers wonder if this is a symptom of disease, a sign of water retention, or poor circulation. Don't worry! As long as this swelling occurs only when you walk, it's just the centrifugal force of your arm movement forcing blood into your hands. For greater comfort, leave your rings at home. If the feeling of swollen hands disturbs you, try walking with your elbows bent for a while. When you stop walking, your hands should resume their former size and shape!

Sudden Storms

Summer showers can come on quickly and without much warning. While the always-prepared types may carry a rain jacket in a pouch, most of us simply get soaked. Is it a problem? Not according to Murray Hamlet, director of the Cold Research Program at the U.S. Army Research Institute of Environmental Medicine in Massachusetts.

"If you're not in danger of getting lost and being exposed for a long period of time, getting soaked doesn't put you at risk for hypothermia," says Hamlet. "Just cover up as best you can and keep walking. The exercise will keep your body warm enough."

Worried about catching a cold? Save your energy. Wet hair or clothing and raw weather may aggravate existing symptoms but they won't make you sick, says Richard Clover, M.D., of the University of Oklahoma Health Sciences Center. According to Dr. Clover, when it comes to colds, you should worry more about whom you shake hands with than the weather. Colds are caused by viruses, which are often transmitted by something as simple as a handshake.

If the sudden storm includes lightning, beware of standing under isolated trees, in open fields, near tractors or heavy equipment, or near water. Those are the places where most people in the United States have been hit—1,953 people were killed between 1959 and 1987. Thirty-one were killed at telephones. If you find yourself in a wide-open space with thunder booming and daggers of lightning slashing the skies, don't lie flat on the ground. Drop to your knees, bend forward, and put your hands on your knees.

If a storm is brewing and you literally feel your hair stand on end, a close hit may be imminent. Take precautions. Lightning can hit miles from the parent cloud. Find the lowest spot or shelter under a group of trees, not an isolated one. If you're walking with a group, spread out. You'll present less of a target.

Angry Dogs

During the summer months, many dogs are allowed outside by owners who aren't aware that their friendly house pet may become a snarling wolf dog around strangers. But dogs are territorial, and they often learn to consider the sidewalk and street around their home as their turf. In fact, that's where most bites occur.

Don't ever underestimate the viciousness of a strange dog. Most bites occur with people who have their own pets or had them as children, according to Alan Beck, Sc.D., director of the Center for Applied Ethology and Human/Animal Interaction at Purdue University School of Veterinary Medicine. People who have had an affectionate relationship with a dog tend to assume they can approach a strange animal.

If you can avoid areas where you know dogs are loose, do so. Or you may want to call the local authorities and find out what the leash laws are and report violations. If you do come face-to-face with a strange dog, avoid eye contact. It's seen as a challenge by the dog. If the dog's ears and hackles (the fur along the back of his neck and back) are up, if he is growling or baring his teeth, slowly back off. If he persists in coming toward you, yell at him: "Go home!" Put something between you and the dog. Offer a stick or even a cassette player, rather than your hand or arm for protection. A commercial dog repellent can be very effective. Don't be afraid to use it.

If you happen to be walking your own dog and you see a stray dog coming, turn around and walk the other way. If a fight does ensue, stay out of it, or you'll most likely get bitten. Try distraction. Throw something at them—your hat or a stick. According to Dr. Beck, squirting them with a water pistol often works. It's the next best thing to the old bucket-of-water trick.

Pesky Yellow Jackets

Ever wonder why yellow jackets seem to be dive-bombing you with more tenacity toward the end of the summer? The pesky critters are searching for sugar to feed the emerging queens and males in the nest, according to Peter J. Landolt, Ph.D., entomologist with the U.S. Department of Agriculture's laboratory at the University of Florida. They are attracted to flowery perfumes, and the color they like best is yellow! So leave that Hawaiian shirt at home!

Don't try to swat them if they're disturbing your peace. If you squash the venom sac, a substance is released that calls in all their buddies for an attack. Just keep walking. Chances are, if they can't find any sugar on you, they'll move on to sweeter pastures.

If you do get stung, be prepared to flee. Yellow jackets can strike again. Head indoors, into water, or into the woods. They'll have trouble following you into a thicket.

To deal with the pain out on a walk, a cool stream would be convenient. At home, an ice pack rubbed on the area can prevent the venom from spreading and cut down on swelling. If you're allergic to bee stings, they can be dangerous. Carry your insect-sting kit. Symptoms of an allergic reaction to a sting are chest tightness, hives, nausea, vomiting, wheezing, dizziness, swollen tongue or face, fainting, or shock. The more rapidly these symptoms appear, the more life-threatening they are. Have someone take you to an emergency medical service immediately.

Side Stitches

While walking briskly, you suddenly experience a stabbing pain in your side. A torn muscle? A gallbladder attack? Probably not. Side stitches are caused by a spasm of the diaphragm, a muscle between your chest and your abdomen. The muscle is crying out for oxygen because your expanded lungs and contracted abdomen are blocking normal blood flow. Not to worry. At the first sign of pain, stop walking. Using three fingers, press on the area where the pain is greatest until it stops hurting. Or gently massage the area. Often these simple techniques are enough to relieve the pain. Don't hold your breath! As your breathing resumes a regular pace, the ache should also subside. And you can resume your walk.

Remember to warm up by walking slowly when you start out. Going too fast too soon can cause your diaphragm to cramp, just like any other muscle that is not warmed up properly.

Shinsplints

You're walking through the park on the nice, flat macadam path, heel-and-toeing along, when suddenly the front of your lower leg begins to burn. Or maybe when you got up this morning your shins were sore from yesterday's walk. Nobody is exactly sure what shinsplints are, according to Marjorie Albohm, associate director of the International Institute of Sports Science and Medicine at the Indiana University School of Medicine. But don't worry, we do know what to do about them.

If possible, walk on a soft surface. If you can't change to grass or dirt, try upgrading your shoes. Look for walking shoes that feature plenty of shock absorption and arch support. After you've done a little slow walking to warm up, stretch your calf muscles. Stretching relieves stress on your shins. Lean against a pole or wall, place one foot back, and gently lower your heel to the ground. Repeat 20 times with each leg.

When pain hits, apply ice and elevate your legs for 20 to 30 minutes.

Sometimes you can avoid shinsplints by strengthening the muscles around the shin. One easy way for walkers to do this is to spend some time walking around on their heels. If you've been working out on a stationary bike all winter, you've also been building protection from shin pain.

How can you tell when it's not a shinsplint but a stress fracture that you're dealing with? A fracture has a specific point of pain on or around a bony area, about the size of a dime or quarter. You literally are able to put your finger on it. If you even suspect a fracture, see your doctor.

Chafing Thighs

Shorts feel great in the summertime, except for one thing. Take away the protective material that long pants provide and sweaty thighs rubbing against each other may cause chafing. The solution? Try rubbing some petroleum jelly on your inner thighs. You'll be protected from moisture and friction.

Bathroom Urgencies

Everybody can identify with the little kid bundled in the snowsuit who tells his mom at the last minute that he has to go to the bathroom. Being a half mile from home can be the summer equivalent of a snowsuit if you're out for a walk and the urge to "go" hits. Don't worry, the first sign of the need to empty your bladder is an early warning signal, according to Lester Klein, M.D., at the Scripps Clinic Urology Division. That signal usually fades if you keep walking. You have time to play with. The next time you feel the urge, your body is saying "Hey! Things are getting serious here." And you'd better start heading for home. The third sensor is pain. Don't let things go that far.

You have to learn your body's personal limits. Most people can walk for an hour without a problem. If you can't, you may have to make smaller circuits near your home or stop at a restroom facility in a park. On a hot day, try drinking water an hour or so before your walk to avoid dehydration. You'll probably be able to empty your bladder of excess water just before you walk. If you're going for a short walk, under an hour, rehydrate when you return. If it's going to be more than an hour, take water along and make sure you're able to empty your bladder when you need to.

If you have health problems, check with your doctor before walking outside on a hot day. He may recommend mallwalking. (Bathroom facilities are usually available.)

Sunscreen Sting

To protect your skin, summer and winter, wear a sunscreen. In the summer, when you're more likely to be sweating a lot, sunscreen may rub off, or worse, roll or be rubbed into your eyes. Take tissues to wipe it away, or wear sweatbands around your forehead and wrists.

Sunscreens may not be harmful to your eyes, but they can create a painful burning sensation. Look for sunscreens that are waterproof or water-resistant. They are less likely to sweat off during a walking workout.

Creative Urges

Walking enhances creativity. That's great, right? When you're out walking, you may be bombarded with wonderful ideas. The quandary is, should you carry a pen and paper to write them down? Can your walk be as stress reducing if you're busy solving your own or everybody else's problems, or redesigning the kitchen?

It's probably true that walking puts you in an optimal mood for problem solving, according to Robert Thayer, Ph.D., professor of psychology at California State University, Long Beach, and author of *The Biopsychology of Mood and Arousal*. And if that's your goal, by all means carry paper! However, if you're suffering from anxious thoughts or are under a lot of stress, it's probably best, says Dr. Thayer, to leave your paper at home and try to forget your problems. Allow the walk to distract you. Concentrate on the scenery or perhaps on your breathing. Allow intruding thoughts to surface, but don't focus on them. In effect, don't worry, keep walking!

Headaches
A Prescription for Relief

There aren't too many people who can say they never get headaches. Most people, especially those who get them often, have a set way of dealing with them, like two aspirin and a nap, or a hot shower, or just toughing it out. Here's Maggie Spilner's personal account of an alternative headache remedy she literally stumbled upon:

Every once in a while, I am the unlucky recipient of a migraine headache. When I get them, I always wonder how people who get them often survive. My first thought is aspirin, my second is suicide. The pain usually begins at the base of my skull, and before long I can't tell which is worse—my pounding head or my churning stomach. I remember spending one night staring at the seconds passing on a digital clock for 4 hours, incapable of thought or action. Once I had to call a friend to come over and cook supper for my kids, because the thought of smelling food was overwhelming.

Walking It Off

But shortly after I became the walking editor for *Prevention,* in 1986, I tried something new. I was at a family gathering, sipping a glass of wine, when my head began to pound. I slipped away from the party, took a couple of aspirin, and lay down. (Aspirin doesn't work for me with these kinds of headaches. It's just a knee-jerk reaction that I follow with a prayer.) But I was so very uncomfortable, I just couldn't lie still. In the past year, walking had become an everyday sort of thing. I decided to try doing just that. At the very least, it might distract me from concentrating on my pounding head. I stumbled down the stairs and out the back door. My shoulders were hunched and my sweaty hands were clenched against the pain. I literally staggered up the street. Too dazed to decide on a particular destination, I just walked up and down the block, thinking only about keeping my legs moving.

Two things happened. First of all, the walking helped to reduce my nausea by bringing up gas that was being created by tightness in my stomach. As the tension began to dissolve, the normal relaxation effect of walking dropped my shoulders and eased my scrunched-up neck. I began to breathe deeply, another automatic relaxer. After about 45 minutes of walking, the nausea and headache were gone!

A Two-Edged Sword

Intrigued by my personal discovery, I called Seymour Diamond, M.D., director of the Diamond Headache Clinic in Chicago, to ask if moderate exercise is commonly prescribed to treat the symptoms of migraines. According to Dr. Diamond, exercise is a two-edged sword for migraine or cluster headache sufferers. For some people it relieves pain; for others, it intensifies it. He recommends that his patients try it to find out if it works for them.

How does it work? Dr. Diamond feels that the body's natural painkillers (known as endorphins), which are released during exercise, may be helping. And also that the general relaxation effect may also contribute to a lessening of pain.

There is nothing quite like the peace you feel when a devastating headache subsides. Next time one strikes, see if a little walking can move you toward that relief a little sooner. It's important to be conscious of your posture and your tense areas. Gently roll your shoulders to loosen them. As they relax, feel the tension in your neck ease up. Stand tall. Try not to walk with your head down, or leaning forward, as that will just add strain to your neck and lower back. Take deep breaths and let your arms swing naturally. If the pain of your headache increases, stop walking.

Heart Health

Improve Your Odds

Every 60 seconds, someone in America dies of a heart attack. Heart disease is the leading cause of death in North America, outnumbering cancer and accidents combined.

The old news is that regular exercise reduces your risk of heart disease. The new news is that you don't have to work yourself into the ground to get this benefit. Walking regularly is all it takes.

A study of 5,930 men and women, for example, showed that those who regularly performed an easy-does-it exercise like walking had more healthy-heart factors going for them than sedentary people. In general, moderate exercisers were less overweight and had lower blood pressures and lower cholesterol and triglyceride levels than their less-active peers.

A major study involving over 12,000 men who were at risk for developing heart disease was done at the University of Minnesota

Walking to Recovery

R alph Riemer, 45, was working as a respiratory equipment technician at St. Mary's Hospital in Rochester, Minnesota, when he began to have chest pains. He'd had similar symptoms for weeks, each time he walked up a long ramp at the hospital. This time though, the pain didn't disappear when he sat down to rest; his arms and neck started to ache, too. Riemer headed for the emergency room, where his fears were confirmed: He was having a heart attack.

Tests revealed that Riemer had two blocked arteries. Both were opened with balloon angioplasty. Then, at his doctor's behest, Riemer began doing something he'd been postponing for years: He started to exercise.

Within days of his heart attack, he was given an exercise treadmill test. A week later, he started working out on a treadmill at a nearby cardiac rehabilitation center. From there, he started walking around his neighborhood. At first, he put in about a mile a day. Eventually, he worked up to 5 miles a day, at least three times a week.

"I start everyone off walking; it's integral to our cardiac rehabilitation program," says William Freeman, M.D., Riemer's doctor at the Mayo Clinic. "Most people we see are very out of shape. So we have to ease them into exercise very slowly. Our incremental walking program, which continues for at least four to six months after the heart attack, does just that. Many patients enjoy walking so much that they continue indefinitely."

The American Heart Association agrees that many heart patients can benefit, as long as they have their doctor's go-ahead.

Reimer has lost 30 pounds; his cholesterol and triglyceride numbers are now in the safe range; his resting pulse rate has dropped 30 points. "It's nice to have a second chance," he says. I haven't felt this good in years."

School of Public Health. The researchers spent seven years monitoring the men and found that the men who were least active had a 30 percent greater chance of death from heart attacks than moderately active men. Moderately active means walking—as well as bicycling, fishing, bowling, gardening, yard work, home repairs, dancing, and swimming. When you're talking about walking, that doesn't mean 12-minute miles. That means a comfortably brisk pace for as little as a half hour a day. It's a good idea to fall in love with walking. Walking loves you back!

A Lifetime Habit

In a world of moderate-but-mighty workouts, walking has emerged as the favorite. Maybe because the news got around that a brisk walk is as good for your cardiovascular system as more strenuous exercise, like jogging, or because experts have been saying that just a few minutes a day, three or more days a week, is enough to do your heart a lot of good. But probably it's a favorite because it's an exercise that can become a way of life. People can keep walking for the rest of their lives. And when it comes to exercising for a healthier heart, that's exactly what's needed.

If you don't get any exercise, your chances of having a heart attack are more than tripled, according to studies from the University of North Carolina at Chapel Hill. The studies confirm that a lack of fitness is itself a major independent risk factor for heart disease. To put that risk factor in perspective, the Chapel Hill researchers point out that an inactive person's risk of heart disease is the same as that of someone who smokes a pack of cigarettes a day.

Reducing Mental Anguish

Being fit makes a physical workout less of an effort for our hearts. There is evidence that aerobic fitness also makes it easier for our hearts to withstand psychological stress.

Both fit and unfit people were subjected to the mental stress of an arithmetic test. Meanwhile, researchers at the University of Toronto monitored both the rate and the electrical activity of their hearts.

"Even with this mild challenge, we saw a reliable difference in the electrical activity of the heart," says John Furedy, Ph.D., head of the laboratory where the study was run.

The change was in the amplitude of the heart's T wave. This "wave" occurs when the heart is pumping and pulling new blood in. The change indicated that, in less fit people, the heart overreacted to "fight or flight" biochemicals, such as adrenaline, that are produced during psychological stress.

A Doctor's Walking Prescription

Dean Ornish, M.D., author of *Dr. Dean Ornish's Program for Reversing Heart Disease,* is a firm believer in moderate exercise. "The equivalent of walking a half hour to an hour a day, according to the latest research, causes the greatest reduction in mortality," he notes.

Dr. Ornish recommends 3 hours of walking a week, either ½ hour a day or 1 hour three times a week, to maintain heart health. Other doctors say that less strenuous programs can be helpful.

Take Steps to Protect Yourself

Want to manufacture your own drug to combat stroke and heart disease? You can do so by taking a daily walk. According to John Stratton, M.D., of Seattle Veterans Administration Medical Center, regular vigorous exercise increases the activity of a natural clot-dissolving protein produced in your blood vessels—tissue plasminogen activator (TPA). Blood clots can block arteries, causing heart attacks or strokes.

TPA is the body's natural defense against blood clots. The formation of a clot actually triggers the release of TPA, which works to break down the clots. TPA is so effective in its dissolving abilities that researchers have programmed bacteria to produce it in the lab, and it is sold as a drug to treat heart attack victims.

A lower risk of heart attack may be linked to higher levels of TPA in the blood. In a study by Dr. Stratton and his colleagues, a group of individuals ages 25 to 74 who exercised aerobically for six months increased their TPA levels by an average of 29 percent. More research is needed to determine exactly how rigorous your exercise needs to be to provide this protective effect.

The American College of Physicians, for example, recommends the following program for heart health.

■ Walk briskly for a minimum of 20 minutes a day at least three times per week. Better yet, walk every day.

■ Let your physician advise you of a safe target pulse rate for your exercise.

■ Even if you're subject to angina attacks—chest pains associated with heart disease—you may be able to safely begin a walking program. But it must be done under a doctor's supervision, in a medically supervised setting, if possible, especially if you take medication. (The doctor may recommend monitoring your pulse rate on the basis of a stress test if you have heart disease.) At the first sign of a problem, see your personal physician.

■ If you have a history of angina, don't use weights on your walks and avoid walking outdoors in very cold weather, especially if it's windy. (You can still do your prescribed workout—in the local mall.) Also, don't carry anything weighing more than a few ounces along for fitness walks. Any added strain on the upper extremities can trigger chest pain. If you have chest pains while walking, *stop*—call your doctor immediately. Don't continue your walking program until you've discussed the pain with him or her. If you have been prescribed nitroglycerin, make sure you have it with you.

High Blood Pressure

Coaxing It Down

For years, research has been slowly piling up to show that regular exercise, like walking, may lower blood pressure by 5 to 20 points. Two studies have suggested that your walks may have far more power to lower blood pressure, and do it in more inter-esting ways, than anyone thought.

"Results of this new research could substantially change the way we treat moderate and borderline cases of this very serious problem," says hypertension researcher John Martin, Ph.D., of San Diego State University. "Exercise seems to work more directly in lowering blood pressure than previously had been thought."

Gain without Loss

In one of the new studies, Dr. Martin and his colleagues put 19 sedentary men with mild hypertension (high blood pressure) through either an aerobic exercise program or a "placebo" regimen (slow calisthenics and stretching). After ten weeks, the blood pres-sures of the men in the aerobic group dropped dramatically—from an average of 137/95 at the beginning of the study to 130/85 at the end. That's a change from mild hypertension to high-normal blood pressure. "These drops were significant because they brought our test subjects' readings down out of the range where drug therapy often is considered," Dr. Martin says. The placebo group, on the other hand, actually had a slight increase in blood pressure. And later, when they were placed on the exercise program, they showed similar reductions in blood pressure.

This big improvement in the exercisers was expected, but something else was a pleasant surprise. "Scientists have known for years that losing weight could lower blood pressure," says Dr. Mar-tin. "And they thought that exercise could lower blood pressure only if it also produced substantial weight loss. But that appears not to be the case. Our study found significant blood pressure re-ductions even though participants did not experience sizable de-creases in weight or body fat."

If these findings are borne out by other research, it will mean that exercise has not one but two mechanisms for beating mild hypertension.

Then there was something else. Previous research suggested that it was vigorous exercise that brought blood pressure down. But in this study, the subjects weren't exercising strenuously enough to make profound gains in aerobic endurance. Despite that fact, significant reductions in blood pressure still occurred. Systolic blood pressure (the first number, the measurement of pressure as the heart contracts) fell by 6.4 points and diastolic pressure (the second number, which measures arterial pressure while the heart is at rest) came down by an average of 9.6 points.

"People in our study exercised at levels well within their comfort zone. Their exercise consisted of either walking, cycling, jogging, or doing any combination of these activities for approximately 30 minutes, four times a week," says Dr. Martin. "The subsequent reduction in blood pressure suggests that physical activity of even fairly light intensity may be more helpful against hypertension than previous research has led us to think."

None of this means, though, that reducing body fat and increasing aerobic fitness are not advisable strategies for lowering high blood pressure. "Our research simply suggests that exercise may have valuable effects in normalizing blood pressure that work independently of these two other mechanisms," Dr. Martin says.

Workouts vs. Wonder Drugs

Another study was conducted in conjunction with Johns Hopkins University School of Medicine. In it, 52 men between the ages of 18 and 59 with mild hypertension were asked to exercise regularly for ten weeks while taking either blood pressure medication or a placebo (inactive pill). Sure enough, blood pressure dropped in all the subjects (including those who didn't take medication)— from an average of 145/97 to 131/84. Again, this decrease was achieved without substantial weight loss. The real news here, however, is that the data suggests that aerobic exercise may not be the only kind of workout that can help lower blood pressure. Three days a week, for 50 minutes per workout, the participants in this study walked/jogged or rode a stationary bike and—surprisingly enough— did weight training. It's surprising because weight training tends to raise blood pressure during the actual lifting and so has long been considered too risky an exercise for people with high blood pressure.

"The findings suggest that weight training need not be dangerous if the lifting is kept fairly light," says one of the researchers, Mark Effron, M.D., now with Sinai Hospital in Baltimore. "All of the lifts in our study were performed at 40 percent of a participant's maximal capability, which is a level reported to be associated with acceptable rises in blood pressure." The weight training was done for 30 minutes each session in a circuit fashion, where lifts were done on 20 different variable-resistance machines.

"While we did find that blood pressure was elevated more just after weight training than after the aerobic exercise," says Dr. Effron, "the difference in measurement was only slight.

"What's more, pulse rates were lower during the weight training than during the aerobic activities, so the overall demands being put on the heart by the two types of exercise proved to be roughly the same. That's a significant finding. And it's very encouraging news for the strength conscious."

Also significant in this study is the discovery that blood pressure drugs administered in addition to exercise do not lower blood pressure any more than exercise alone. "Patients engaged in a regular walking program may not need drug therapy for control of mild hypertension," the authors of the study conclude. That's big news for the estimated 40 million Americans with blood pressure readings in the moderately high range (a diastolic pressure of 90 or more). Not all these people could do without medication, but moderate workouts could help many of them get off their drugs or avoid using drugs in the first place.

"They should get complete medical clearance from their doctors first, of course, but if a walking program is approached sensibly, it can be a highly recommendable option to standard drug therapy," Dr. Effron says.

One more interesting piece of evidence uncovered in the study: Although both exercise and the drugs lowered blood pressure equally well, exercise alone actually proved superior to one of the drugs (propranolol) in affecting cholesterol. Exercise lowered total blood cholesterol and low-density lipoprotein (LDL) cholesterol (the heart-clogging kind) and raised high-density lipoprotein (HDL) cholesterol (the beneficial type). (This has been demonstrated in other research, too.)

The Whys of Success

So why is it that high blood pressure yields to a daily walk in the park? Why should firming up the muscles help loosen up the arteries? You might think just the opposite would be true.

"We're not sure yet, but there are some theories," Dr. Martin says. "It may well be that the amount of inactivity many of us have been accustomed to is simply unnatural from a biological stand-point. A certain level of physical movement may be necessary to keep the body's blood pressure–regulating mechanisms working as they should.

"We know, for example, that small arteries can begin to shut down through lack of physical activity and that regulatory hor-mones from the kidneys can be adversely affected. Add the effects of psychological stress that can result from too sedentary a lifestyle and you can begin to see just how extensive the ill effects of too little activity can be."

So if you have high blood pressure and you've been given a green light by your doctor, there's no reason not to take your con-dition "by the horns and wrestle it to the ground" with a sensible walking program. Plan to walk about 30 minutes at least three days a week. And don't forget to implement other blood pres-sure–beating tactics like cutting back on sodium, alcohol, tobacco, and stress.

Added Incentive

So walking can wrestle down blood pressure naturally—and with no side effects other than greater energy, a firmer physique, and a shot in the arm for self-esteem. It's great news.

But the news becomes even greater in light of an important new discovery from researchers at the University of Michigan Hos-pital in Ann Arbor. They found that borderline hypertension—either 140 to 160 systolic or 90 to 95 diastolic—appears to pose greater risks to the cardiovascular system than previously had been thought. A random sampling of 946 people between the ages of 18 and 38 found that those whose blood pressure was in the borderline range (approximately 12 percent of the total group) had signifi-cantly greater cardiovascular abnormalities than the people whose pressure was normal.

Levels of total cholesterol, triglycerides, and insulin all were higher, while HDL cholesterol was lower in the borderline group. The borderline group also showed signs of having less flexible arteries than the normal group, and their hearts showed signs of having lost elasticity and hence pumping power.

"We used to think of borderline hypertension as a gray area, but we now have reason to believe it's darker than we had thought," says study director Steve Julius, M.D. "People with borderline hypertension are likely to be at a significantly greater risk for suffering from cardiovascular disease than people whose pressures are normal. They should make concentrated efforts through exercise, weight control, and restriction of sodium, dietary fat, tobacco, and alcohol to bring their pressures down. Only if these strategies fail should pharmacologic [drug] treatment be considered."

Hiking
Heading for the Hills

If you've been walking the same routes day after day, passing your neighbors' houses so regularly you could deliver the U.S. Mail, maybe you'd enjoy a break from your routine. Maybe it's time to head for the hills!

Hiking means getting away from city streets and enjoying Nature in all her pristine glory. But if you have the idea that hiking means Maine to Georgia on the Appalachian Trail, and nothing less, relax. Hiking is not backpacking. It simply means getting out in the wilderness a little bit and adding a little adventure to your walking routine. You can hike for an hour or for a week. But lots of walkers need to get used to this idea. They feel a little intimidated by hiking clubs and wilderness outfitters.

Getting Ready

Here are some suggestions for beginners to get the feel of hiking without the fear of becoming lost in the woods.

Pick a park. Your nearest state park is a good place to get your feet wet hiking (figuratively speaking). Most have a selection of short, tame trails that won't have you wandering too far from civilization. An easy way to locate one is simply to look at a road map. State parks usually stand out as green areas on the map (state and national forests may also be marked that way). If you're more ambitious, you might want to pick up a guide to state and national parks and forests at the library or a bookstore.

A call to the park ranger ahead of time can help you find out if the area you've chosen has the right hiking trails for your ability. He or she may be able to recommend one that's particularly nice—a trail through blooming laurel in June, or past oodles of ripe blueberries in July, for example. Picking up a trail map at park headquarters can ensure that your first step is in the right direction.

Start small. If you've never hiked before, choose a short jaunt of 20 to 30 minutes on a level trail, to get the feel of it. If you like it, you can tackle longer or more difficult hikes later on. Mount Everest isn't going anywhere. And remember, a mile walk over hill and dale can take two or three times as long as a mile cruise down city sidewalks, so plan conservatively.

Hoof on down to the local hiking store. Most stores that specialize in hiking and recreation equipment have employees with enough experience hiking local trails to make recommendations. They can refer you to the local hiking club, too, where you can hook up with other beginning hikers or benefit from the experience of veterans. The stores usually sell trail maps of hiking areas in your neck of the woods, and guidebooks to go with them. They also sell books that list good walking trails all over the country.

Tap your map. As you get better at hiking, you'll probably want to leave the well-trampled areas and roam a little farther afield. But you'll still want to know where you are! A good map can tell you everything you need to know about a prospective hike: Where can I park? Will the trail cross a stream? Is the hike level or uphill?

Most trail maps have a legend in one corner that identifies the symbols for trails, roads, streams, and other features. They'll have a scale of miles so you can estimate the length of a particular hike.

The maps and guidebooks also tell you which color the trail blazes are. What in blazes are blazes? They're splashes of paint or markers on the trees along the trail. Follow them like ET followed the Reese's Pieces and you're sure to stay on track.

Until you're comfortable finding your way around in the wilds, play it safe: Always turn back if you're not sure of a particular trail. An outing with an experienced hiker is a good time to practice your map reading. He or she can teach you how to read "topo" (topographic) maps. They're the best kind because they show the ups and downs as well as the easts and wests.

Practice self-gratification. Just walking in the woods can be its own reward. But many hikers look for a bigger payoff: a spectacular view, a waterfall, a rushing stream, or a campsite at which to picnic. Maps and guidebooks usually provide those details about the trails so you can plan your route accordingly. Here's another hint: Look for circuit hikes—routes that loop around so you can start and end at the same spot without covering any ground twice. You'll get to see more than if you hike out to a destination, then backtrack on the same trail. And you'll feel as if you've really been somewhere.

Pamper your feet. Comfortable, sturdy walking shoes are fine for easy, level hikes, but lightweight hiking boots with cushiony socks are better once you graduate to more rugged trails. Remember that it can be much cooler in the mountains; pack accordingly. Dress in layers so you can put on or peel off clothes as the temperature changes. If you're going to be out for hours, take a poncho.

A day pack can hold the extra clothes and other necessities: a plastic water bottle, your maps and snacks, or a picnic lunch. Al Fresco's Restaurant is charming, and there's never a wait. Sandwiches, nuts, raisins, granola bars, and apples all travel well.

Hike on vacation. Don't forget your vacation as a way to expand your hiking horizons. That's when you have the time to travel to some truly breathtaking destinations. National parks and forests have well-worn, well-marked trails, knowledgeable rangers, and some of the most striking panoramas you can imagine.

Hill Striding

Getting Fit Faster

You're walking along at a brisk, 4-mile-per-hour pace, your arms swinging, head held high, feeling great and talking a blue streak to your walking partner. All of a sudden, you notice that your heart is thumping and your conversation is stalling between gasps for breath.

What happened? A hill. While it began so gradually that your eyes hardly noticed, your body certainly did! As a matter of fact, while you were gabbing your way up that grade, your body was revving up to a 45 percent increase in calorie burn!

To get fit in record time, find the path of most resistance. Walking uphill is a great way for walkers to increase their level of cardiovascular fitness and burn more calories in a shorter amount of time. Just look at these figures: If you walk at a 4-mile-an-hour pace, after 2 miles (½ hour) on a level grade, you'll have burned approximately 225 calories. Change to a 5 percent grade—the ground is rising 5 feet for every 100 feet you travel—and you'll burn 325 calories. Make that a 10 percent grade and you bump your calorie burn up to 425, and at 20 percent you're burning 625 calories every half hour!

Make Sure You're Up to the Challenge

Many people avoid hills for fear of overexerting themselves. And it's true that walking uphill places greater strain on the cardiovascular system. So be sure to proceed slowly at first and slow down if you feel any discomfort.

Start out with a very gradual slope. If a steep grade is all you have, stop as often as you need to catch your breath. Try walking uphill for a few minutes and then turn around and walk down. Expect to feel some muscle soreness after your first few tries at hill walking, particularly in the front of your leg and your Achilles tendon.

Continued problems with fatigue and shortness of breath should be evaluated by your physician, according to Peter Hanson, M.D., director of cardiac rehabilitation at the University of Wisconsin Hospital and Clinic. But being able to carry on a conversation comfortably is a good way to check on your level of exertion. Walking alone? Have a few words with yourself. If you're gasping to get them out, you're going too fast.

It's a great feeling to master a hill, to go from having to stop every 20 yards to rest to striding all the way to the top nonstop. Psychologist and weight-loss expert John Pleas, Ph.D., suggests selecting a particular hill to conquer and naming it something challenging like "Mini Mt. Everest" or "Energy Incline."

If you live in the Midwest and anthills are about the closest thing to an incline you ever see, then you might want to consider stair climbing as a boost to your walking workouts. Stairs are the equivalent of a 50 percent incline, so you'll want to go slowly. And remember to stretch out those calves afterward.

Walking up hills is great when you really want to work up a sweat and you don't have much time. Have to cram your usual 4-mile routine into a ½-hour time slot? Do a 2-mile stint uphill and consider yourself exercised!

Injury and Overuse

Avoiding the Down Side

Walking is the safest, simplest exercise available. Yet, while its hazards are few, what you don't know *can* hurt you. Here are four problem areas of pain or discomfort, other than blisters, and what you can do to help prevent them. (See the blister chapter, beginning on page 14 for tips on prevention and treatment.)

Banishing Heel Pain

When you get up in the morning, do your heels feel painful and sore as you hit the floor? Heel pain that is most noticeable in the morning or after long periods of inactivity is often plantar fasciitis (*PLAN-tar fassy-EYE-tiss*), an inflammation of the ligament-like tissue on the bottom of the foot that helps to keep your arch in good form. Your arch is your body's built-in shock absorber.

When you walk, your foot pronates slightly, which means your arch flattens and your foot leans inward. If you pronate too much, the tissue can get overstretched and pain and tenderness result.

This type of heel pain can be prevented by wearing good, stable walking shoes that do not allow a lot of pronation, according to Stephen Weinberg, D.P.M., attending podiatrist in sports medicine at Columbus Hospital in Chicago. A good walking shoe should provide ample arch support and the lacing system should fit comfortably but snugly, helping to hold your foot straight.

"Good arch support is more important in a walking shoe than lots of cushioning for shock absorption," says Dr. Weinberg. That's because walking does not pound the body or the foot, as does running. However, when you walk for exercise, you spend lots of time on your feet and that puts pressure and strain on your natural shock absorbers.

Sidestepping Shinsplints

If you've ever been an overeager walker, you know what shinsplints are—those burning pains in the front of your lower leg or shin that can leave you limping for the nearest park bench. Shinsplints are a going-too-fast-too-soon injury. Your muscles start cramping up from overuse.

You have to let your body tell you how fast is too fast. That can be frustrating at times. You may feel as though you ought to be ready for a long fast walk, and yet 10 minutes after you start, your shins are burning up.

Listen to them. Slow down. You must increase your speed and distance gradually. Sometimes it's hard to assess just how far you've come along. If you are not checking your speed and distance regularly, you may not realize how much you've improved your stamina and skill. You may push yourself just to keep up with someone a little faster.

Your shin muscles are hurting because they are usually weaker than your calf muscles, which are cramping up and pulling on the muscles in your shin. When you feel pain, you can slow down and keep walking, or you can stop and do some calf stretches. Find a tree or wall and lean against it with your hands, keeping your feet a little less than arm's length away. Keep your heels on the ground and you should feel a gentle pulling in your calves. Or you can sit on a bench and put your feet up and stretch your toes back toward your knees.

If you're really uncomfortable, you may have to head for home and apply ice to your shins with an ice pack for 15 to 20 minutes.

If you're getting ready for a walking race or vacation, you may want to strengthen your shin muscles a little faster by exercising them beyond what your walking program provides. Sit on a bench, strap on an ankle weight, and slowly lift your leg (do both legs). Or when doing the dishes or some other stationary job on your feet, raise yourself up and down on your toes. Alternate standing on your toes with flexing your toes back up toward your knees. That will stretch and strengthen your shin muscles.

Protecting Your Knees

Knee pain in walkers is often the result of some structural problem, like knock-knees or bowlegs, according to Dr. Weinberg. Sometimes an orthotic (custom-made arch support) can help to correct the problem.

Be sure your shoes fit well. Blisters or calluses may cause you to walk differently to avoid pain, and thus put stress on your knees or hip joints.

Walking on inclines is hard on the knees, causing pain on the inside of the knee. Keep to level surfaces if walking hills has given you some problem. It's the downhill ride that's tricky. Walking uphill, according to Willibald Nagler, M.D., chief physiatrist (doctor of physical medicine and rehabilitation) at Cornell Medical Center in New York, is virtually risk free to your knees, but walking downhill is not. The knees are stressed, and the pelvis tilts to balance the body, which may lead to low back pain. People walking downhill tend to misstep more easily due to forward momentum, leading to strains and sprains.

"Walking downhill is the single greatest way known to man to create muscle soreness," says James M. Rippe, M.D., director of the Rockport Walking Institute.

Of course, if you're going to go up, you're probably going to have to come down sometime. Take it slowly, watch your step, and rest if your muscles feel tired or strained.

Beating the DMS Blues

DMS, delayed-onset muscle soreness, occurs when you fail to condition your body gradually to endure greater stress and strain.

It usually occurs within 24 to 48 hours after exercise that goes beyond your current level of conditioning. It may increase for two or three days and is usually gone after about a week. For walkers this usually means sore calf muscles or shins, but it can also affect your arms, buttocks, hips—whatever you're moving that you haven't worked hard for a long time, if ever.

To avoid DMS, you need to be consistent in your walking workouts and only gradually add miles or speed. If you pay attention, you can enjoy a smooth, pain-free progression to higher and higher levels of fitness.

Some of us are just not methodical by nature. We tend to exercise in spurts. We may walk every day for a week, then skip a week, and then do a 6-mile jaunt. Then we wonder why we can hardly walk across the room, much less around the block.

DMS can be disconcerting to people who are starting out as well as to those of us who know better and just overdid it. Although not harmful, DMS is painful. And you may miss a few days of exercise because of it. If you're a beginner, you may become discouraged and quit.

Robert Willix, Jr., M.D., a sports medicine physician and director of the Willix Health Institute, uses walking as a part of a health-maintenance prescription for his clients. If they experience DMS, he advises that they take one day of rest and then do a shorter, lighter workout with a day of rest in between sessions.

"Don't stop walking," says Dr. Willix, "or you'll just have the same experience all over again."

If the pain is in your shin, Dr. Willix recommends aspirin, because you may be experiencing a form of tendinitis rather than muscle soreness. "Aspirin reduces inflammation and should be taken every 4 hours, regardless of pain, for two days. You're treating the inflammation, not the pain," he says. "If you find that the pain gets worse when you continue to walk, stop, and see your doctor."

Many people who exercise for fitness or fun will experience DMS at one time or another as they get used to understanding their bodies and their limits as well as their egos! When that happens, rest assured that the pain will go away in a few days. Don't let it discourage you. It's just a signal that you've reached your current limit and pushed a little too hard. Ease up, but keep walking!

Intermittent Claudication

Check Yourself

Intermittent claudication is a tongue-twisting term that means your blood vessels are blocked with fatty deposits and your blood is not circulating as well as it might.

If your legs ache when you walk but feel better a few minutes after you stop, even without sitting down, then you may have this serious problem, says Philip Osmundson, Ph.D., of the Mayo Clinic's Division of Cardiovascular Diseases. If your leg aches don't go away within a half hour, or if you have to rest in order to continue your walk, claudication probably isn't your problem, he says.

If you even suspect blood flow blockage, see your doctor. Anyone with intermittent claudication should be receiving regular medical care. The doctor will tell you to quit smoking and will probably recommend a program of regular exercise, such as walking. While walking can be painful, it is also helpful in keeping the condition under control, says Dr. Osmundson. The trick is to walk until you reach the point of pain, then rest and walk again. Regular walking revs up the circulation in the blood vessels around the afflicted area over time. (See also Terrain Therapy, beginning on page 182.)

Journal Keeping

Provide Your Own Inspiration

Daily walking logs are really "save-your-life" diaries. By keeping a written record of your walks, you may be literally saving yourself from all manner of physical ills and lengthening your life as well as enhancing your sense of well-being. Recording those daily walks shows you mile by mile, hour by hour, how far you've come!

People in the *Prevention* Walking Club often say that keeping a log helps them to stay motivated. Watching those miles stack up on paper is tangible evidence of the sometimes hard-won internal battles of "to walk or not to walk." And somehow, there is a reassuring sense of fullness and security when you can look back to a certain day and know: "Yep, walked 3 miles that day around Trout Creek Park. It was drizzling and foggy but the mist off the stream was eerily beautiful. Felt relaxed and peaceful."

Creative Logging

There are several ways you can expand your record keeping beyond just how many miles or how much time you spent walking. Enhancing your walking journal can enhance your pleasure and personal awareness. This, in turn, can motivate you to walk more. How about keeping track of your weekly weight, your resting pulse, or your time for a mile? Even if you're not trying to break records, the results can be interesting. Another way is to add some subjective observations about your mood, feelings, what you mused about on your walks. What great ideas did you spawn? What problems did you solve? What daydreams did you drift through? That may make for some exciting reading in a future quiet moment!

A third way to increase the value of your log is to make notes about your routes. If it's the same route, what are some changes that take place? Increase your powers of observation. If you change your routes, document them so you can go back to or take a walking partner on the best ones. There's no better way to get to know a neighborhood than to walk through it.

Buy a special notebook or pad of paper to designate as your daily walking log. (*Prevention* Walking Club members get a yearly log as part of their walking club handbook.) Keep it in an easily accessible place. Don't lose it in your desk or under a pile of . . . well you know . . . anything. Buy a special pen or pencil that you use just for writing in your walking journal. Tie it to the notebook if you have to, so nobody walks away with it.

Get in the habit of jotting down your time and distance as soon as you walk in the house. If you walk at work, keep a small notebook for recording your walks, then transfer the notes to your journal later. When you get more time, expand on your impressions.

A Gentle Reminder

Once a week or so, maybe just once a month, take a moment to sit down and read through your log. Savor it as a moment of privacy and quiet, a reckoning between you, your walking goals, and your log. This is where you have recorded your moments of truth. The first truth—I walked or I didn't walk. The second truth—I walked 1 mile or 2 miles or 3 miles or 10 minutes or an hour. The third truth—I felt great; I felt lousy; I went faster; I slowed down. This may all sound pretty melodramatic. But the fact is, it is so easy to kid ourselves about what we want to accomplish and what we actually accomplish.

How many times have you heard yourself complain about how a certain remedy or method never worked for you? But when you really examined your efforts, they were laughable! You didn't follow instructions, or maybe you didn't even read them all the way through. Or you read them and followed them, but not for the prescribed length of time. And then you gave up and blamed something or someone else for your failure.

Your log contains a special magic, a power to encourage and inspire you to go beyond even your own idea of what you expect to accomplish. Fill in dates for every day of the week. Leave the spaces blank where you did not walk. That way you can see at a glance how well you're doing. Your log can become your impartial ally on your footpath to better health.

Love

That Special Walking Partner

L ots of people love to walk, but how many walk for love? At *Prevention,* we received so many letters from walkers who said they felt walking enhanced their relationships, we thought it was worth looking into. So we followed our noses from the experiential paths of our readers to the hallowed halls of scientists and psychologists and found out, once again, that walkers are on to something good!

You may already know that if you're having trouble staying motivated to walk, finding a partner can help. A study that looked at 51 men enrolled in a hospital-based walking program at St. Francis Medical Center in Peoria, Illinois, found that they were twice as likely to stick with it for a year if their wives walked, too. But what you may not be truly aware of is this: Walking—in often subtle ways—can help build relationships.

If, for example, you're having trouble finding quiet time to communicate with a special person in your life, scheduling walking time together could solve that problem and give you both the benefits of exercise to boot. Since it is true that good relationships contribute to good health, then walking with someone you care about on a regular basis provides a double dose of good medicine!

Time for Talk

Kathy and Joe Hlavaty, of Williams Township, Pennsylvania, lead extra-busy lives. Joe's a schoolteacher and coach, Kathy works in a nursery school. They have two children. And they also help run a dairy farm. "Taking walks together is one way Joe and I find time to communicate, without the distractions of the house and the farm and the kids. It's hard for us to sit still and carry on a conversation. There's always something we feel we should be doing!" Kathy says.

Gloria McVeigh, a *Prevention* editor, once remarked that when she got married, a trusted friend suggested that she and her husband take a walk together every day. "It was the best advice I've ever gotten," she says. "While I've watched other marriages crumble, ours has remained strong. And I give a lot of credit to those long walks and talks that helped us struggle through tough times and stay in touch with each other."

Walking through Tension

Cynthia Strowbridge, a New York City psychotherapist, encourages her clients to walk together, especially if they have been experiencing tension in their relationship.

"The tension can be dispersed through the exercise, rather than channeled into an outburst of emotion," says Strowbridge. "And walking together can often ease communication in other ways. First of all, it's natural not to have constant eye contact while you're walking. Sometimes when you're staring each other down, you're staring feelings down! And it's also natural to have silent pauses while you walk. Those same pauses in a more sedentary setting can be awkward and anxiety producing."

Then there's that relationship-enhancing "other dimension" to walking that's often overlooked. We tend to think of communicating strictly in terms of talking. But have you ever walked in silence with someone close to you—and felt a strong feeling of connection?

"I've often had people tell me that they have experienced more profound feelings of relating than they've ever known when they have walked in silence together," comments Strowbridge. "We forget how intimate it is to be wholeheartedly with another person in silence. Being in step together, out of doors, can be amazingly healing to the body and mind."

Strolling toward Understanding

It may be easier to experience this silent connectedness while walking because, in part, going for a walk together gets you away from distractions like TV, telephones, and household demands. It's like retreating to your own private island where the two of you can

Sex in the Seventies?

Not the 1970s. Your seventies! Although popular opinion holds that older people have little or no interest in sex, Dr. Phillip Whitten, a behavioral scientist at Bentley College in Waltham, Massachusetts, feels that's a myth.

"Most people retain an interest in sex well into old age," says Dr. Whitten.

Interested, yes. But active? Maybe. The deciding factor may be vigorous physical activity. In a study of 160 Masters swimmers between the ages of 40 and 80, the physically fit swimmers had sex lives similar to those of people 20 to 40 years younger. (Masters competitions, which are available in many sports categories, including racewalking, provide competitive opportunities for men and women over the age of 25.) Not only were the swimmers more active sexually, they enjoyed sex more than their less active peers.

Dr. Whitten admits that the study does not determine whether the differences in sexual activity are due more to psychological or biological factors. "The most important factor may well be psychological," he says. "These people were proud of their bodies, and they felt younger."

What does all this have to do with walking? We can't say for sure, but if you're interested in sex, Dr. Whitten suggests being physically fit is the best way to ensure that you'll continue to enjoy it, whether you're 40, 60, or 80. There you have it. Another benefit to add to your list of reasons to keep walking!

clear your heads and air your thoughts and feelings without interruption. Jerilyn Ross, associate director of the Roundhouse Square Psychiatric Center and president of the Phobia Center of America, feels even more strongly about walking to enhance relationships since she started her nightly jaunts with her brother.

"We were having trouble getting together to just talk. We're both night owls, so after his family is in bed and my work is done, he walks to my house, we walk back to his house, and then he drives me home. We talk and get exercised, too."

"Couples, family members, and close friends have so little time to be together without disruptions," says Ross. "Disciplining yourselves to set aside time to be together without distractions enhances your sense of commitment to each other."

Ross also thinks that walking removes barriers to communication. "Sometimes the only time you can say what you need is when you don't feel the pressure of looking directly into the other person's eyes. Walking provides you with that opportunity naturally," says Ross.

"This has become a very special time with my brother. And I've never slept better!"

Mallwalking
Undercover Work

It's never too hot, too cold, too windy, or too wet. It's never too dark or too sunny. While that may sound like a recipe for instant boredom to the more adventurous types, for more and more walkers, it's the answer to a prayer.

Mallwalking in America is booming. Shopping centers around the country are opening their doors hours early to accommodate people who want to walk in air-conditioned or heated comfort all year long. This growing army of people who enjoy walking indoors is looking for safety, comfort, and companionship on the road to better health. According to research conducted by Avia, the athletic-footwear company based in Portland, Oregon, mallwalkers are primarily 40-plus, with women outnumbering men three to two. They are dedicated walkers, exercising from three times a week to daily. By conservative estimates, according to Avia research, there are half a million regular mallwalkers in the United States.

Senior citizens with health problems that prevent them from tackling difficult weather conditions are especially enamored of malls. Not only do they get to take their daily exercise in a safe, warm environment, but they usually end up staying for breakfast and friendly conversation as well.

Two Mallwalkers Walk down the Aisle

If you ask Jim Padalino of North Collins, New York, about the benefit of mallwalking, he may tell you "a lowered resistance to romance."

Jim met and courted his wife, Mary, while participating in a YMCA-sponsored walking program at the McKinley Mall in Hamburg, New York.

"We were having supper at the mall one night, and he asked me to marry him. I said yes, and people around us went 'Yeah!' " said the happy bride. Their romance became so popular that the mall's managers decided to give them their wedding and honeymoon.

"We thought it was only fitting. They met here, they became engaged here, and if they wanted to get married here, we wanted to plan and pay for the wedding," explained mall marketing director Leslie Suppa. The Padalinos accepted the offer and were married in the mall's lovely gazebo.

Twelve restaurants supplied the food, and several shops provided the dresses, tuxedos, hairstyles, and accessories. There were 300 invited guests, but over 700 people showed up.

The Padalinos met five months before the "big event" when Mary, 59, joined the walking program. Jim, 74, had been walking for two months. He began walking at the invitation of a friend who was recovering from a stroke.

"Mary was a fast walker and was always passing me," says Jim. "She finally slowed down so I could catch her."

The couple continues to walk at least three times a week. Mary has lost 25 pounds and has lowered her blood pressure since beginning the program. In fact, she modeled in a fashion show at the mall.

Jim can't guarantee that you'll find a spouse by walking, but he's sure that you'll find friendships, fun, and better health.

Joining the Fun

If you're interested in finding a mallwalking program, call the mall offices near you and simply ask if they have such a program. Don't be shy. They are sure to know what you're talking about, and if they don't have one, they may be able to tell you who does.

Malls often involve local hospitals or city health bureaus in their programs. The hospital may send nurses to take blood pressure, check cholesterol levels, and give health tips.

Generally, there is a nominal charge for joining a mallwalking club. You may be asked to pay a dollar and put your name and address on file, plus any important medical information and emergency numbers. That way, if anything happens to you, someone can take quick action. You may be given a button or some form of pin to wear for identification purposes when you walk. According to Melvin, Simon and Associates, the nation's largest manager of malls, most mallwalking programs average 150 to 200 participants. One group, at the Eastland Mall in Tulsa, Oklahoma, boasts 825 walkers!

Malls that have programs usually open their doors early on specified mornings so that walkers can take advantage of the long, empty corridors. There is usually a guard on duty—a boon for people who feel their neighborhoods are unsafe for walking alone. Some malls even provide coffee or juice and muffins. Others may open a coffee shop just to serve the walkers.

You'll find anything from casual strollers to catch-me-if-you-can speedwalkers. They usually follow a prescribed route, marked out either by arrows and footprints or on a diagram provided by the mall. The usual route follows a ¼- or ½-mile loop. You can circle the course until you reach your desired mileage for the day. And no stopping for lights, cars, or big dogs!

The benches provided for shoppers provide convenient resting places for walkers. And there is always access to bathrooms and water. Starting to sound inviting?

About the only hazard of mallwalking is slipping on a too-slick floor. Be sure to wear shoes with decent traction and be careful at the entryways on snowy or rainy days.

Some people use the malls as the mainstay of their walking program. While mallwalking may not appeal to you as a steady diet, it can be a nice backup track on days too hot or too humid for safe or comfortable walking or on icy days when streets and sidewalks are too dangerous to navigate. Rather than let your walking program suffer and risk losing all that conditioning you've gained, head to your local mall to work out. If you're not up to socializing, it's a great place to wear headphones—no motor vehicle traffic. And with all that fluorescent light, you're not likely to get mugged!

Mini-Walking Vacations

A Fast Getaway

M any people find walking vacations are a wonderful way to relax and regenerate. But not everyone has the time or money to travel or take off for a week—or even a weekend.

We think mini-walking vacations can give you that same sense of peace and of being released from your normal, stressed-out time frame. You can recapture that childhood feeling of having no place in particular to go, nothing more pressing to do than wander.

Before You Start

Here are a few guidelines to follow for a successful mini-walking vacation adventure.

Plan on spending at least 3 hours. This is time when you will be free from any obligations. A vacation walk should be lots longer than your normal exercise routine. It's more of a saunter, with time to stop and smell the roses.

Choose a starting point no more than 10 minutes' driving time from your home. You want to spend your 3 hours walking! Besides, it's fun to be on walking terms with nearby places that you normally only drive through.

Park your car in a safe place. It's also good to be near a spot where you can get some good food or drink when you return. Although you may not have a big appetite when you return (exercise often helps control appetite), food never tastes better than after a long walk.

Take a local map along. When you're walking and you're under any kind of time constraints, taking a wrong turn or getting lost, even temporarily, can ruin your day.

Carry a small day pack or fanny pack. It should hold water, your map, a crushable hat, sunscreen, sunglasses, a few plastic bandages, and your wallet.

Take a friend. If you can, it's always nice to have a walking partner, preferably someone who is as comfortable with silence as with conversation. And remember, this is a vacation! Not a time to dump your troubles on even a willing ear, much less be dumped *on*.

A Prime (Mini) Example

Here's a personal account from *Prevention* Walking Club's Maggie Spilner.

My favorite mini-walking vacation started at a local country store, called the Goosey Gander. They have a side business as caterers and are the only place around that has an old-fashioned snow cone machine. I asked permission to park my car in their lot for a few hours and headed across the street to picturesque Honeysuckle Road.

It was a hot summer day, but my walking partner and I headed up the side of the mountain, and the woods kept us cool. With no particular destination in mind, we made decisions at every turn based on curiosity and what looked interesting. We were inspired by a man who had created a remarkable garden in a field of boulders and high-tension wires. We marveled at secret "mansions" tucked away in shaded glens. Like two kids, we picked the houses we would live in "when we grew up." About 2 hours into our walk, we passed a shaded bridge over an icy mountain stream, took off our walking shoes, and soaked our feet.

I've been on walking vacations in England, British Columbia, San Diego, and Vermont. The sense of delight and freedom that we felt was as potent as any walking vacation I've experienced, hundreds of miles from home!

After 2½ hours, we headed back to the Goosey Gander for some ice-cold lemonade, hoagies, and fresh peach pie. What was half a Saturday stretched behind us like a weekend retreat. Cost: about $6. Planning time: about 20 minutes.

Find a friend and plan your mini-walking vacation together. Or take turns making plans, surprising your partner with secret destinations and special culinary delights, anything from Thai cuisine to your favorite hot dog stand. Keep working with the same map, gradually covering all the areas surrounding your home. Don't put it off; do it next weekend. Walk out the back door and *voilà!* you're on vacation!

Moonwalking
A Lightweight Fantasy

Imagine yourself on a long, long walk. Your legs are tired. Your day pack is starting to feel like a steamer trunk. You begin to fantasize about being lighter and lighter. How easy life would be if you weighed only, say, 50 pounds instead of 150!

To Alan Bean, an astronaut who walked on the moon in 1969, that was no fantasy. On the lunar surface, with one-sixth of the earth's gravity, his 150-pound body, plus 150 pounds of spacesuit and gear, in effect, did weigh only 50 pounds. "My legs didn't feel tired," Bean says. "They thought they had the day off!"

However, there are some drawbacks to this unique walking holiday. Because of the difference in gravitational pull, it's hard to keep your balance. "You tip over before you realize what's happening," says Bean. Imagine your body careening softly to the ground and landing in a slow-motion splash of moondust.

And talk about high-tech walking gear. Your "walking shoe" on the moon has to be able to protect you from intense heat. You can forget about that comfy sweat suit, too. Your moon togs will have to have built in air-conditioning.

Oh, and there's one more thing any man (or woman) headed for the moon ought to know. Due to the weak gravitational pull, ordinarily strenuous activities take about as much energy as lying in bed. That may not sound bad until you realize that whatever muscles you brought with you are going to go home a little weaker from lack of exercise...no matter how hard you try to work out.

So, back to earth, and that day pack turned steamer trunk. Maybe it's time to stop and take that pack off and rest till it feels like a day pack again. Lie down, stretch out, and enjoy the sensuous feeling of your body sinking into a soft patch of grass. And thank gravity for that!

Music

Tunes That Move

Have you ever sat in an auditorium, gritting your teeth and trying to stay awake while an orchestra performs some classical masterpiece? Listening while in a stuffy concert hall is no way to appreciate good music. Wake up and walk with it instead. Twentieth-century technology has made the symphony pocket-size and portable. With a cassette player you can take those concertos and

Tone Down Your Tunes

Headphones should come with a warning label. Pedestrian safety concerns aside, listening to personal cassette players may have a negative effect on your ears if used without caution. Not only that, the potential for permanent hearing loss increases if you're listening to music while you are exercising vigorously, according to Richard Navarro, Ph.D., chief audiologist at the Miracle Ear Hearing Centers in Hollywood, California. Dr. Navarro studied the effect of headphone use on hearing while an associate professor of audiology and speech pathology at the University of Nevada at Reno.

Research has found that hair cells that line the inner ear swell and eventually fall out when both vigorous exercise and the adrenaline response to loud noise restrict blood to the inner ear.

In a random survey of people using Walkman-type headsets, audiologist Barbara Brunner of Gallaudet University in Washington, D.C., found that listening volumes ranged up to 102 decibels. That is well above the 80-decibel cutoff considered safe for long-term exposure.

Dr. Navarro recommends listening to a personal cassette player for no more than an hour a day while exercising and never at more than half the maximum volume. If you are already exposed to other sources of noise, even 1 hour a day may be too much, he notes. Brunner suggests that if you cannot carry on a conversation while listening to your cassette player, then your safety, as well as your hearing, is at risk.

Editor's note: After all these dire warnings concerning health and safety, you may wonder why we recommend walking to music at all. You have to make to make an informed decision based on your personal experience and environment. Are you exposed to loud noise during your workday? Do you live in an area where you are concerned about walking on the street or in the park? We all have a variety of personal risks to contend with. There are few sports anyone would ever try if they feared continually for their safety. We think music can add excitement and energy to your walking workout, and that you can be safe if you take precautions. But you are taking certain risks. If you're worried, then the old axiom—better safe than sorry—is probably the best road to take!

sonatas out of the auditorium and into the natural world that was often their inspiration.

If you've never listened to music with headphones, you don't know what you're missing. The sound from these miniature devices envelops you as though you were sitting center stage in a musical production.

Catch the Mood

The tempo of the music should match your stride and your mood. Some people like rock and roll for fast walks, classical music for meditative strolls.

Walking to music can help you maintain a brisk pace. How many times have you been striding briskly along, then found yourself lost in thought, walking at a snail's pace? Listening to a brisk beat can keep your walk snappy even if your mind wanders.

There are plenty of walking tapes on the market that have been developed with specific paces in mind. You can choose 15-minute, 18-minute, or 20-minute miles, and so on. Some walking tapes have encouraging voices spurring you on, some contain warm-up and cool-down phases, and some even feature stretching instructions.

Listening to music while walking seems to give people a special lift. A marathon walker from Kutztown, Pennsylvania, once philosophically opposed to wearing headphones, now dons them regularly for his training walks. "I feel like I have my own personal sound track," he says. "It makes me feel larger than life."

A fitness walker from San Diego, California, says walking with music gives her "a tremendous feeling of exhilaration and aliveness—an instant high."

A Note of Caution

Headphones can distract you from traffic or other dangers on the road. It's best to wear them only during the day and only in parks or on trails where you won't have to worry about cars or bicycles. Headphones won't completely block out sounds around you, but they can be dangerous if not used with discrimination.

Nutrition

Boosting the Benefits of Walking

Question: What does walking have in common with good nutrition?

Answer: The long-term payoff is the same. If you walk on a regular basis, you reap great benefits in terms of better health, higher energy, and improved self-image. You reap the very same benefits from eating right.

In fact, most committed walkers sooner or later take a long, hard look at what they're eating. What kind of diet, they ask themselves, should they follow in order to enhance the health-giving powers of walking?

It's funny, but in letters from *Prevention* Walking Club members, we often see this pattern develop. Once they start walking on a regular basis, club members automatically begin paying attention to what they eat.

Craving Carrots . . . No Kidding

The act of walking seems to lead naturally to a desire to eat a wholesome, healthy diet. The *desire* to eat right is not enough, however. You need to know which food choices are the right ones. You also need a certain amount of determination and commitment to make those choices and stick to them—the same kind of determination that turned you into a regular walker in the first place.

Feel yourself tensing at the thought of giving up your favorite foods? You'd be surprised how quickly changes in eating habits become routine, even enjoyed.

Ask anyone who's switched from whole milk to skim milk. At first they thought skim milk tasted terrible, but after gradually working toward skim by drinking 2 percent and then 1 percent milk, they adjusted to the flavor and texture of skim. Now they think whole milk is repulsive—like drinking cream! It may be hard to believe now, but imagine yourself craving a sweet, raw carrot or a tangy apple instead of a hot fudge sundae! It *could* happen, you know. In fact, it may very well happen almost automatically once you realize how the right food choices can boost the healthful benefits of your walking program into orbit.

Let's take a look at how some of the special health benefits of a regular walking program can be enhanced by the right food choices.

Helping Your Heart

Walking regularly is one of the best things you can do to keep your heart healthy. But you'll be sabotaging those walks if your regular *après* walk lunch is a burger and fries.

When it comes to heart health, most Americans simply eat too much fat. And most cardiologists recommend reducing the amount of dietary fat. But by how much?

According to guidelines issued by the American Heart Association (AHA) and the National Cholesterol Education Project (NCEP), 10 percent of a person's total fat intake should come from monounsaturated fats (like olive oil), another 10 percent should come from polyunsaturated fats (like corn oil), and *less* than 10 percent should come from saturated fats (like butter.)

The trouble with these guidelines is that they're a bit complicated for most of us to figure out. "You need a minor in mathematics to walk through a supermarket and figure out what you should eat," says William Castelli, M.D., director of the landmark Framingham Heart Study. And even if you can read the labels, they may be misleading. Many products listed as "cholesterol-free" may be high in saturated fats.

The solution?

"If you reduce all dietary fat, you automatically knock down saturated fat intake, because about half of the fat we eat is saturated fat," says Dr. Castelli.

Think grilled or baked instead of fried. Enjoy a bowl of air-popped popcorn instead of a bag of potato chips. Switch to 1 percent milk or skim milk. Get acquainted with low-fat salad dressing.

Besides becoming a dietary sleuth and ferreting out fat from your diet, eating more fruits and vegetables helps, too. (After all, you have to eat something!) The soluble fiber in fruits and vegetables helps lower cholesterol. Some favorite recommendations of the nation's cardiologists are broccoli, bananas, beans, and bran.

As for meat, stick to fowl or fish whenever possible. Fish and shellfish are stocked with omega-3 unsaturated fats that may open your arteries and keep your blood flowing.

Keeping Blood Pressure Down

High blood pressure is a serious medical condition that requires a physician's care. And one of the things physicians tell people with high blood pressure is to get moving. For many people, walking seems to help reduce blood pressure levels.

To boost the power of walking to bring that pressure down, you may want to reduce the amount of salt in your diet. Although doctors don't know why exactly, they do know that sodium contributes to high blood pressure.

Regularly consuming excessive amounts of salt, which is about 40 percent sodium, can bring on high blood pressure in some people, according to George Blackburn, M.D., Ph.D., associate professor at Harvard Medical School and chief of the Nutrition/Metabolism Laboratory with the Cancer Research Institute at New England Deaconess Hospital.

"It's worth noting that about 50 percent of the people with high blood pressure are sodium sensitive," advises Dr. Blackburn. "If you have high blood pressure, you need to discuss your diet with your physician."

Even if you don't have high blood pressure, there's preliminary evidence that a high-salt diet may damage blood vessels regardless of blood pressure. Most Americans have developed an unnatural craving for salt. Try to cut back. Remove that saltshaker and try some of the new herb blends for seasoning. Don't just settle for blandness.

Remember the skim milk story? One day you may reach for your favorite bag of chips or movie popcorn and find the salty taste overpowering.

Building Better Bones

While it has been widely accepted that walking can help stem the loss of bone in older, postmenopausal women, the idea of taking calcium supplements to assist in countering that loss has been widely debated. The big emphasis was on estrogen replacement.

But a study published by the *New England Journal of Medicine* in 1990 suggests that extra calcium in the diet can prevent bone loss in older women. Researchers at Tufts University found that extra calcium had the greatest effect on those who were getting the least amount of calcium to begin with. In general, older American women tend to receive far less than the recommended 800 milligrams of calcium a day.

Earlier studies that concentrated on women who had just recently gone through menopause seemed to indicate that extra calcium didn't make all that much difference. But the Tufts study looked at women who were well past that phase of their lives. For these women, calcium made a difference even after bone loss had started.

It takes only about three servings of calcium-rich foods a day to reach the recommended 800 milligrams. If you're not a milk drinker (one glass has about 300 milligrams), you can boost your calcium intake with yogurt, broccoli (there it is again!), turnip greens, kale, low-fat cheese, or tofu. You may also want to ask your physician about taking calcium supplements.

And make sure you get enough vitamin D. The so-called sunshine vitamin aids in the absorption of calcium. As a walker, you probably don't have to worry about this particular vitamin—spending 15 to 60 minutes outdoors while the sun is shining can meet your daily requirement.

Assessing the Big Picture

If we move on to other areas of health where a regular walking program plays a positive role—cancer prevention, diabetes, stress, weight control—the nutritional picture pretty much remains the same. Rather than repeat ourselves, let's get that big picture in focus.

Americans tend to think of meat as the main part of their meals. While they don't need to give up meat—and the valuable nutrients, especially iron and vitamin B_{12}, that it provides—they do need to stop thinking of it as the centerpiece.

Start thinking of meat, chicken, or fish as the side dish and make vegetables and legumes the main focus, and you'll go a long way toward healthier eating. Cut back on fat; increase your consumption of fruits, whole grains, and vegetables; limit sweets and highly processed foods that fill you up but give you little nutritional value. Eat a wide variety of fresh, wholesome foods and eat them in their most natural state when possible. And if you feel you can't meet your nutritional needs through your daily meals, take a balanced vitamin and mineral supplement.

Remember, you're a walker. Just by walking, you boost your mental and physical health in many ways. A famous nutritionist once rated the most important things to do to live a long and healthy life. He said the most important thing was to have a positive attitude. The second most important thing was to get sufficient exercise. (A well-exercised body can handle the stresses of life better as well as occasional dietary indulgences.) Third on his list was healthy eating.

In simpler terms: Don't worry, keep walking, and learn to love veggies!

Orienteering

Fast Thinking on Your Feet

Orienteering seems like the perfect opportunity to act out a dozen childhood fantasies—evoking memories of Tarzan and Jane, treasure hunting, commando, and hide-and-seek.

With nothing but a map and compass, you're off to find that chest of doubloons, and in a hurry, too, before somebody else gets there. In this game, however, the treasure is a series of orange and white kitelike markers called controls. And your finding them doesn't deprive anyone else of a similar pleasure.

Meets, sponsored by various orienteering clubs around the country, are usually held in forested areas like state, local, and national parks. Started in Scandinavia around the turn of the century and imported here around 1967, orienteering will probably boom in the United States as walkers discover its unique excitement.

Something for Everyone

Everybody connected with orienteering in this country will tell you that beginners are welcome at all meets. But when you're tempted to try it for the first time, you may be scared off by the competitive atmosphere and the fact that you are getting timed along with much more advanced orienteers.

Don't be! Most other sports distinctly divide people into pros and amateurs, men and women, adults and children. If you're not a pro, you do not show up at Yankee Stadium on a Sunday and expect to play an inning or two. But at an O-meet (short for orienteering), you will find experts and beginners. You'll see men, women, and children, all running, walking, and otherwise scrambling over the same courses at the same time. Don't let the presence of high-level competitors intimidate you. The delightful thing about orienteering is that there is something for everybody, and you can start from scratch at your first meet.

Here is what you do need to know and what you can expect your first time out.

First of all, what do you wear? Sturdy walking shoes or hiking boots are a good idea. Pants should be long, to avoid poison ivy and scratches from underbrush. And because a beginner's pace will be erratic and you'll be heating up and cooling down a number of times, layered clothing is a good idea. Meets generally run rain or shine. If you're an Eeyore type and like mucking about in soggy woods, you'll love a rainy O-meet.

You may want to take a canteen and a few snacks, like fresh or dried fruit. (Just be sure to carry something for trash, if necessary.)

Checking In

When you arrive at the site for the meet, head for the registration table, which is usually open for a couple of hours. People stagger their arrivals, going out on the course at different times.

You will be required to sign a form and pay a fee, usually $2 or $3 per map. You must decide what course you want to try so you can be given the proper map. White courses, usually 2 to 3 miles long (provided you don't get lost), are for beginners. Yellow courses are for advanced beginners, and the orange are for intermediate. If it's your first meet and you feel comfortable out in the woods, you may want to try the yellow course. White may seem too easy, as it tends to follow an established path. Orange would be a challenge to someone totally new to orienteering.

The beginner courses are mostly on level ground, close to major map features like lakes and paths or roads. They don't require many decisions about which is the best and fastest route. Once you hit the trail, you have only one thought: getting to the next marker.

You can usually rent a compass to help you find your way. You may have to leave a deposit, either cash or perhaps your car keys. You may have to wear a whistle, which is to be blown only in case of an emergency, such as being hurt or lost. Orienteering whistles cost about $1.

Setting Out

At the registration table, a volunteer hands you a card with your name on it, printed with a bunch of numbered boxes. You keep this card inside your map and punch the appropriate box every time you reach a new control (those orange and white markers hidden out there in the woods). The punches, attached to the controls, make different-shaped holes, to foil any ideas of cheating. You can't fake it; you have to find the right markers.

You must turn this card in when you finish, even if you do not complete the course. It's the only way officials can know that you are not still out in the woods when the volunteers are getting ready to pack up and go home.

Mastering Maps

At this point, you have to realize that technically this is a timed competition. Although you can choose not to be timed, the spirit of orienteering is that it is a race, whether against your own time or somebody else's. That is why you will not be given a map with your route marked until you reach the starting point. There you are given a folded map and must wait for the go signal. Then and only then do you get to see your route. At some meets, you transfer your route to your own map from a master map.

A number of volunteers are stationed around the registration tent to help beginners. Join a group and get your crash course in map reading.

The instructor at our first meet was Mark Frank, at that time the director of the Delaware Valley Orienteering Association Education Program and a board member for the United States Orienteering Federation.

Mark pointed out the most important aspects of the map: the scale (to judge distance), the brown contour lines (they show you how steep the hills are), and the legend (which explains what all the other colors and lines and dots and dashes stand for).

According to Frank, an experienced orienteer can look at a map and visualize it three dimensionally. He rarely uses a compass to find his way unless he is hopelessly lost and wants to go home. The real art is being able to know where you are simply by identifying the features around you with a specific area on the map.

After instruction, if you need it, on how to use a compass, you head for the starting point. A volunteer will write a starting time on your card and tuck it into the clear plastic folder that covers both your map and a clue sheet that lists the controls and what natural elements they are hung on. He or she will hand you the folded map and direct you to wait until your starting time is called out.

If you are competing, any glance at your map before your start would be reason for disqualification. But as rank beginners, we immediately opened our map and tried to get our bearings. We didn't want to be standing there for 10 minutes while everyone else tripped over us.

Eager to be off, and feeling that our compass skills were

stronger than our map-reading skills, we lined up our compass and set off toward the first control.

Lost in the Woods

How wrong can you be! Forgetting one important instruction about using the compass, we set off in exactly the wrong direction. Nobody uttered a word, not even a chuckle, when we returned to start over half an hour later. One thing a beginning orienteer can be pretty sure of is that if you can't find the control, it's probably you, not the control, that's lost.

A word about being lost: Orienteers who are competing do not want to talk or be talked to. Sharing any information about the course is more than taboo—it's against the rules of competition. You may feel a bit odd if you become obviously lost (perhaps throwing up your arms, sitting down on the nearest rock, and crying like a baby) and friendly-looking people crisscross in front of you but decline to offer you any help.

It's not that they are sadistic; it's just that they are being true to the orienteering creed: "It is forbidden to obtain outside help or collaborate over running or navigation."

If you get confused and need some help but are not at the whistle-blowing emergency stage, ask somebody who is obviously moving at a casual pace. Families are a good bet, because anybody who is traveling with a partner is not competing.

The Game Heats Up

As soon as you find your first control, you'll be hooked. The treasure hunt will have begun and you may be surprised at the excitement you'll feel and your desire to pick up your pace to find the next one.

There will be two letters on a white card above the white and orange control marker. These letters should correspond to letters on your clue sheet for that number control. If they don't, don't use the punch. You are at the wrong control and have somehow slipped up in navigation. Or you may have run into another course's marker. If it's the right control, punch your card (right through the plastic), and then start orienting yourself toward the next leg of your route.

Avoid getting bunched up with other people. If you are a beginner, it may feel safer to stay within sight of other orienteers, but you won't learn a thing if you're just playing follow the leader. Either run ahead or sit down and take a break if suddenly you have to stand in a line to punch your control card.

Rising to the Challenge

Don't feel bad if you get lost a few times. It will teach you more about orienteering than if you happen to make it straight through the course without a struggle, in which case the course was probably too easy for you.

Choices are what make orienteering a real challenge. Which way shall I go? Which is faster, staying on the path or going through the brush?

Although beginners don't usually have too many choices to make, we mistakenly followed one trail that took us to the edge of a dam. We could either retrace our steps and take a dirt path to the bottom of the dam and across the footbridge, or we could inch our way down the rock embankment along the dam. We chose to inch, carefully, as there was a 30- or 40-foot drop to shallow rocky water at the highest point. When we reached the footbridge, we looked back and, to our horror, saw that a family and two silver-haired women were following in our footsteps!

It wasn't our business to tell them what to do, but we were thankful when they thought better of it and headed back toward the path.

There were a couple of steep inclines to deal with on the advanced beginner course (yellow), so be prepared for a little climbing and sliding. But there shouldn't be anything too difficult for a conditioned walker, unless you get off course, as we did.

When you've punched in at all the controls and you're heading for the home stretch, the final marker, remember that for some people, this is a timed competition. They may come barreling in and dive for that last punch. Don't get in their way. It's not sporting and, besides, it might hurt.

When you finish, hand in your map so your time can be tallied and so the people running the meet know you're out of the woods. If you want to take your map home with you, you'll have to wait until your time's been tallied.

After you finish is a good time to stand around and chat with the other orienteers or eavesdrop on other people's experiences. You can learn a lot about the different possibilities and choices you can make: what you did wrong, what you might do better next time. It's an opportunity to rerun your course mentally and change your game plan.

Sharing experiences also helps to generate enthusiasm and arrive at an understanding of what draws people back to orienteering. We heard one competitor exclaim that as he was running through a difficult area he fell down several times. But as Frank, a 12-year veteran of orienteering, pointed out, he had a smile on his face when he said it.

There are orienteering clubs all over the United States. Joining one is probably about the only way you'll find out about when and where events are being held in your area. To locate the club nearest you, send a self-addressed, stamped envelope to Robin Shannonhouse, U.S. Orienteering Federation, P.O. Box 1444, Forest Park, GA 30051.

Ozone Alert

Protect Yourself

In the summer of 1989, ozone levels rose above the Environmental Protection Agency standards of safety in more than 60 percent of the towns, cities, and rural areas tested.

There is some evidence that exercising outdoors when ozone levels are too high may produce such symptoms as coughing and discomfort when taking deep breaths. Recurrent exposure may even lead to chronic respiratory problems. All in all, then, it seems only prudent to avoid unnecessary exposure. Here's how.

■ Be aware of the pollution alerts in your area. They are based primarily on ozone levels. Check your newspaper or radio or contact your local health bureau for information.

■ When there's a pollution alert in effect, take your walk inside a local mall. Or, if you have access to a motorized treadmill, use that. Ozone levels drop by about 50 percent indoors.

■ Exercise early in the day. It takes several hours of sunlight to make ozone. If the sun is rising at 5:30 A.M., try to get your walk in by 8:00 or 9:00.

■ Not an early bird? Walk after dinner, or before a late dinner. Ozone levels drop off in the early evening. (Check with the health department in your area for the safest times to exercise.)

■ Try not to exercise along busy streets that are tree-lined. On hot summer days, trees can trap pollution under their leafy boughs. You'd be better off away from cars anyway and somewhere where the wind can clear away polluted air.

■ Remember, every time you leave your car at home and walk, you're doing yourself, your neighbor, and the environment a favor.

Partners

Two-Stepping
for Better Performance

Partners are of tremendous value in sustaining any exercise program, including walking. Although there are many programs people can do alone, studies have shown that very few people start or continue them without a friend or a spouse. They need social support. Even when people join a group, they generally do it with a friend.

The thing that keeps people walking, especially on days that they don't particularly feel like it, is knowing they have a partner waiting to walk and talk with. Sure, some days you feel so great that every step of a walk makes you high. You're not walking, you're floating! But there are lots of days when having someone to walk with keeps you from turning around and heading back home after 10 minutes.

Choosing Wisely

Since walking should become an almost daily activity for the rest of your life, if you want to reap its physical and mental benefits, it's helpful to incorporate as much of your *life* into walking as you can. What we mean by that is, don't go searching far and wide for a partner—look to your husband, your wife, your child, your parent, or even the family dog. That way, each time you exercise, you also strengthen the relationships that are most important in your life, those that help maintain your sense of happiness and well-being.

Some days you choose your walking partners, and some days they choose you. It's important to be open and flexible to whoever happens to walk your way! Let's talk about some ways of adapting to walking partners.

Pairing Up with a Pet

It's not for everyone, and we would never recommend that people go out and buy a pet just to help maintain their weight or their blood pressures, but from personal experience as well as reading hundreds of letters from *Prevention* Walking Club members, we're not sure if there is any more reliable walking partner than a dog.

They *always* want to go for a walk (unless the weather is *really* bad, in which case maybe you should reconsider, too!). They tend to be very enthusiastic about walking. They remind you, if you've forgotten, when it is definitely time to go for a walk. They are good company. They almost never complain. They are great listeners if you want to talk. And if you decide you really want to wear your headphones and listen to music, they will not be insulted or feel slighted.

Of course they need to be trained to a fitness walking routine (see the dog chapter, beginning on page 41). But it really doesn't take very long and the rewards are well worth the effort of training.

Walking with Kids

Children are a part of most of our lives whether they're our own, a friend's, or our grandchildren. Children are not usually walking partners by choice.

Maggie Spilner, of *Prevention* Walking Club, has found this to be true with her own kids. If she says, "Do you want to go for a walk?" they say, "Where to?"

"If there is no particular goal," she says, "forget it. I had a wonderful 3-mile walk with my 9-year-old son, Robin, when I offered to walk to the Dairy Queen and back. Generally speaking, my kids are in bed when I'm out walking in the early morning. I used to bribe them with doughnuts, but I realized the walking was not enough to undo the evil of the doughnuts. Now I simply walk with them whenever we have to get somewhere that is important to them, like little league games or video arcades or the baseball card store. (I'm basically along to carry the cash.) I get an extra walk in, and they get some needed exercise. And we get a chance to talk and play together—something that's often hard to do in a house with two TVs and a Nintendo."

When walking with kids, you're the adult. You're the one who will have to adapt. Walk slowly enough to match their pace. Don't walk so far that they'll never trust you enough to go with you again. Don't take it as an opportunity to lecture to a captive audience. Kick back and try enjoying their company.

Walking at Work

The workplace can be fertile ground for finding walking partners. Everybody gets a lunch break, and a noontime walk can be the ideal stress reducer.

Try to accumulate a list of possible walking partners—some

that like to stroll, for days when you don't want to get all worked into a sweat, and some for those ½-hour hill strides that are worth 1½ hours of level walking. Walk with people you work with and you can discuss business or just get to know each other better and develop a more easygoing rapport outside the pressures of the office.

You should take your walking shoes to work as well as a nice, comfy pair of socks. Walking in dress shoes or work boots can wreak havoc on your feet. Besides, taking a moment to slip into your comfortable walking gear sets the mood for a relaxing, energizing walk.

Try to find partners who are generally equal to you in stamina. Don't try to keep up with anyone who is really too fast for you or refuses to slow down to a pace comfortable for both of you. It's not worth the risk of injury or soreness to try to keep up with someone else. If you're a fast walker, don't demand anyone keep up with you. If no one can match the pace you prefer, you may have to walk alone at that speed.

Walking with Your Partner

If your husband or wife or boyfriend or girlfriend and you would like to walk together but you are very unevenly matched in speed or endurance, the stronger partner can go out and put in a couple of miles first, push herself, and pick up her partner for the second half or the cool-down. Gradually allow your partner to get in better condition. (Although don't forget that temperamentally, he may never want to go your speed or mileage.) You can also wear a weighted vest or belt to pick up your heart rate and slow down your pace to match a partner's.

But even if you want to walk briskly, you should still be able to carry on a conversation with your partner. If either of you is gasping for breath, you need to slow down. That's one of the great things about walking for exercise. It's companionable. You can talk and still get your workout done.

Generally speaking, your partner's height compared to yours is not important. Mutt and Jeff types can walk together comfortably if they want to. Shorter legs may have to move a bit faster, but not uncomfortably so. Don't try to take longer strides; you may pull muscles. Just take more short ones. If you have to jog to keep up with your partner and he or she won't slow down for you, consider finding a new partner (for walking, that is.)

To review, if you're looking for a walking partner, look to the people closest to you first. Try to find somebody you can support and who can support you. You probably won't have to look too hard or too far. Ask at home. Ask at work. Be positive about your own commitment. If weight loss is your primary goal, find someone else who wants to lose weight. If relaxation is on your agenda, find someone who also wants to reduce their stress level. The more in sync you are mentally, the easier it will be to get together to work out!

Pedometers

Counting Your Steps

Your wristwatch tells you that you've been walking for an hour. Your pedometer tells you how far you've walked. And together they tell you whether you've been a tortoise or a hare. (Two miles an hour rates tortoise; 4 miles an hour approaches hare.)

The pedometer is a compact little device that hangs from your belt. If you listen carefully, you can hear the soft tick, tick, tick of its internal pendulum swinging back and forth with your every step. If you enjoy measuring your accomplishments in tangible numbers, pedometers can be a fun walking accessory.

Purchasing a Pedometer

You can find pedometers at sporting goods stores or in mail-order catalogs like L. L. Bean. As walking becomes increasingly popular, more department stores are carrying them.

Once you locate a store that sells pedometers, you have one more decision to make—shape.

The round pedometers have a hand that circles around the face, measuring off miles. You have to pick them up to be able to read them. The square ones usually have a digital readout on top that is readable by glancing down.

Both types hook onto your belt with a metal or plastic clip. They should be placed at your waist, about halfway between your hip and your belly button, for the greatest accuracy. Check the clip out to see if it's going to sit still. It needs to fit snugly or it will move around and tilt sideways or worse, fall off.

Pedometers come in all sizes, with varying degrees of accuracy and readability. The electronic type are more expensive and often give more information—like the date and the time. And they can sometimes count calories for you or beep to pace you. However, they seem to malfunction. In fact, once we sent away for the same electronic pedometer *three* times, and we could never get it to work. Either we were breaking it as soon as we started pushing the buttons or we couldn't follow the instructions. At any rate, it seems the simpler, the better. If you love electronic gadgetry, try one. You may have better luck.

Get Ready, Get Set

In order to get an accurate reading from your pedometer, you must set it to the length of your personal stride. The packaging on most pedometers will tell you how to calculate that measurement.

One simple way to determine your stride length is to measure off a distance of 10 to 25 feet. As you walk the distance, count the number of steps you take. You'll probably get a more accurate reading with a longer distance, as you'll tend to relax and even out your stride. Divide the distance you walk by the number of steps you take to travel it. For example, if it takes you five steps to walk a distance of 10 feet, then your stride length is 10 divided by 5, or 2 feet. Pedometers can usually be set anywhere from 2 to 6 feet. Once you've set your pedometer, leave the setting alone. It's best not to lend it to anyone else, as the more the setting is changed, the less likely it is to retain its accuracy.

Pedometers work better on level ground. On a hike, you change your stride length and bounce around a lot, and the reading is affected. But if you're wearing the pedometer around town on sidewalks or roads, you'll get a pretty good idea of how far you've traveled.

Getting Adjusted

To check your pedometer, mark out a specific 1-mile route with your car. Then try to walk it as closely as possible. If your pedometer is way off, take it back, or try adjusting the stride length until your pedometer reads a mile when you know you've walked one.

If you wear a watch and time your walks, you can use the two together to find your walking pace in miles per hour. If you walk a mile and it takes you 15 minutes, divide 15 into 60. You're walking at a 4-mile-per-hour pace. Twenty minutes is a 3-mile-per-hour pace. Incidentally, 20-minute miles are considered marching time in the army and 15-minute miles are double time. Hut! Two! Three! Four!

Personal Safety
Protecting Yourself

That barking dog you pass on your walk each day has gotten out of his pen and is in your path—snarling. What do you do?

You are walking down the block and spot someone across the street closely following your progress. How should you react?

The answers are clear-cut and can protect you from attackers and wandering dogs who don't want to be anybody's best friend.

National Crime Prevention Council (NCPC) data show that close to 90 percent of rapes, assaults, and robberies happen to people who are alone. So the first rule of personal safety is: Buddy up.

"When you add one more person to your party," suggests Leonard Sipes, director of information services at NCPC, "it will substantially reduce the probability of attack."

Strategies for Safety

Even if you are out walking with another person, don't hesitate to use these other tactics to keep attackers at bay.

- Walk with purpose. Make believe you are a linebacker.

- Look unapproachable.

- Take off those headphones, especially if you're out walking at dusk or in a secluded spot. "By wearing headphones, you are eliminating an extra sense you really need in case of trouble," says Mary Conroy, author of the self-defense primer *Every Woman Can.*

- Vary your walking routes and times, even if only slightly. Would-be attackers are often aided by the regular schedule you keep.

Know how to recognize and avoid danger, too, says Conroy. Be on the lookout for:

- A person approaching who has one hand in his pocket. He may be reaching for a weapon.

- Someone giving you a longer-than-usual look. Fellow walkers or passersby who mean no harm exchange cursory glances or greetings and move on.

- A car following you at your pace. Turn completely around and walk in the opposite direction if you are suspicious. It will cause a predicament for the driver, who probably won't want to maneuver his car to keep on your trail.

Go with your gut feeling if you are getting bad vibrations in any situation. They are more reliable than you think.

"Women have wonderful intuition if they would only use it,"

stresses Conroy. "I've had many women say to me, 'A half-block away I knew he was going to grab me.' " If you feel uncomfortable, cross the street and try to walk to safety.

Better Not to Bear Arms

Self-defense and law enforcement experts don't recommend carrying weapons for two reasons: You may not have the proper training to handle them, and they could be used against you in a scuffle.

Some walkers feel better, though, carrying a small shriek alarm in their pockets. If they feel threatened, a push of a button causes a piercing alarm, which could startle an attacker or alert others.

Unfortunately, there is no 100 percent guarantee that these defensive measures will forestall an attack. If someone is still willing to take a chance on attacking you, what's the best way to respond?

"If somebody comes up to you and says, 'Don't move. Give me your wallet,' don't move and give him your wallet," advises Sgt. Donald Wactor, a veteran crime prevention officer with the Orange, New Jersey, police department. "If the person threatening you gives you a command, do that and nothing else. Your life is worth more than the property you have on you.

"The only time you should resist," says Sgt. Wactor, "is when you are in a desperate situation and fighting back might be the difference between life and death. And that is a decision you will have to make in a few seconds at that time."

The Jaws That Bite

If you are unfazed by stray dogs and the threat they pose, you are a prime candidate for a bite.

Many dogs will nip at you if they believe you are treading on their turf. And as a walker, you may be doing just that.

"The most common biting situation occurs with pets who are not confined to the yard," says Alan Beck, Sc.D., director of the Center for Applied Ethology and Human/Animal Interaction at Purdue University School of Veterinary Medicine. "Dogs allowed to run into the street soon feel the sidewalk, street, and alley are well within their territory.

"Walkers coming down a public thoroughfare that the dog has laid claim to will be approached with the same aggressiveness as if they were entering the owner's living room. Half of all dog bites occur," he adds, "on the street, sidewalk, or alley adjacent to where the animal lives."

So how do you tell if the dog in your path does not have the best intentions?

"Back off slowly when the ears and hackles [hairs along neck and back] go up or if the dog growls or bares his teeth," says Dr. Beck.

If it's too late to retreat, our dog-bite expert—who has never been bitten himself—offers this advice.

- Put something between you and the dog. Walkers might carry a short, thick stick that can be used as a "bite stick." Offer the stick instead of using a hand or arm for protection.

- Assert some dominance. Yell "Go Home!" with command in your voice.

- Avoid eye contact. "Sometimes just doing something else, such as tying your shoe or playing with a camera, is all that is needed to divert a dog's attention," says Dr. Beck.

- Use a commercial dog-repellent spray. One popular brand contains ground red pepper that temporarily burns the animal's eyes, nose, and skin. "The dog feels enough pain to be distracted," explains Dr. Beck. "It's similar to what women can buy to ward off attackers."

Don't ever trust a strange pooch, *especially* if you are a veteran dog owner and believe you can handle any canine.

According to a study Dr. Beck conducted with the postal service, persons who had pets as children or adults had a higher bite rate than non-pet-owners.

"We rated letter carriers by how many chances they took—whether they would reach down to try to pet a dog or back off," says Dr. Beck.

"Sure enough, carriers who have owned dogs take many more chances. They think they know dogs and are less likely to yell or retreat. They put themselves in vulnerable situations."

They are also less likely to use a dog repellent.

End of Tail, or . . . Tale

Although dogs are likely to be the four-legged creatures you see most on your travels, don't be surprised if you spot a raccoon along the way.

These crafty animals are infiltrating streets, parks, and backyards in cities and suburbs. Don't let the cute masked face fool you—the ones you encounter may have rabies, especially those found in the southeastern and Mid-Atlantic states.

"There is just enough rabies among raccoons to make any exposure not worth it," warns Dr. Beck. "And it's not as if you're doing them any big favor if you pick them up or pet them."

You may be tempted to touch, especially if you discover a very young animal or one that may be lost or sick. "Even if it's not rabid," Dr. Beck advises, "the chances of rehabilitation or doing anything useful for the animal are small. Just leave it alone."

Walking is the safest fitness activity there is. Don't let any person or animal make you forget it.

Photography
Taking Pictures on the Hoof

Many walkers develop a reverence for natural beauty and a sensitivity to their surroundings, whether rural or urban. Sometimes that special appreciation leads to a desire to capture some of the images they see during their solitary strolls and share them with others. Photography and walking are two pastimes that can easily go hand in hand.

You may believe that you need special telephoto lenses and tripods to take satisfying outdoor photographs. Wrong! Sensational scenic pictures can be taken with do-everything-for-you cameras that are available today for amateurs. In fact, attempting to grapple with sophisticated equipment too soon can permanently dent a budding walking photographer's enthusiasm.

A few simple tips from the experts can help you capture the delights of your walks through the eye of your camera.

Use Light for Effect

Walkers have a built-in advantage when it comes to lighting. Most walkers head out the door at the best times of day for picture taking: in the early morning, late afternoon, or early evening. "The long shadows cast by early and late sun create interesting contours and patterns," says Ralph Venk, D.D.S., president of the Photographic Society of America.

If you capture the images of dawn and dusk, you'll tap into a beauty that the rest of us miss while sleeping, eating, or watching TV.

That doesn't mean it's wrong to shoot at noontime. You just need to understand the effect of strong overhead light. "When taking pictures of people, be aware that bright sun can make them squint and can cast facial shadows, making wrinkles look deeper," warns John Hamel, photo editor for *Bicycling* magazine. Using a flash can fill in these shadows. Or place people in the shade. Either way, make sure they're not looking directly into the sun.

Choose the Right Angle

"The difference between a good photograph and an okay snapshot depends primarily on the thought that goes into a picture before you click the shutter," says Dr. Venk. "Most pictures would improve immensely if the photographer took a few minutes to think before shooting." Ask yourself: Am I in the best spot?

People generally view the world from two angles, standing up and sitting down. So find a place to put your camera that will offer another way of looking at the object. "A special viewpoint for a walker might be the one belonging to his feet, if they had eyes," says Rick Baughn, university photographer at Indiana University–Purdue University at Indianapolis. "What would they be seeing that

I'm not? Cracks in the pavement, beautiful autumn leaves littering the sidewalk, bugs scurrying around? A puddle might look like a lake from down there. Put the camera flat on the pavement and snap away. You'll definitely get a new perspective."

Fill the Frame
with What's Important

Including too much in the picture is a common problem among amateurs. To avoid a cluttered photograph, you must develop a roving eye when looking through the viewfinder. Look carefully at the whole image and notice any distracting objects in the surrounding area. "Focus on one image and keep it simple," says Dr. Venk. "Move in closer to isolate your subject."

Establish Depth in Landscapes

A photograph will not automatically reveal the interest and depth that you see with your eye in a panoramic landscape view. You can help it suggest near and far by creating planes of depth. Include something in the foreground—some flowers, a tree. A branch jutting across the top can further establish a natural frame.

When you were a kid, the hardest part of taking a picture was probably getting the object of interest fully recorded on film. You learned to "center," to put the person or object right in the middle of your viewfinder. "In general, avoid such fastidious centering," says Dr. Venk. You're usually better off moving the main subject a little (or a lot) up, down, or sideways.

Freezing fast-action shots requires more advanced features than autofocus cameras provide, but you can take slow-action shots by using a simple technique called panning.

While your friend is walking, situate her face on a particular spot in your viewfinder. Move your camera smoothly as she moves. Do not slow the camera as you click the button. The result? Her face should focus clearly, while her arms and legs will blur. The final effect may be humorous—she'll look like she was walking at a fantastic pace!

As a regular walker, you have the special opportunity to stretch both your legs and your creative impulse simultaneously. A camera may turn out to be your favorite walking companion!

Posture
Benefits of Walking Tall

Maggie Spilner was one of those teenagers that teachers and parents were always telling to stand up straight. She says, "Even my friends would come over and grab my shoulders and try to push them back. At 13, I was 5 feet, 8 inches tall and towered over most of the boys as well as the girls my age. I gave up trying to stand tall. It wasn't very rewarding. I couldn't hear what was going on in all those inner circles down on the ground floor, and besides, it was too tiring and my back ached from the effort.

"That's why, when someone remarked to me that I had nice posture, I turned around and waited for the sarcastic punchline. No one had ever told me I had good posture! Then I remembered someone had made a similar remark a few weeks before, and I'd assumed I had misunderstood.

"I had myself firmly envisioned as an inveterate slouch until I was videotaped walking on a treadmill. I was astounded! My back was straight. My stomach was pulled in. My chin was up.

"David and Deena Balboa, co-directors of The Walking Center of New York City, were analyzing my walking technique. They'd first seen me a year before and told me that basically I walked like a duck with a sunken chest. Since then, I'd taught myself to stand tall, straighten my stride, and raise my head.

"I'd read that walking can improve your posture by strengthening the muscles in your back and abdomen. And I had been concentrating on keeping my chest up in order to breathe more easily from my diaphragm. But somehow I hadn't expected it to work on *me*. The feedback from the videotape was really great. Because of it, I've been able to change the hunched-over image I had of myself to fit my actual, new carriage."

The Posture/Pride Connection

According to the Balboas, proper walking technique will do more than strengthen muscles and lead you to better posture. As psychotherapists, they've found that improving your posture can help you face the world more confidently. In other words, self-esteem tends to make you stand taller, and standing taller enhances your positive feelings about yourself. It's a two-way street.

Has anyone commented on your posture since you started walking? Ask for feedback from friends, or check your mirror. If you have the opportunity, have someone videotape you while you walk. You may be in for a pleasant surprise, as Maggie was, that another walking benefit has sneaked up on you.

If people say you tend to slouch, then keep that in mind when you go for a walk. The Balboas suggest imagining there's a string coming out of the top of your head, pulling you tall and straight. Tuck in your buttocks, raise your chest, breathe deeply, and walk tall. Forget any notions of ramrod posture. It's important to stay relaxed at the same time you pull yourself up by your imaginary string. Rigidity will only impede your natural walk. So pull yourself up, but hang loose on that string at the same time. Allow your hips, your arms, your legs, your whole body to move around that center line. As David Balboa always suggests, think dance.

The Posture/Pain Connection

While standing tall can fill you with the pride of a positive self-image, slouching can fill you with equally powerful but less desirable feelings—pain.

Dianne Schlegel is acutely aware of the problems that can be caused by poor posture. She spent nine years in pain. Pain that forced her to quit her secretarial job and to feel that there was no hope for her health.

Schlegel loved to walk. But walking seemed to aggravate the problems she had with neck and back pain. She tried lots of different things to help herself, including buying two different mattresses and seeing doctors and physical therapists who prescribed exercises, electrostimulation, and massage. Some treatments seemed to help, but the pain returned when the treatment stopped.

Then she read about walking expert David Balboa in a *Prevention* editorial by Bob Rodale. In the article, Balboa was referred to as a sort of body mechanic. Grasping at straws, Schlegel resolved to get in touch with him.

When she met with Balboa, he studied her while she walked. "I noticed right away," says Balboa, "that she walked with her body pitched forward, creating tremendous strain on her lower back. Her neck was jutting out and her shoulders were hunched. And she held her hips very rigidly."

What Balboa saw was not mysterious. When he imitated her walk, Schlegel gasped, "Gee, that looks painful!" And she listened carefully while he gave her instructions for better body positioning while she walked.

"I couldn't believe how good it felt to walk again after just a few instructions," she says. "My whole body felt exercised, from my shoulders to my toes! And there were no spasms afterward. My back muscles were tired, but not in pain. At first, it took a lot of concentration to allow my hips to move freely, leave my back foot on the ground longer, and roll off my toes, keeping my back centered over my hips. But now it's second nature. David constantly told me to slow down, feel the rhythm. He advised me to picture my legs as starting a few inches above my navel and to glide as I walked, not bounce. That mental image really helped me to use my hips more and not just lift my legs at the thigh."

A Dose of Relief

Day after day, Schlegel practiced her new walk diligently, constantly checking her posture, walking tall, making certain she wasn't bending forward at the waist. Within three weeks, she had the new style down pat. "And I knew it was the answer," she says,

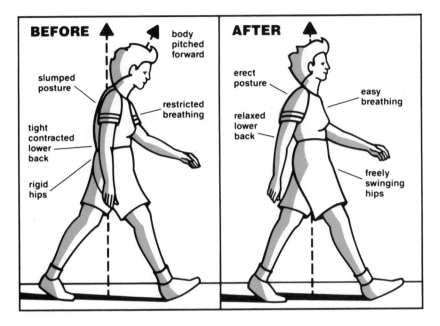

BEFORE — body pitched forward, slumped posture, restricted breathing, tight contracted lower back, rigid hips

AFTER — erect posture, easy breathing, relaxed lower back, freely swinging hips

The proper walking form can help eliminate painful back spasms and other physical discomforts.

"because on days when I was tired and I slipped back into my old, poor posture mode, my back would hurt again. When I stood tall again, the pain left!"

If you suffer from acute or chronic back pain, see your family doctor. He or she may want to refer you to a physiatrist (doctor of physical medicine and rehabilitation), orthopedic surgeon, or back pain specialist. But according to Hubert L. Rosomoff, M.D., medical director of the University of Miami's Comprehensive Back Pain and Rehabilitation Center, 99 percent of all back pain sufferers do not have a serious health problem. Their pain is the result of muscles that are deconditioned, strained, or stressed—the kind of pain that can be addressed by attention to posture and body mechanics.

Most people who have back pain, says Dr. Rosomoff, are not suffering so much from back injury as from strain or tension of the whole musculature around the hips.

Even if you are not currently suffering back strain, take a minute to check out your posture. Remember, your top half should never get out in front of your bottom half. Your legs and torso carry you. Don't try to drag your body around by your neck!

Presidential Walking Awards

Go for the Red, White, and Blue

The Presidential Sports Award program was instituted in 1972 to encourage people age 15 and older to become more physically active throughout life. The emphasis is on regular, consistent exercise—not stupendous speed or distance. The only competition is the one you have with yourself. There are now 51 categories of awards, and of all the awards given in the last two years, fitness walking has outpaced all other categories, with close to 4,000 people earning the Fitness Walking Award.

For several years, *Prevention* magazine has been working side by side with the President's Council on Physical Fitness and Sports (PCPFS) in Washington, D.C., to promote their Presidential Sports Award for Fitness Walking. Thousands of *Prevention* readers and *Prevention* Walking Club members have applied for the award, which boasts more participants than any other sports category. The readers who participated kept a record of their walking activity and applied for the award when they reached a specified walking goal. Recently, *Prevention* and the PCPFS created two new categories for the Presidential Sports Awards: Race Walking and Endurance Walking.

Winning the Awards

And what will you receive if you reach your Presidential Sports Award goal? Well, most important, you get all the health benefits associated with regular exercise.

To commemorate your accomplishment, the Amateur Athletic

Union (AAU), which administers the program, will send you a personalized certificate of achievement signed by President George Bush, suitable for framing; a letter of congratulations from the council's chairman, Arnold Schwarzenegger (also suitable for framing); a beautiful blazer patch embroidered in red, white, blue, and gold with the name of your sport; a sports bag identification tag imprinted with an awards logo; and a "shoe pocket" to hold your valuables and emergency identification while you're walking.

Going for the Goal

Prevention and the PCPFS both know that some people need extra motivation to keep exercising regularly. The Presidential Walking Awards can provide an inspiring goal for the estimated 60 million people who enjoy walking to stay in shape. Here are some of the comments from *Prevention* Walking Club members who walked for the Presidential Fitness Walking Award.

From Arleen Nicoletti, Millbrook, New York: "I made it and what a great feeling to have done it!"

From Mary Lou Sabroski, Duluth, Minnesota: "I'm excited to have completed the walks! It was a real challenge for me to do them all!"

Robin Weidenhammer, Reading, Pennsylvania: "Thank you for giving me the incentive to walk some weight away! The incentive to walk faster was just what I needed. Besides the physical improvements, my mental outlook is better, too. Thank you for helping me to a better way of life!"

From Dorothy Barnhill, San Diego, California: "This was a great challenge, and I loved it. It greatly increased my stamina and my walking speed. Thanks for this award."

From Sam Flaherty, Portland, Oregon: "I enjoyed working on this award. I'm diabetic, and my walking prescription is 2½ miles per day, so it fit right in! Thanks for the challenge!"

From Paul Bakker, St. Charles, Missouri: "While working toward this award, my wife and I started walking together. So we have both been introduced to a new form of entertainment, and I have lost 18 pounds."

Setting New Goals

The new Race Walking Award and the Endurance Walking Award provide new goals for people who have already achieved the Fitness Walking Award, as well as offering a different kind of challenge for people who enjoy walking for fitness.

Racewalking is coming of age in America, and the 1992 Olympic Games schedule includes the first racewalking events for women. (Men's racewalking has been an Olympic event for many years.) Judged racewalks are becoming more available, and racewalk clinics are springing up around the country. Racewalking is for people interested in speed, high-intensity workouts, and competition. (Although the racewalk technique can be enjoyed at slower speeds, the Presidential Award requires an average of 12 minutes per mile or better.)

The Endurance Walking Award challenges those walkers who like to spend hours on the road wandering through country trails, or urban hikers touring the cities. Part of the requirement is to take

The First Lady Loves to Walk

Most people know President George Bush likes to run to keep in shape. But not too many Americans are aware that Barbara Bush keeps Secret Service agents on their toes during her daily walks.

The First Lady walks 4 to 6 miles a day, depending on the time available, and keeps up a pace of "15 minutes per mile or better." When asked what she liked best about walking, Mrs. Bush quipped, "The feeling I have when it's over!" But she went on to say she loves being outdoors, walking with her dogs, listening to books on tape, or just relaxing.

at least five 10-mile walks and at least one 15-mile walk; speed is not important for this award.

Getting Started

To get you started walking toward your Presidential Walking Award, we've included a Presidential Sports Award log for you to photocopy (see "To Get Your Award" on page 142). Read through the specific requirements below for each type of walking award. Choose the award best suited to your program and start recording your walks in the log. When your log is complete, send your log and check or money order for $6 to the address provided in order to receive your award.

If you're a *Prevention* Walking Club member, remember to include your membership number to receive your special pin.

If you have not been exercising regularly, please check with your doctor before beginning a vigorous walking program.

Making the Grade

To ensure your getting the greatest physical benefit, the requirements for each category should be met within a four-month period.

To earn the Fitness Walking Award, you must:

1. Walk a minimum of 125 miles.

2. Walk continuously at a pace of at least 4 miles per hour (a mile in 15 minutes).

3. Credit no more than 2½ miles a day to your total.

To earn the Race Walking Award, you must:

1. Racewalk a minimum of 200 miles.

2. Racewalk continuously at least 3 miles each outing. Only 5 miles on any day may be counted toward the total. Miles counted toward the 200-mile total must be spread over at least 40 outings.

3. Walk an average time of 12 minutes or less per mile.

To Get Your Award

After completing the requirements for one of the awards described on pages 140 and 141, fill out and sign your log. Send it, along with a $6 check or money order (payable to AAU/Presidential Sports Award) to: Presidential Sports Award, AAU House, P.O. Box 68207, Indianapolis, IN 46268. Allow up to six weeks for delivery.

DATE _____ MILES _____

I hereby affirm that I have completed the requirements for the Presidential Award in _____ Walking. I obtained my log from *Prevention* Magazine Health Books.

Signature _____

Prevention Walking Club Number _____

Name _____

Age _____ Sex _____

Address _____

City/State/Zip _____

_____

4. Follow the basic rules of racewalking. (Keep one foot on the ground at all times and keep the supporting leg straight as it comes under the body.)

5. Participate in at least three judged events.

To earn the Endurance Walking Award, you must:

1. Walk a minimum of 225 miles.

2. Make sure your endurance walks are continuous for at least 5 miles. (No more than one 10-mile or 15-mile walk can be credited each week.)

3. Make sure that during the four-month period, at least five of the outings are 10 miles long, and at least one is 15 miles long.

4. Include four 1-hour walks a week.

The Prevention Walking Club

We'll Coach You and Encourage You

In April of 1986, *Prevention* magazine began a walking club to encourage and inspire its readers to take our recommendations for a healthy lifestyle seriously. For a small annual fee, members receive a handbook with a daily log, a membership patch and card, and quarterly newsletters. We offer an incentive system of prizes and patches that members can apply for as they accumulate mileage. The response from our readership was astounding! Over 100,000 people signed on in the beginning!

Eager for Information

We received thousands of letters from our members extolling the benefits of their new-found fitness habit or remarking how happy they were, as lifelong walkers, to be recognized at last. Research was finally beginning to prove what many had known from personal experience—walking is a nearly perfect exercise.

At first, members could send us their logs to qualify for fantastic gifts for walking 250, 500, 1,000, or 5,000 miles. But after a while, we realized that only a small portion of members were interested in those material rewards. Most simply wanted the best, most up-to-date information about the benefits of walking. They were interested in the feel-better results of walking regularly. They wanted tips on technique, gear, walking vacations, and ways to share members' success with weight loss, stress reduction, or coping with diabetes, arthritis, and other chronic conditions.

Success Loves Company

Today the club is still going strong, with more than 70,000 members. *Prevention* holds a walkers' convention every year, the All-American Walkers Rally, where members and other interested people can spend three days together attending seminars with leading walking and health and nutrition experts, browsing through an expo filled with walking-related products and healthy foods, and enjoying fascinating and fun walks—on the beach, through local theme parks, at sunset, sunrise, and in between.

Volksmarches (see page 194), racewalks (see page 145), even walks that result in haiku are usually a part of the festivities, as is a banquet to honor people who have changed their lives and the lives of others through walking. Destination cities such as Tampa, Florida, and San Diego and San Jose, California, have drawn thousands of people together for weekends of walking and camaraderie.

You can join the *Prevention* Walking Club and receive the *Walker's World Handbook,* the *Walker's World Newsletter* (now bimonthly), and other club benefits. Write to the *Prevention* Walking Club, 33 East Minor Street, Emmaus, PA 18098 for information. It's a great way to stay inspired and motivated to maintain your walking program.

Racewalking

Fast and Challenging

I t's the darndest-looking sport. With a quick-paced waddle, race-walkers look like people trying to run with blisters on their feet.

But don't laugh. Racewalking, a featured event in the 1988 Summer Olympics, is gaining popularity among people who walk or run for fitness. And for good reason. It's a great aerobic sport that's easier on the bones and joints than running and burns more calories than regular walking.

Racewalking can help you not only trim excess weight but also tone key muscles. Calves become shapelier. Upper arm, shoulder, and back muscles strengthen, improving posture. Best of all, race-walking zeros in on problem areas—the abdomen, thighs, hips, and buttocks. And that funny-looking hip action can whittle your waist and firm your lower torso.

So what are you waiting for? A little inspiration? Step-by-step instructions? Encouragement and support? Then read on.

A Beginner's Racewalking Clinic

You don't have to race to racewalk. As veteran coach Howard Jacobson says, "It's the style that counts . . . proper racewalk style promotes a high degree of fitness, even if you're not out to set records."

To cash in on the benefits of racewalking, you'll have to invest some time and effort to learn the technique. You'll need to focus on your body: Pay attention to your stride, your posture, your breathing. In time, says former national racewalking coach Gary Westerfield, you will achieve an efficient style that will make you feel "like you're floating along . . . almost like you're dancing."

There are two rules for racewalking that govern technique. First, one foot must be in contact with the ground at all times. Otherwise, technically, you'd be running. Second, you must keep your knee straight when it is directly under the body and over your foot. Straightening your knee automatically sends your hip jutting out.

Here is the one-two-three of proper racewalking form:

1. "Get hip" to the feel of racewalking. Stand with your feet together. Relax. Now straighten one knee, allowing your hip to slide back and bending your other knee. (If you've ever carried a baby on your hip, this will feel very familiar.) Shift your weight from side to side, straightening one knee and then the other, allowing your hips to adjust by moving slightly to the side. This is the motion you want to incorporate into your walk. Try a walk around the room this way.

2. Concentrate on landing on your heel, with your foot at a 45-degree angle to the ground with your toe up and your leg straight. The idea is to roll onto your foot, making sure your knee is straightened as your body becomes centered over your leg. Having the toe up assures that your leg will be straight. Then you start to bend it as you push off with the toe of your other foot.

3. Combine steps 1 and 2. If you try walking around the room with this heel-and-toe motion, while keeping your hips straight, you'll notice that you bob up and down. Instead, let your hip relax and move out as your knee straightens. You won't bounce up and down. Instead, your head will maintain an even line and you'll feel that gliding effect.

4. Move your hips from front to back, using your hip as an extension of your leg. In doing so, you can add from 4 to 8 inches to your overall stride length. That's why someone racewalking next to you and taking the same number of steps will seem to glide past you effortlessly.

5. Bend your arms at the elbows and let them swing from the shoulder. You'll find you can actually add momentum to your walk by pumping your arms. Just be careful to stay relaxed. A lot of people hike their shoulders up around their necks as they try to go faster.

6. Coordinate your arm swing with your stride. When your foot is forward, the arm on that side is back; when the foot is behind you, the arm is out front.

Perfecting the Technique

Racewalking takes practice. Plus all the help you can get from friends and fellow racewalkers. According to Henry H. Laskau, three-time Olympian who won 42 National Racewalking Championships, racewalking form is difficult to master on your own. And it takes time. He estimates that it takes the average person six to eight weeks to get the technique down. Laskau advises learning the technique very, very slowly. Technique and form come before speed and distance, he says. Also, it's advisable to get input from a pro. If you don't know one, try some of these avenues.

■ Attend a racewalking clinic where you can get feedback from experienced racewalkers. There are active racewalking clubs in almost every state. You can receive a directory by mailing a self-addressed, stamped envelope to Sal Corrallo, TAC (The Athletic Congress), P.O. Box 120, Indianapolis, IN 46206.

■ Find a partner who is willing to train with you so that you can monitor each other's technique. Check each other on the angle of heel strike, for body lean (never backward and no more than 5 degrees forward), and on whether or not you're straightening your leg, says John Gray, author of *Racewalking for Fitness.*

■ Read a good racewalking book, like Gray's or Howard Jacobson's *Racewalk to Fitness,* which is generally considered the classic how-to-racewalk manual. Jacobson has years of racewalking and coaching experience. His book has a "you-can-do-it," friendly approach. Jacobson tells you how to start, how to train, how to enter races if you wish to compete as well as how to deal with hecklers. (He's the kind of guy who likes to heckle back.) The book is now available in paperback for $9 plus $1 for postage and handling. Send your check to Walker's Club of America, Book Department, Box M, Livingston Manor, NY 12758.

The Value of Video

You might also try training in front of the TV with a racewalking video. And why not watch the best? Martin Rudow, U.S. Olympic coach from 1985 to 1988, introduces racewalking techniques for fitness walkers and competitive athletes in his video, "Racewalking Technique." Excellent treadmill photography of racewalkers really shows you how the hips and legs move. It's available by mail order only; send $21.45 (which includes postage and handling) to Technique Productions, 4831 N.E. 44th Street, Seattle, WA 98105.

Anne Kashiwa, coauthor with James M. Rippe, M.D., of Rockport's *Fitness Walking for Women,* is also co-creator of a racewalking video. With the help of Tim Lewis, who holds the world racewalking record for the indoor mile, she introduces the benefits of racewalking and demonstrates the techniques in a slow-motion treadmill sequence.

"You can take apart the total racewalking technique and add one motion at a time to your regular fitness-walking workout." says Kashiwa. The key element is practice, she says. "You'll know when you're getting it right. You'll feel that very gliding, fluid motion. That's the reward of concentrating on this technique of walking." The video, "Yes! We're Walking!" by Fit Video, is available for $19.95 at local stores.

Confessions of Two Racewalking Converts

Why are people of all ages finding challenge and reward in this curious sport?

To an uninformed spectator, racewalking may seem all strain and no gain. After all, if you're walking for general health and cardiovascular conditioning, speed is not important. (It's consistency that counts; just walk at a comfortable pace for 30 to 40 minutes, three to four times a week.)

So why racewalk? Some do it for the competition; some to challenge their bodies to a higher level of fitness. The good news is that people of all ages can racewalk. And for those who do, the rewards are well worth the effort. Here are two cases in point.

Viisha Sedlak: Fit at 40

When Viisha Sedlak was in high school, her track coach told her she had no athletic ability. Today, at age 42, she is the number one female Masters (over 35) racewalker in the world. She holds three world records—the 5-K and 10-K track records and the 5-K road record, which she gained at *Prevention*'s 1990 All-American Walkers Rally in Tampa, Florida.

Sedlak began running in her early thirties. She was one of half a dozen women ever invited to run in the LaRochelle Six-Day Race, considered the world championship of long-distance running. To help her train for these ultramarathon races, she turned to racewalking. In time, she found that she enjoyed racewalking more than running. So she stuck with it.

"I find racewalking more intellectually challenging than running," she explains. "You cannot let your mind drift. You must stay focused on your form in order to enhance the efficiency of the walk.

"Another advantage of racewalking is that it really improves body tone. I have trimmer thighs, buttocks, and waist than when I was a runner. And I'm impressed with the effect it has on posture— mine as well as that of women I've coached. Because of the vigorous arm swing, the muscles in the upper back are strengthened and the shoulders open up and straighten. People become less round-shouldered."

Sedlak counsels people on weight loss and nutrition and conducts racewalking clinics. "My biggest thrill is to see a woman who's 50 or 60 years old compete and cross that finish line with hundreds of other athletes," she says. "One thing I've learned is that we all create boundaries for ourselves. The boundaries I break through in a six-day race are essentially the same boundaries any sedentary person breaks when they walk their first mile. People who have been sedentary all their lives start saying, 'I can do it! I can be an athlete.' "

Marilla Salisbury: Racing at 80

"Sunbonnet Sue" knows all about success in racewalking. That's the nickname Marilla Salisbury's husband, Earl, gave her because she dons a calico bonnet when she racewalks. Salisbury, 80, can walk a 13-minute mile and won eight gold medals in the World

Association of Veterans Games in Melbourne, Australia. She says it's becoming more difficult to find competition.

She is the quintessential late bloomer. She didn't start race-walking until she was 72 years old. At 70, she was, in her words, "a sedentary lump." Her body was so crippled by arthritis she could not tie her shoes. She had so much difficulty turning her head, she nearly had to give up driving.

Then, during an afternoon drive in San Diego, she and her newlywed husband came upon a fitness center and, out of curiosity, decided to check it out. Impressed with the friendliness of the staff, they signed on. For two years, Salisbury worked with weights to strengthen and limber up her body. Then she graduated to running. At the age of 72, she won her first gold medal in her first race, a 10-K. "The mayor was at the race and he was so excited when I finished, he ran down to hug and kiss me," she recalls.

Fearful that running might aggravate spinal deterioration, Salisbury's doctors suggested that she give up running and take up walking instead. That's when she discovered racewalking.

Now she travels to track meets around the world accompanied by 83-year-old Earl, who incidentally took up shot put, discus throwing, and javelin a couple of years ago. So far, she has competed in Masters meets (competitions for women age 35 and up and men 40 and up) in Chile, Italy, mainland China, Australia, Puerto Rico, and South Africa.

To prepare for these meets, Salisbury maintains a strict training schedule. She lifts weights three nights a week. Three mornings a week, after warming up for 30 minutes on her indoor treadmill, she joins "another girl" at a nearby track where they racewalk 15 to 20 laps. The other girl is 71 years old.

When she's not training or globe-trotting, Salisbury speaks at convalescent centers. "It's distressing to see people younger than me dependent on wheelchairs, especially when I know many of them could be doing what I'm doing. You have to stay active to keep going," she says.

Masters Competition

Lots of people who rejected competition in the high-pressure arena of high school or college athletics find an urge to give it a go later in life. And Viisha Sedlak and Marilla Salisbury both feel Masters competitions offer an ideal opportunity to test their mettle. Masters competition is fun. Master athletes are extremely supportive. The races are a wonderful place to get friendly advice.

"The sport is so young right now. There is opportunity for people to be very successful in Masters' competitions," says Sedlak.

If you'd like more information on Masters track meets, you may want to subscribe ($18.75 per year) to *National Masters News*, P.O. Box 2372, Van Nuys, CA 91401.

Rainy-Day Walking

Go On, You Won't Melt!

It's been raining for two days, and you're feeling disgruntled and irritated. This morning your newspaper was soggy, you discovered a leak in your second-floor bedroom, and when you tried to let the dog out, he took one look at the raindrops and beat it for your favorite chair.

Sitting at your desk at work, you're worried that the bucket under the leak may fill up before you get home. The prospect of a soggy sandwich at your desk looms before you. Usually your lunch hour would find you taking a brisk walk to energize your sagging spirits, but who walks in the rain? Sure, Thoreau mucked about in the woods rain or shine, but he was tuned in to a different drummer. You're a confirmed fair-weather walker and not even the promise of a hot lunch will lure you out into this slop. But walking on a regular basis has added a certain rhythm to your life, and you miss it, even after just two days. You feel tense and the air inside seems stuffy and dead.

Damp Weather Shoe Sense

So it's spring and the world is "mudluscious and puddle wonderful" (as e. e. cummings described it in "in Just-spring"), but what about your walking shoes?

Be sure to dry them thoroughly when they get a soaking, but don't put them too close to any heating element, as they may shrink or warp. Stuffing them with newspaper or paper towels will help to soak up the moisture and help to retain their shape.

Leather shoes can be wiped clean with a mild detergent, which should be followed by the appropriate wax polish. An application of mink oil will give added protection from soggy terrain.

It's a good idea to have at least two pairs of walking shoes, so that you can switch from day to day, allowing each pair to dry out slowly, whether wet from perspiration or puddles.

Enjoy the Splash

Putting the enticement of a fresh deli sandwich before you, you drag on your raincoat, grab your umbrella, and plunge outside.

At first your muscles are tense against the coolness, your head is bent over, and the umbrella totally blocks your view as you foray up the street. But gradually, as that familiar, steady rhythm of walking renders its surprisingly soothing effect, your muscles loosen up and an awareness of your surroundings begins to creep in.

First, perhaps, it's the syncopated tapping of the rain on your umbrella that seeps into your consciousness. And as you tune in to that sound, you notice the rain zinging on a drainpipe and then the cacophony produced by water rushing into a storm drain.

Soon the smells reach you: the distinctive acrid smell of wet pavement, or the incredibly rich, sweet smell of rain-drenched flowers. Lifting your umbrella to peer in front of you, you catch the dance and swagger of raindrops across blacktop and the rainbowed rivulets of water streaming into tiny whirlpools by the curb.

By now you've forgotten whatever it was that kept you from venturing out in "foul" weather. You're standing taller, breathing deeply, and treading briskly. You return to the office refreshed and rejuvenated. Are you keeping a walking log? If so, write a few inspiring comments, so that next time you won't allow a little rainy weather to keep you from the pleasure of your daily walking habit.

Splash Sense

You're not going to let a little rain dampen your enthusiasm for walking. If you decide to tough it out, here are a few foul-weather tips to see you through.

- Step around puddles. Standing water may be deeper than you think.

- Avoid the white stripes on roads. When wet, they can be more slippery than the road surface. Stay on asphalt and concrete surfaces.

- Wear bright clothing. You won't be as visible to drivers on rainy days.

- Wear garments that breathe. While a plastic slicker may keep the rain out, you may get so sweaty inside, you'll think you weren't even wearing a raincoat.

- Forget your rubber boots. They don't breathe. Leather holds out water better than cloth or nylon mesh. Rippled soles are best for traction.

- If you can't stand the rain pelting you in the face, carry an umbrella. You can still get a nice, brisk walk in, even if you aren't swinging those arms fully. Walking with an umbrella is better exercise than watching TV, no matter how slowly you do it!

Shoes

The Fit and the Foot

Before walking became America's favorite fitness activity—with 30 million people claiming they walk for exercise at least three days a week—you'd have been hard-pressed to find anything called a walking shoe. If you were a walker before 1985, you probably wore a sneaker, a running shoe, or a comfort shoe on your regular outings. Comfort shoes were sturdy-looking, supportive, and a bit on the grandmotherly side. Sneakers were thin, practically archless, and did little to hold your foot steady. Running shoes were probably your best bet, and many people still choose them for walking. But running shoes have a flared heel, designed to offset the impact of the runner's weight as he pounds the ground. A walker walks heel to toe, and that heel flair gets in the way. Walking shoes do have specific characteristics that make them great for walking. But if you've never owned a pair, probably the only thing that will convince you for sure is to try them.

What Makes a Walking Shoe

Any well-known company that produces a walking shoe has explored the technical features walkers need—like a firm heel counter, to keep your heel from wobbling, a beveled heel to make you more steady and comfortable as you come down on your heel, sufficient resiliency in the sole to cushion your foot, good arch support, and a sturdy lacing structure that helps to keep your foot from leaning in or out (pronation and supination are the official terms).

Of course, these companies are all battling for your feet, so they promote the special characteristics of their own product—like a rocking sole that helps you roll through the heel-to-toe walking motion, or an extra-wide toe box to accommodate lots of movement and the spreading of your toes when you push off.

Recognizing that no technological feature will do you much good if your shoe doesn't fit well, some companies have made their shoes available in more widths and lengths. There are varieties in leathers and mesh, some more breathable than others. Some shoes are even waterproof, which is great for people who walk with their dogs over wet, dewy grass in the mornings. Some walking shoes are very athletic-looking, while others could go straight to work. Some have thick and not-too-flexible soles. Others, more suitable for very fast walking, are thin soled.

The important thing when picking a shoe is to think about your own needs. What kind of walker are you? Where will you be walking—on what surface? There are shoes for mallwalking, racewalking, walking on country trails, hiking, and those that double as tennis shoes. Go to a shoe store where you can talk to salespeople who know their products. Explain your needs and try on several different brands of shoes. Let your feet make the final decision. While we can't tell you the perfect shoe, we can tell you a lot about getting a good fit.

Your Guide to a Perfect Fit

In a survey done by the Gallup organization in 1984, 73 percent of the people surveyed said their feet hurt. That means if your feet don't hurt, you can consider yourself exceptional and count your blessings. If they do hurt, you can put up with it, curtail activity, see a podiatrist, buy orthoses, use little pads here and there. There are endless possibilities and sometimes they work.

When Charles S. Smith, a professional shoe fitter for 20 years and author of *Ten Steps to Comfort,* came to Rodale Press, he said that many problems with foot pain could be solved by properly fitting shoes. We were skeptical. When he said that getting a proper fit is often as simple as getting a shoe a half size larger, we laughed out loud.

"That's such a simple answer, Charlie. Why don't more people catch on?"

"Because they're holding on to a whole lot of myths and misconceptions about what correct fit is. They *think* their shoes fit, so they figure the problem must be with their feet. Usually by that time it *is* their feet, because they've abused them with shoes fitted too small."

But, we inquired, shouldn't you be able to tell when you first try a shoe on whether it's going to hurt or not?

Not necessarily, according to Smith. And he went on to explain why. We were listening with half an ear when a colleague (I'll call her Mary) came along who was having terrible problems with her foot since she had begun walking regularly.

Mary started having pain in the ball of her foot and her heel after two months of walking. She'd gone to her doctor, who advised her to take aspirin and to stop walking so much. He said she had tendinitis. Mary slowed down a bit, but her foot still hurt, so she went to a podiatrist. The podiatrist x-rayed her foot and gave her a cortisone shot for inflammation and a special pad for her shoe for extra cushioning. The shots worked, Mary said. But when they wore off, she had to go back for more.

Her podiatrist also suggested that she needed an orthosis, a custom-made support for her foot. He said that her increased activity caused some defect in her foot to become more apparent. Orthoses were made, but Mary couldn't stand to wear them. They hurt too much. She'd devised her own adjustments with some shoe inserts but was still having pain when we called her over to meet Smith.

He immediately measured her foot and told her she needed at least a half size bigger than she was wearing. He recommended she purchase comfortable shoes in the proper size. Mary got the shoes and took them, along with a pair of hiking boots in her usual size, on a walking vacation, where she trekked 10 miles a day. The hiking boots, she says, almost killed her. The new shoes, in the larger size, saved her. She's been wearing those shoes, walking an hour a day for over three months now, and no longer experiences any pain whatsoever!

Needless to say, Smith was not surprised. He sent us many testimonials from people he had helped with proper fitting. In all cases, a size change made the difference between pain and comfort. He said that in many shoe stores, there often are no qualified or experienced fitters. And even if there are, people often argue about their correct size, so the fitter may just give up and let them buy a poorly fitting shoe. Smith maintains that the public needs to be educated so they can work with the shoe fitter instead of against him. They can avoid unnecessary medical expense, and they can walk without pain.

Now, walkers are a step ahead of the game here because walking shoes, unlike pumps (heeled or flat), *are* styled and built for comfort rather than fashion. Good walking shoes have firm heel counters, wide or flared heel bases, multiple laces, padding, cushioning, and flexibility. But all that technology will be worthless if they don't fit.

So what are some of the beliefs that stand between you and a pair of comfortable walking shoes?

Myth #1: A size is a size is a size. The fit of a size 8 shoe will vary considerably with style and features, even in the same brand. Always have both feet measured, and use the larger of the two sizes as a *starting* place. You may have to increase your size number to get a proper and more comfortable fit.

Myth #2: If a new shoe feels roomy, it is too big. Somewhere we got the notion that a shoe should feel tight. Maybe it's because some styles cut for fashion, like pumps, flats, or loafers, fall off if they're not tight. And if you wear them, you may have to compromise on comfort. But a walking shoe should have sufficient room to allow for adequate space when your foot flexes. You may not experience discomfort until you've worn them for a while. Shoes fitted too small will restrict the normal exercising of the muscles and tendons, causing pain and cramping.

Also keep in mind that your foot can swell to a whole size larger when you walk, and that you'll be wearing thick socks to soak up perspiration. Take your thick socks with you when you go to purchase your walking shoes.

Myth #3: The heel of a shoe should fit snugly. Many people think the heel of a shoe should not slip when they try it on in a store. They try to slip their foot out at the heel by contracting their foot, and if they can, they think the shoe is too big. They end up buying a too-snug heel that leaves too little toe room, and they get blisters. (Blisters are generally caused by tight shoes, not loose ones.)

According to Smith, you should be able to stick a pencil between your heel and the back of the shoe to guarantee proper fit. The heel does not *fit* by being narrow or tight. It begins to fit after the shoe has been flexed repeatedly. The heel will "cup," or turn in at the top, and begin to fit your heel by conforming to the curve of it. Once you understand this, you realize that you won't feel the actual fit of a shoe until you've been wearing it for a while. In the store, you're making an educated guess.

Professional shoe fitters are aware of this adaptive characteristic of a shoe and that's why they take a shoe and bend it several times when they take it out of the box. They are starting that heel cupping process for you, not just "softening up" the shoe.

Myth #4: Tight shoes will stretch to fit better. Or a variation of that theme: Shoes need to be broken in.

Discard those ideas with your Band-Aids and corn plasters. The only thing you're breaking in with a too-small shoe is your foot. And as we've already noted, a shoe actually gets *shorter* in terms of space available to your foot when you're walking in it, although it may get a bit wider. But the change in width can be controlled by adjusting the laces. No well-fitting shoe made for comfort should ever put you through a Band-Aid and blister phase. It should feel great right from the start.

Myth #5: The last pair of shoes your mom bought you for high school should still fit today. According to Smith, this is one of the toughest misconceptions to shatter. Foot size changes with age or weight gain or loss and with alterations in exercise patterns. You don't expect your prom dress or tuxedo to fit you today, do you?

Myth #6: Bigger feet are uglier, more clumsy, a definite social disadvantage and something to be embarrassed about. Lots of people, especially women, feel uncomfortable about large shoe sizes. They tend to blush and become self-deprecating when they have to give their shoe size. One friend with big feet told me people used to joke that he'd be really tall if so much of him weren't folded under! This is something you just have to work through your own psychological mill. There are no studies showing that people with big feet are actually clumsier or that women with small feet have more fun.

Don't let this kind of social conditioning of your self-esteem prevent you from taking a larger shoe size that may mean comfortable and pain-free feet!

Finer Points of Fit

Now, three more tips for choosing comfortable shoes.

You probably know that one of your feet is larger than the other. Make sure you fit the larger foot! It's better to add a half insole in the front of the shoe on the smaller foot than to cramp the larger foot in a too-small size. And a half size too small, even though it's only ¹⁄₁₆-inch difference, can mean pain for your foot!

Also pay attention to the shape of the toe of your shoes. The wider and higher the toe box, the more comfort for your foot. And don't be afraid of extra space between your toes and the end of the shoe. It does not mean the shoe is too big if you can press on the toe of the shoe and hit nothing but air space. You need that extra room during the motion of walking. If you are buying a shoe with a more tapered toe, there should be more space beyond your toes than if you are buying a shoe with a very rounded toe box. Your foot will not be comfortable if you squash it into a parabola shape. Shoes that taper to a point originated in the thirteenth century because it was believed that the point would repel witches. That belief was taken to the extreme when the points became so long they had to be tied to the knee so you wouldn't trip over them. Pointy shoes have remained in vogue as a matter of aesthetics. They have nothing to do with foot comfort or fit!

And finally, find a shoe store where you know you'll be getting the assistance of a professional shoe fitter for any special problems you may have. Consult your Yellow Pages for stores with nationally recognized quality shoes. The ads may even list professional fitting service. Be flexible and open to new suggestions when you find a good fitter. Armed with what you know now, the two of you can make a great team for fitting you with a shoe that will satisfy your tastes and your need for total foot comfort.

Searching for Shoe Shape

A survey conducted by the American Academy of Podiatric Sports Medicine (AAPSM) in 1989 revealed an increase in walking-related foot injuries. Many of those injuries may have been related to poorly fitting shoes, according to William Van Pelt, D.P.M., a Houston podiatrist, president of the AAPSM, and conductor of the survey.

The injuries cited as most common were complaints about pain or pressure along the outside borders of the foot. Other problems were toe irritation or pain, ankle sprain, Achilles tendinitis, pressure on the big toe, pain on the inside of the ankles or on the bottoms of the feet behind the toes, irritated bunions, and pain on the bottom of the heels (plantar fasciitis).

What a lot of people don't realize is that size is not the only

Time for a New Pair

A lot of people forget to pay attention to the shape their shoes are in. If the laces still tie, they're still good. But the fact is, the resiliency of certain materials decreases with age, providing less shock absorbtion. If your ankles tend to turn in or out when you walk, the heels of your shoes will wear unevenly, making the problem even worse, and making it easier for you to strain or sprain your ankle. The soles of your shoes lose their traction, making you more vulnerable to slips or falls. Some walking shoes are even guaranteed for only a certain number of miles!

Your feet deserve the best treatment you can afford for them. They take a lot of abuse. Take care of them, and they'll help to keep you healthy and happy for as long as you live. Give your walking shoes periodic checks and don't wait till you wear them out to purchase a new pair. Actually, you should have two pairs. While you're using one pair, the others need to dry out to prevent fungus, odors, and blisters from annoying you.

factor to be considered in shoe fit. A little-known sizing factor concerning foot type also has to be considered.

According to Dr. Van Pelt, there are three basic foot types. About one-third of us have a high-arched foot that tends to be curved. (If you drew a line around your foot while standing on a piece of paper, the shape would be curved, toward the center of your body.) It's called a C-shaped or banana-shaped foot type. Another third have a foot that is more gently curved. And a final third have a flat foot, with feet shaped "like railroad boxcars."

Shoes come in three different "lasts." The last is the shape the shoe is centered around. If you hold a shoe upside-down and look at the overall shape of the sole, you can determine a straight-last, curve-last, or standard-last shoe.

Why do manufacturers build their shoes on a particular last? "This is pretty much a matter of standard and habit," says Dr. Van Pelt. The first shoe designers probably looked down at their own foot or their wife's foot and decided that was the shape of all feet. Often, manufacturers just keep using the same lasts.

"You can have a perfectly adequate shoe that fits the person in both length and width, and it will still cause irritation or injury because it is not built for their foot type," says Dr. Van Pelt.

"Unfortunately, most people don't know anything about lasts. And it's not marked on the shoe. People need to know that it is important not to put a round peg in a square hole. If you put a C-shaped foot into a straight-lasted shoe, you're going to have uncomfortable points of pressure. That can cause pain in the foot, and because of muscle contractions, pain all the way up the leg as well.

"The public can make educated guesses about the last of a shoe. First, put a piece of paper under your foot when you are sitting down. Bend over, and without exerting too much pressure on your foot, draw around the outside edges. That will tell you your foot shape. Match that shape to the bottom of any shoe you want to purchase."

Socks

Keeping Feet Sweet

Baby boomers remember when socks were taboo. The only material that got close to their feet was the leather of their loafers. After the bobby-socks era, socks got lost in the shuffle of sandaled hippies or dock-sidered preppies.

But in the 1990s, socks are not only hot fashion accessories, they're also high-tech sports equipment. And, as with a lot of things, until you've experienced the higher-priced versions, you probably don't know what you're missing.

If you're still wearing 100 percent cotton tube socks from the grocery store, and are still happy about it, chances are you've never experienced a Thor-Lo or a Rockport, two current Cadillacs of the walking sock world.

Think your walking feet could stand a little pampering? A little extra cushioning? A drier, cooler home to live in? Well, we're going to help you hop into the right sock. At *Prevention,* we walk-tested 12 different brands of manufacturer's recommended socks for walking. The comments of our testers were mostly "Hmmmm," "A-a-a-a-a-a-hhhh" and "O-o-o-o-o-o-h, how soft and cushy!" As a result of our "on the hoof" survey, we think you could try just about any high-tech walking sock and have happier feet. Here's some useful information to help you sort through the sizes, styles, and materials.

Sizing Them Up

The fit of your walking sock is as important as the fit of your shoe. Too tight and you'll constrict your toes. Too big and the extra fabric will bunch up, causing discomfort, friction, maybe even blisters. Your sock should slip on comfortably but fit smoothly over your entire foot, with room or stretchability for the toes to move. Forget the one-size-fits-all type. They may be okay for growing kiddie feet, but *you* have a sock size.

Sock sizes were set by the National Association of Hosiery Manufacturers in 1974 after launching an extensive survey of human foot dimensions. The sizes, based on nine specific measurements of the foot and calf, serve as guidelines for industry standardization. The consumer relies on manufacturers' packaging, which relates sock size to shoe size. Individual manufacturers' charts may vary because there are no industry-wide standards for sock-to-shoe sizes, so check each chart. Generally, sock sizes are larger by a size or two than shoe size. And one sock size accommodates two shoe sizes.

How far the sock extends above the foot has to do with style, not size. Traditionally, athletic socks were midcalf (also known as crew). But today, sport socks are available in anklet size (covers the ankle bone) and footsocks (does not extend above the ankle bone). It's a matter of personal preference and where you want your tan line.

Natural vs. Synthetic

Natural fibers like cotton and wool *used* to be the preferred material for socks because they are breathable and absorb perspiration. That was before synthetics like orlon, polypropylene, and Coolmax were developed, with their ability to wick moisture away from the foot, keeping it drier and less likely to blister or to generate odor. Synthetic fibers tend to release the moisture for evaporation. Cotton absorbs moisture into the fiber. When socks become sweat-soaked, they become hard and matted during use, intensifying friction.

Synthetic fibers also retain their shape and texture longer. After a few machine washings, cotton socks without added resilient synthetics (like nylon or Spandex) become limp and lifeless, dry, matted, and shapeless. Synthetics stay soft, puffy, and fluffy and bounce back to their original shape.

Despite new research on the resiliency and blister-preventing qualities of synthetics, many consumers still hold on to their affection for cotton. If you're one of them, you should know that Cherokee, Bill Rodgers, or Burlington PrimaSport Walking Socks, all of which we tested, are primarily cotton, with nylon and/or Spandex added for better fit and shape retention.

Double-Lay-R socks use Dupont's Coolmax fabric, which has superlative wicking action. Their sock is also constructed with two layers, which not only reduces friction but allows for more effective transportation of moisture and evaporation. (Walkers and hikers have long known the value of wearing two pairs of socks, but often the results were too bulky.) Their socks are guaranteed to keep you from blistering, or your money back. (Our tester said they felt "like silk.") A less expensive Coolmax sock is ASICS Walking Sock—only one layer.

The Techno-Socks

Some walking socks go beyond cool, dry, and snuggly into the realm of high-tech walking features.

Easy Spirit's Performance Sock, made of high-bulk orlon

acrylic and stretch nylon, is fully cushioned (on the sole, top, toe, and heel) with a terry pile surface to help reduce shock. Our tester said these socks felt like she was "walking on air."

Thor-Lo PADDS Foot Equipment Walking Series features Spandex around the arch for arch support and generous protective padding on the heel and ball of the foot. A low-density pad on the top of the foot protects the instep from friction from the laces. It's the kind of sock that seems to make *any* shoe comfy. But be careful. If you get addicted to Thor-Lo's, you may have to buy shoes a half size bigger to accommodate that extra padding. Our tester already had several pairs at home. "They last so much longer than my other socks, and they feel terrific!" she said. "They're well worth the extra dollars."

(Thor-Lo's run $7 to $8.25 a pair. Along with Double-Lay-R at $8.95, they're at the high end of the price range. Most other socks we tested ran $4 to $6 a pair.)

The Rockport Walking Sock, made of Orlon and Spandex, also pads the heel and ball area and hugs the instep. An added feature is the "bulb" toe area, which gives extra room for the toes to spread during the walking motion. The crew style features a graduated tension weave in the calf area, which Rockport claims gently helps to pump the blood out of the walker's foot and back into the calf, so legs and feet won't cramp or tire as easily.

NaturalSport has a high-tech sock aesthetically designed to match their AerobicWalker shoe. Made of Orlon and nylon, the socks come only in anklet length. They're double welted at the top (folded over double), which keeps them snugly in place around the ankle and prevents stretching or fraying. Our tester's comment: "They fit like a glove."

Sweet Socks

With all these new materials for socks, sweaty feet stay a little (maybe a lot) drier. But for those of us who never consider taking off our shoes around our friends for fear of losing them (our friends, not our shoes), wicking action may not be enough. All of Burlington's PrimaSport athletic socks, including the walking version, have a chemical called Bioguard applied to the sock material during the dyeing process. Guaranteed to last for the life of the sock, this antimicrobacterial agent may help to keep really sweaty feet sweet. Tested by independent laboratories for uniform application, the chemical has never been reported to produce any kind of irritation to the foot. And *our* tester, chosen specifically for his not-so-sweet feet, says so far, so good.

Wear and Care

No matter how great your socks are, it's still a good idea to wear a clean, fresh pair for every walk and take an extra pair if you'll be out for more than an hour or if you know your feet sweat excessively. Moisture is the major culprit of the blister-making process. (It's good to alternate your shoes every day, too, so they can dry out. The socks wick the moisture away from your foot, the shoe picks it up from there.) Follow the manufacturer's instructions for

What the Seal Means

You may see the American Podiatric Medical Association (APMA) Seal of Acceptance on the packaging of various socks. This seal means the manufacturer applied to the association for review. The APMA is not an independent testing laboratory (they don't go out and test hundreds of socks and rate them). But if a manufacturer submits a sock, a committee reviews the product, wears it, cuts it apart, and reviews its advertising claims. Then a second committee works with the manufacturer to form an agreement on educating the public about maintaining healthy feet. In order to secure a seal of acceptance, the manufacturer must participate in this education process.

If the sock you choose does not have an APMA acceptance seal, that may simply mean they haven't applied for it, not that they have been tested and rejected. Socks we tested that have APMA acceptance are Thor-Lo PADDS and the Rockport Walking Sock.

care. In most cases, that just means popping them in the washer and dryer. Socks made out of cotton may need to be treated a little more delicately, with a cooler dryer, to retain their softness and shape.

Our testers loved the comfort of these super socks. But many were resistant to the higher prices. When reminded that these socks would probably last longer and retain their shape better than cheaper brands, they agreed they were worth the extra bucks. You'll have to see for yourself. The socks we've mentioned should be available at major sporting goods and department stores. Happy sock hunting!

Spirit
Healing for Body and Mind

Whether we're reading poetry by Walt Whitman, essays by Ralph Waldo Emerson, or letters from *Prevention* Walking Club members, we learn there is more in a walk than meets the eye. Walking may be good for the body, but it also provides food for the spirit. And in today's fast-paced world, that's something worth walking for.

Walking in beautiful, natural surroundings seems to have a special regenerative power for the spirit. And there seems to be a distinctly different flavor to traipsing through the woods or walking on open roads with long-distance vistas: two wonderful and separate pleasures.

On Forest Path

In the woods, there is a sense of closeness. You feel an intimacy with the rocks, the trees, the leaves, the smell of damp earth.

You can touch everything around you, feeling the textures under your feet and with your hands. Since your view is limited, you concentrate on what's immediately nearby.

You usually have to keep an eye on your feet, too. This can give you a feeling of being closed in or harried if you're not careful. Don't walk too fast. Take time to look around. When you slow down, you see so much more—like tiny wildflowers that barely catch your eye unless you actually stop to look for them. If you carry a small magnifying glass, those tiny wildflowers will reveal intricate patterns, symmetry, and color.

On a Clear Day . . .

On an open country road or a hilltop or other open space, you get this sense of exhilaration, of expansiveness. You can see great distances and you instinctively feel a part of all that space and immense beauty. (After all, you're walking through it! You are part of the landscape!) You can take your eyes off your feet and soar with the birds for a while.

In *The Power of Myth,* coauthor Joseph Campbell relates how Buddhists deliberately achieve this effect within their temples. The temples are situated on hillsides. The visitor walks first through small, intimate gardens, then climbs stairs and very suddenly passes by a screen or turns a corner and is confronted by a wide view of the countryside, inducing a feeling of tremendous energy and expansion. Campbell defines this feeling by quoting an ancient Hindu scripture: "When before the beauty of a sunset or of a mountain, you pause and exclaim 'Ah,' you are participating in divinity."

By walking in beautiful natural settings, you give yourself the opportunity to regenerate body *and* spirit. If you open yourself to it, the sense of the sheer power and beauty of existence may flood over you.

Along with all the physical benefits to your body and mind, you bring this special healing power of nature to your soul. Take time to go walking for this special benefit. You don't have to travel to exotic places to do it. Find a beautiful park or neighborhood with a view, or a local trail, and take a slow, leisurely walk with a friend or alone. The natural rhythm of walking will relax you and the healing power of natural beauty will refresh you.

Stress

Learning to Step Away

Stress has become synonymous with modern living. In a world that puts ever-increasing demands on our minds and emotions, and less demands on our bodies, we're continually thrown out of balance. The results are probably more far-reaching than we like to admit. From anxiety, tension, and illness to divorce, drug and alcohol problems, and crime, stress plays a part, pushing people to their physical and psychological limits.

While we may have very little control over some of the external causes of stress in our lives, there are things we can do to relieve the effects of that stress. Eat well, sleep well, maintain positive relationships, and *exercise.*

If you go for a walk today, you will feel better. It is as simple as that. Walking gives you psychological benefits immediately. And if you keep walking, measurable physiological benefits follow like fruit follows flowers.

Everybody can benefit from exercise, according to James M. Rippe, M.D., cardiologist and a leading physiology researcher at the University of Massachusetts Medical School in Worcester. And his research backs up that conviction.

Dr. Rippe tested 36 walkers for anxiety, tension, and blood pressure levels before, during, and after 40 minutes of walking. Results showed immediate decreases in tension and anxiety as well as blood pressure, regardless of how fast or slow the participants walked.

"The interesting point here is that psychological benefits, like reduced anxiety and tension, may be separate from physiological benefits," says Dr. Rippe. "The psychological benefits may kick in sooner."

Adrenaline Shock Absorber

One of the reasons stress has a negative effect on our bodies is that it triggers the body to produce adrenaline to cope with perceived danger—real or imagined. If you don't take action, though, adrenaline accumulates, causing muscle tension and feelings of anxiety. There is an easy, readily available way to "take action," however. Read on.

When New Jersey advertising executive Robert Milo was given a prescription for tranquilizers to cope with stress, he feared their addictive power. Instead of taking the medicine, he went to see psychologist William Rosenblatt, at the Biofeedback and Stress Management Center in Morristown, New Jersey. There, he says, "I found the best tranquilizer ever—walking."

Walking is a positive way to move you into action and use adrenaline. It also causes the release of calming brain chemicals called endorphins—natural tranquilizers.

Walking gives people a sense of control, Dr. Rosenblatt says. "When people exercise, they see that they can control (indeed reverse) their physical reactions to stress—even if they can't control the stressful situation. As a result, they can cope better emotionally."

Work was a major headache for Milo. Now his hectic day is cushioned by morning, lunchtime, and sometimes evening walks. "I'm a lot happier than I used to be!" he claims. And his long laugh after that last comment lets you know he means it.

Special Soothing Strolls

While any kind of walking will help to reduce stress, there may be some days when you're especially interested in expanding those stress-reducing effects. Here are some tips for extra soul-soothing strolls.

While many walkers report that walking provides an excellent opportunity to mull over problems, experts say that you're better off leaving your problems at home if you're trying to counteract stress. Enjoy your walk, and give your mind a rest.

How do you leave those problems behind when you step out the door? Turn your walk into a mini-meditation. The beneficial effects of meditation as a stress reducer and immune system booster have been well-documented. Adding some meditation techniques to your walk may take you another step away from the negative effects of stress. While there are no scientifically controlled studies examining the benefits of combining meditation and walking, many stress-reduction specialists feel it's a winning combination.

David and Deena Balboa, co-directors of The Walking Center of New York City, suggest these simple meditative steps for enhancing the stress-reducing value of walking.

■ Release yourself from any goal or objective. A walk for the purpose of unwinding and reducing stress is not a fitness walk with a target heart-rate goal.

■ Walk somewhere where you can maintain a sustained rhythm without interruption—a track or a long, peaceful pathway without breaks or crossways.

■ Consciously relax your shoulders. Keep your head erect to avoid contracting the windpipe and shortening your breath.

■ Lower your eyelids slightly to decrease the amount of external visual stimuli.

■ Allow your arms their full range of motion. You will naturally begin breathing more deeply, which automatically releases tension.

■ Take a few really deep breaths. When exhaling, allow yourself to sigh gently but audibly to release tension and emotion.

■ To clear your mind, focus on your breathing, not to control it but simply to watch it.

■ Become aware of the swing of your arms and how you move your feet.

■ Periodically check your shoulders to make sure they're dropped and relaxed.

The Zen Perspective

Focusing on your breathing and your body while you're walking brings you to a state of "mindfulness," according to George Bowman, Zen teacher at the Cambridge Zen Center in Massachusetts. That means you are open and aware in the moment, free from regrets of the past or anxieties about the future.

"Pay attention to the rise and fall of the feet and of the breathing until you reach a place where the mind quiets, until, in the most fundamental sense, you're just walking," Bowman advises.

Sidestepping Stress

There's another way to bring the beneficial effects of walking to bear in your life. Instead of just using walking to wash away the effects of stress and protect against its onslaught, there are many times when you can take a walk to *avoid* stressful situations in the first place.

Here's a list of stress-busting walking strategies. After a while, if you begin to let these strategies become a natural part of your life, you can stop thinking of them as avoidance measures, and start thinking of them as smart steps to positive living!

Feed your feet, not your face. If anxiety, boredom, or force of habit have you running to the refrigerator for comfort, slow down! You're just making your life more stressful by adding excess weight. When you know your hunger is motivated by stress, force yourself to take a brisk walk around the block or the hallways instead. Walking will relax you and may help you lose the urge to eat under duress.

Relieve "eyeball" pressure. Facing an uncomfortable personal confrontation? Take your spouse, your boss, your kid, or your friends for a walk-and-talk session. Meeting with people face-to-face, where constant eye contact is required, can generate extra anxiety and tension, especially if the subject matter is stress producing to begin with. Whenever you can, plan walking encounters. Not only do you relieve stress by making continual eye contact unnecessary, you both get to walk off some of the tension as you talk.

Chill out! You're angry. But do you really want to say those things you're screaming inside your head? Or will they just cause more stress in your life? Take a 5-minute walk break. Stomp your way around the block. Growl or groan out loud, if you can. Often we unload a week's worth of stress on the unlucky person who places "the last straw" on the back of our camel. After a walk break, you may feel less angry and have a better perspective on the situation, saving you and the other person a stressful and unnecessary argument.

Take walk breaks at work. Coffee breaks can be stress producers. Think of it. The caffeine, the smoke, the company gossip, can all get to you. Escape from the office routine of coffee and doughnuts. Research shows that a brisk walk can give you more energy than a sugary snack. If you can get outside, the fresh air may do wonders for your outlook, too. If not, a brisk jaunt through the halls, maybe a flight of stairs or two, will bring you back to your desk ready to concentrate.

Park in your own driveway. Ever head downtown on a Saturday morning and spend precious time circling the stores, looking for a parking space? Try leaving the car at home, or if too far, parking your car in a nearby residential area and walking to town for your Saturday morning errands. You'll avoid the aggravation of clogged streets, you won't be contributing to air pollution, and you'll get in a relaxing stroll. And you may even save time!

Incubate your best ideas. Sometimes knotty problems can leave us feeling physically tied in knots. Solutions start avoiding us. That's the time when less thinking and more relaxing and mental drifting can be a real asset. Take a stress-free stroll and let your subconscious do a little undercover work. Leave the problem behind, and when you get back, you may just find the answer staring you in the face.

Ease your dental fears. Picture yourself in the dentist's chair. Are your palms sweaty? Your shoulders hunched? Your breathing shallow? Do you start to feel queasy as soon as you get in the car to drive there? Then don't! Drive there, that is. Many people are uncomfortable in the dentist's office. Plan ahead so you have time to walk to the dentist and back. If the office is too far to walk to, park a mile away and walk from your car. You'll be more relaxed when you arrive (tension increases any discomfort you may encounter). And on the way home, you can walk off any excess adrenaline you built up while there.

Avoid parking lot panic. Door dings, kids everywhere, cars pulling in and out . . . parking lots sometimes seem like accidents waiting to happen. Next time you head for a mall or department store, don't automatically head for the center of the storm and try to get the "choice" spot closest to the door. Park as far from other cars, people, and the door as you can. Take a quiet stroll around the perimeter before you race into that bustling shopping arena. A restorative cool-down will be waiting for you on the way back to the car.

Slow down, slow down, slow down. Many of us are in a perpetual state of *hurry*. Our bodies get the message that we're in a continual state of emergency. Learning to prioritize and organize can help. What's really important to you? If you want to walk to relieve stress, try a pleasantly fast pace, not a breakneck one. Studies have shown that exercising vigorously can leave people feeling more anxious, not less. If you can't carry on a conversation without gasping for breath, you're walking too fast.

Plan a walking vacation. Vacations are a sign of status in America. Everybody wants to take one. But we do it so seldom, we're not very good at it. Planning a vacation can be a big headache—all the details, the reservations, the restaurants. How many people come home saying they need a vacation to recuperate from their vacation? A walking vacation, on the other hand, is a truly rejuvenating experience. Tour companies around the country are cropping up that will literally take care of your every need for a weekend or a week or more, at destinations here and abroad. You eat fine food, walk through beautiful, scenic pathways, and meet wonderful people. And all you have to worry about is the day pack on your back. You come home invigorated and refreshed. And looking forward to a walking vacation can add incentive to your regular walking program. Ask your travel agent for brochures on walking tours. (See the walking vacations chapter, beginning on page 189.)

Stretching
Flexibility Feels Fabulous

Walking makes you feel good. It relaxes you and provides you with an amazing number of health benefits. As you maintain a consistent program of walking for fitness, your gentle workouts gradually build stronger muscles.

Many of the muscles that you use to walk may benefit from gentle stretching to prevent tightness and discomfort that may develop as they grow stronger. Another good reason to stretch is that tight, shortened muscles may inhibit your natural walking gait. In addition to exercise, any number of factors can cause muscles to become short and tight—your job and stress for example.

Physiatrist Charles Norelli, M.D., shared several stretches with us that he has found helpful in his practice. These stretches are *not* meant to be used as a warm-up before walking. The best warm-up for more strenuous forms of walking is a few minutes of gentle walking.

Our muscles account for about 40 percent of us. You're probably familiar with superficial muscles like the pectorals, abdominals, and biceps that give body builders their dramatic, armorplated look. But Dr. Norelli's stretches are more concerned with lesser-known muscles that lie deep beneath the surface and have names that sound like prehistoric animals, such as the quadratus lumborum (under the spine) and the psoas major (running from groin to spine).

These stretches should be performed a few times a week. You may find that they enhance your flexibility, relieve stiffness, protect you from back pain, and just plain make you feel good.

These stretches are adapted from yoga postures. For convenience, none of them need to be done on the floor, as real yoga is. They can all be done in your office, in fact. Think of these stretches as a routine to help you prevent your muscles from becoming stressed out and overworked. It is also a broad-spectrum muscle-soothing therapy for a range of common symptoms stemming from modern lifestyles.

Do the stretches slowly, gently, and with concentration on proper form. Don't hold your breath; breathe regularly. Only one to three repetitions of each posture need be done.

Ear-to-Knee Stretch

This valuable stretch relaxes the quadratus lumborum, in Dr. Norelli's view the most overlooked source of low back pain. The quadratus lies deep beneath the spinal muscles and joins the

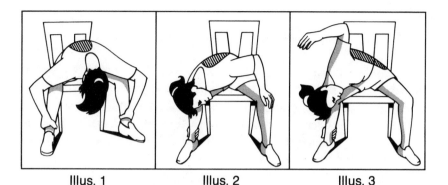

Illus. 1   Illus. 2   Illus. 3

pelvis to the 12th rib. When tight or tender, it can pull you down or off to one side, causing you to shuffle. Or there may be unrelenting pain at the belt level in your low back. Sound familiar?

The causes of a whacked-out quadratus are legion. A common one is prolonged sitting, especially if you have a habit of leaning to one side, as you might do when watching TV or talking on the phone. Awkward lifting, sustained overload from gardening, or scrubbing the floor can also do it. So can a fall. Or even a quick stooping movement when your torso is twisted.

The quadratus is also irritated by poor posture, scoliosis, or having one leg shorter than the other.

The ear-to-knee stretch helps relax this troublesome muscle. If your back tires quickly when you're out walking, a tight quadratus lumborum may be the cause. The more relaxed and flexible these muscles are, the more relaxed and pain free your walk will be.

Sitting in a chair, spread your legs apart, bend over, place your palms on your ankles, and let your torso sink between your knees to loosen your back a bit (see Illustration 1). Then slowly bend your torso to the right, until your right ear touches your right knee. Rotate your head slowly to the right (see Illustration 2). If you are so tight you can't comfortably reach this position, come as close as you can without causing strain. Now slowly raise your left arm until it is just sort of hanging over your head (see Illustration 3). Hold for 10 seconds, then slowly raise your torso. Repeat on the opposite side, with your left ear to your left knee.

Wave to the Sun

Another muscle—a pair, actually—that you probably never heard of is the psoas minor and major, or the "tenderloin" muscles. They are quite long, extending from the thighs and hip joint right up to the lower spine. They can both tighten up from too much sitting (a nearly universal problem these days), causing pain in the middle of the back.

To stretch them, we do a version of part of the Sun Salutation series of postures, which every yoga student knows.

Stand with your feet together, toes pointed directly ahead.

Illus. 4

Bring your left foot backward and right foot forward, taking care to keep the toes pointed straight ahead. Raise your left arm straight overhead; keep your right arm at your side. Now bend your knees slightly and tip your torso back somewhat (see Illustration 4). You should feel a good, gentle stretch under your belt on the left side.

Breathing regularly (as always in these postures), hold for 10 seconds or so, and return. Repeat on the other side. This is a good stretch you can do before and after a long period of sitting. Keeping your psoas stretched will help keep your hips flexible, enabling you to lengthen your stride when you walk and keep your lower back flexible and exercised.

Neck Looseners

Maybe you never notice how stiff your neck is until you get away from your desk long enough to relax and stretch a little. You go for a walk and you realize you hurt every time you turn your head. Or your shoulders are hunched up to your ears.

The neck has three different and important muscle groups. The splenii are the muscles that run up the back of the neck on both sides of the spine. Keeping the head tilted forward for long periods—which many of us do without realizing it—can make the splenii tight and sore. To ease that tension, tuck your chin in, grasp the back of your head, and gently exert forward pressure.

The trapezius muscle is the large coat-hanger–shaped muscle that links your shoulders to your head. You can find the top of the trapezius by feeling the muscular ridges on your shoulders, just to the right and left of your neck. Anyone who chronically holds his arms in an elevated position—while typing, reading, drawing, or operating machinery, for instance—is a prime candidate for "trapeziitis."

To release the tension, sit in a chair and grip the seat with your left hand, to stabilize the shoulders. With your right hand, gently bend your head slowly to the right (see Illustration 5). Repeat on the other side.

Finally, we have the scalene muscles, located just above the collarbone, deep inside. They are called the great foolers because when they start to act up, they can mimic symptoms of a pinched nerve and whiplash, causing pain or numbness in the thumb, the forefinger, the back of the arm, or in the shoulder blade area.

To relax the scalenes, grip the bottom of your chair with your left hand as before. Place the right hand atop your head and pull your head gently to the right. As you do so, guide your head slightly backward (see Illustration 6). Repeat on the other side.

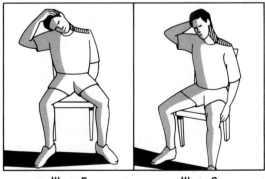

Illus. 5   Illus. 6

Loosen the Lower You

Here's a stretch with some anthropological interest: the oriental squat. It can ease chronic calf pain in racewalkers and speedwalkers and stretch the hips and deep tendons of the back. It'll also make it easier to scrounge around under the kitchen sink looking for the cleanser!

With your feet about 12 inches apart, squat down on your haunches. Fold your arms and rest them on your knees to maintain balance. Your feet should be slightly turned out, with your heels flat on the floor.

If you're the average Westerner, you won't care to squat for very long. But in the Far East and elsewhere, it's a position of comfort. African tribesmen have been observed to squat like this for hours, waiting for game.

Taking the Pinch Out of Your Buttocks

Imagine that you're washing dishes and standing a good bit away from the sink to avoid splashing yourself. If, in this stance, you were to pick up a heavy frying pan (something we don't recommend), you would feel pressure in the glutei muscles of the buttocks. Besides lifting, the glutei come in for a lot of work during walking.

The glutei extend and rotate the thigh and help support the back. When stressed, they can trigger a pain that mimics the irritating jolt of sciatica.

A wonderful stretch for the glutei is the posture Westerners most associate with yoga: the Twist.

The Twist is normally done on the floor, but here is a simpler version you can do in your chair. Cross your left leg over the right and hook your right arm around your left knee to stabilize your legs. Hold onto the chair with your left hand and slowly turn to the left, while exhaling. You should feel a stretch in the left buttock. Repeat on the other side.

Here is another, even simpler version of the Twist. Prop your right foot up on a secure chair or stool, bend your right knee and slowly move your left shoulder toward the right knee. Breathe out and enjoy the stretch. Repeat on the opposite side.

Loosening Your Chest and Arms

Most people need to expand and stretch the chest area. While not directly related to walking, here is a good stretch to do to round out your stretching workout. And besides, it feels great!

Dr. Norelli calls it the "doorway stretch." Stand with your hands at shoulder height. Place one hand on each side of a doorway, or the walls leading into a corner—whichever is most convenient. Your feet should be out just far enough so you can lean into space before you and feel a good stretch in your pectoral muscles. Vary the stretch by raising your hands and placing your forearms on the doorway or walls and again leaning inward.

Summer

Beating the Dog Days of August

Heat and humidity may be making your walking program look like pure tomfoolery. Just yesterday you were thinking of calling it quits till the autumn breezes wooed you out again, right?

It's no joke. Heat and humidity can dampen more than just your spirits. They do stress your body. But there's no need to stop now and give up all the conditioning you've gained so far. Here are some suggestions for reducing the risks of summer heat or finding temporary alternate routes for walking to fitness.

No-Sweat Walking

Talk with your doctor. If you have a specific health problem that makes walking outdoors in high temperatures unhealthy for you, or you just find it too darn uncomfortable to be outside, then do what thousands of Americans are doing—head for the malls. And we don't mean for a shopping spree or an ice cream soda.

Malls across the country are opening their doors to walkers before the stores open. You can walk to your heart's content (and ease) in a temperature- and humidity-controlled environment.

Be forewarned: Mallwalkers take their walking seriously. You'll find everyone from strollers to racewalkers perambulating on these indoor courses. Be careful of wet, slippery surfaces on rainy days. Many malls have varying textured surfaces now, rather than endless linoleum. An added payoff: the change in the terrain of the floor makes your feet and legs use different muscles and you tire less quickly, according to podiatrist Richard J. Robinson, D.P.M., of Santa Paula, California.

Indoor tracks at the local YMCA/YWCA are a good bet, too, though they tend to be less temperature controlled than the malls.

Waterwalking

You can totally immerse yourself in this method of walking. Stay cool in the pool but get your exercise by walking in thigh- to chest-high water. The potential benefits are the same as walking on land but with less sweat and lower risk of injury. The water supports the body's weight, making this an ideal exercise for people with weight problems or arthritis. Unlike swimming, walking allows you to walk and talk with your pool partner while you exercise, which may banish the boredom factor of doing laps across the pool. Your local Y may have a waterwalking program. Or you can walk in an outdoor pool. Of course, you'll need to slather on the sunscreen if you're going to be waterwalking outside.

Experts suggest that if you walk in chest-high water, you try swinging your arms in the water for a total-body workout. Start walking very slowly for the first few minutes and then try to reach a speed that feels vigorous without being exhausting. And don't forget to include a cool-down period!

Staying Cool Outdoors

If walking outside is your passion, there are lots of things you can do to help yourself withstand the hot weather.

Wear a breathable hat to keep the sun off your head and face. A terrycloth hat that you can soak in water is ideal. It can cool your head and block the sun's rays. Visors are okay, but the top of your head may feel hot. Hats that don't breathe trap heat in.

Wear light, loose clothing. Heat loss occurs through the

The 4 Commandments of Beach Walking

Summer takes many of us to the beach for a day, a week, or even longer. A barefoot walk on the sand can be the soul-soothingest kind of exercise, but it can also be tough on the feet and legs. There are three reasons for this, podiatrists say: The looseness of sand subjects the arch of the foot to unnatural stresses, causing it to pronate (flatten) excessively. In addition, when the heel sinks into the sand, it gives the Achilles tendon an unnatural yank. And because most beaches incline toward the sea, beach walkers may walk at an unnatural leg-stressing angle.

The result: stress, strain, and possible injury vacationing walkers can do without. Here are a few tips for those summer walks on the beach to keep your fitness walks soul-soothing rather than body-bruising.

1. Always wear shoes, and if you normally wear orthoses, wear them, too.

2. It's better to walk close to the water, where the sand is firmest and flattest.

3. Stretch out those calves after your walk. They may be extra tight from the unusual surface. And you'll be helping your Achilles tendon, too.

4. Change directions frequently so that if the ground is sloping, both feet will get equal time on the steeper part of the slope.

evaporation of sweat from your skin. The more skin exposed to the air, the more heat is lost. Wear as little as possible, but again, protect your skin with sunscreen.

Drink plenty of water. Unless you're waterwalking, it's better to put the water in your body rather than on it. Carry a plastic water bottle and drink periodically on your walk (sometimes thirst is a delayed reaction) or plan stops near water sources. Avoid sugary drinks. Sugar prevents the stomach from emptying and delays water getting to the tissues.

Walk early in the morning or in the early evening. Morning and twilight workouts help you avoid the steamiest temperatures and most skin-scorching rays.

Don't go out when the weather is very hot and steamy. You risk heatstroke or heat exhaustion. If humidity is low and there's a good breeze, warm-weather workouts should be safe.

Beware of sudden fluctuations in temperature. If you're traveling from a cooler climate to a warmer one for vacation, be careful. It takes the body about 10 to 14 days to adjust to heat and humidity. Take it extra slow.

Take extra care of your feet. When the sidewalks start heating up, the temperature inside your shoes skyrockets. That can mean more sweat, more blisters, athlete's foot, and infections. Be sure to change your socks often and consider using an antifungal foot powder. Switch to a lighter shoe with lots of ventilation. Leather shoes can be ventilated by your shoemaker by punching air holes around the arch to make air rush in as you step.

Terrain Therapy
Healing through Challenge

Terrain therapy is a European concept that goes back at least 30 years. Used in some health spas in America today, it may well find increasing popularity in the future.

What we're talking about is a form of therapeutic walking that makes use of the natural lay of the land to modulate the "dosage."

Terrain therapy is used in clinics in the Caucasus region of the Soviet Union, as well as at the Wildwood Sanitarium and Hospital in Wildwood, Georgia. This is how it works.

Filling the Prescription

Following medical consultation, a patient is given a prescription to walk. Typically, a circulatory ailment or weight problem is involved, and walking is just one aspect of the therapeutic approach.

On the first day, the patient meets a highly trained counselor or walking guide, who has been briefed on the patient's status and prescription. Walking then begins on a perfectly level course, at whatever speed is comfortable.

The guide not only chats with the patient but observes him or her closely for any signs of faintness, disability, or pain. Every few minutes, they stop, and the guide performs a quick pulse measurement. If all is well, based on the parameters given by the consulting physician, walking resumes.

For conditions such as intermittent claudication—in which cramping pain occurs after only a few minutes of walking—the rest stops may be very frequent.

Gradually, the guide begins to introduce the walker to graded paths. This may happen within the first hour, but the patient could wait for a week or more before getting the go-ahead.

A good initial choice might be a stretch of terrain where the path goes very gently upward—rising, say, 4 or 5 feet over a distance of 50 yards.

Using a pace slower than that used on the level, the two begin to negotiate this first, easy challenge.

Pulse check: Everything okay?

How's the breathing?

Calves okay?

If so, the pair continues up the grade a little farther.

Now, here's where a special feature of terrain therapy comes into play.

On Course for Healing

Natural woodland paths often go pretty much straight up hills. Sometimes they zigzag a bit (these zigs and zags are called switchbacks), but the general direction is relentlessly toward the summit. Short stretches are often quite steep.

That combination of up, up, up and unpredictable steep stretches makes most purely natural paths unsuitable for terrain walking.

A terrain therapy course needs to be modified so that: (1) no part is especially steep, and (2) there are numerous *side paths,* perhaps every 25 yards or so, that return the walker to a level track. The level portion continues for a distance, and then slopes gently downward to the beginning level. Or there can be intersections where the walker and guide can choose to either gain a bit more altitude or go down.

The simple line drawing on the opposite page will give you an idea of what the whole course might look like.

The side paths not only give walkers a rest but permit return to a slower heart rate while forward motion continues. And being able to complete a "loop" is much more satisfying than having to go back down the same way you came up.

Climbing Out of Pain

Now let's rejoin our walker, who, over a period of days, is gaining strength. In fact, let's join a man we'll call Bill whom Mark Bricklin interviewed some time ago on the terrain therapy course at Wildwood Sanitarium and Hospital.

"I used to walk down my lane to get the newspaper, a distance of maybe 1,200 feet," Bill said, "and my legs would hurt so bad they felt like they would burst, bones and all. My neighbors would keep their eyes on me as I walked, because they were afraid I would have another heart attack."

When Bill was asked where his legs hurt, he placed his hands on his hips and said grimly, "From here on down."

The odd thing was, this conversation was taking place while hiking on a challenging woodland trail heading toward the top of

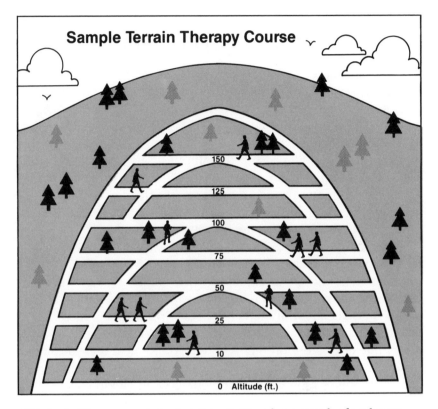

This looks like a mountain, but it isn't. It's a honeycomb of pathways laid out on the side of a hill. Notice that ascent is always at an angle to minimize the grade. Side paths intersect with ascenders and descenders.

Raccoon Mountain, just over the Tennessee border.

Every once in a while, the walking guide would stop to let Bill rest. His guide would take his pulse and nod that it was okay to start hiking again.

Bill had come to Wildwood three weeks before Bricklin met him and was due to return home in another week. Before coming, he'd had two heart attacks. Even mild exercise, like going up a mere bump of a hill on the way to his mailbox, would give him severe intermittent claudication—the terrible pain in his legs he spoke of. Often, he'd get angina pains as well. On top of that, he suffered from black lung, the coal miner's disease that causes severe shortness of breath. Because he had been to so many doctors, he was on more than a dozen medications.

On the Road to Relief

At the time of the interview, Bill had progressed—quite remarkably—to being able to walk 3 to 4 miles on the level, taking brief stops along the way. The pain was gone, and he was off all medication except for the nitroglycerin tablets he kept in his pocket in case of an angina attack.

In discussing Bill's case with staff physicians, Bricklin was told that the walking regimen was part of Bill's total program, which also included medical care and a super-healthy diet of fresh vegetables, fruits, and grains, supplemented with 400 international units of vitamin E and 500 milligrams of vitamin C daily.

Interestingly, Bill said that his chief physician warned him that there was a certain amount of risk in the aggressive cardiac "rehab" program he'd chosen to enter. But determined to do something besides fill his rapidly deteriorating body with more drugs, he decided to go ahead (with the help of some prayer, he added).

Bill's case is not all that unusual, the doctors at Wildwood said. And while circulatory problems may respond most dramatically to the exercise-plus-diet plan, weight-loss clients also get terrain therapy—sometimes as much as 10 miles a day, in divided doses.

Some Need Supervision

Bill's guide, by the way, was equipped with a paging device. In the event of an emergency, he could summon help from doctors or paramedics who were never more than a few minutes away. That's important: When challenging someone who has a health condition—however slowly and sensibly—you still need rapid access to heavy-duty medical care. *Terrain therapy should never be attempted under other circumstances.*

In the Soviet Union, Bricklin saw patients at a country health spa who had just returned from a session of terrain therapy relaxing in a special kind of meditation room. Listening to soft piano music, they reclined in soft chairs and gazed out a big picture window at the big tree-covered hill where they'd just exercised. Many were nodding off to nap-land, just what the doctors wanted. They call it "relaxing in the arms of Nature."

Now, some may be thinking: All this could be just as well

accomplished on a treadmill with an adjustable gradient mechanism. Well, you're right. At least to some extent. But would it really be as bracing . . . satisfying . . . relaxing?

Going It Alone

If clinically supervised terrain therapy can't be part of your personal landscape, though, you *can* get many of the same benefits with a treadmill and trained instructor.

There's also a special fitness adaptation of terrain therapy for people who are basically healthy but simply out of shape.

To enjoy it, though, you must have access to at least one reasonably graded hill—preferably with a sidewalk and a series of side streets that can take you off the incline and onto the level.

When walking uphill, always warm up on flat terrain for a good 15 minutes. On the grade, slow down, shorten your stride, and never keep pushing if you feel faint, fatigued, or strange. You ought not to feel much more challenged than you do when striding briskly on the level.

You may be able to gradually increase your upward progress. That, in turn, will add strength to your legs, increase your stamina, and introduce a new element to your regular fitness routine.

Just remember: The terrain therapy approach, done without medical evaluation and proper supervision, is only for people who are perfectly healthy and experience no unusual symptoms or pain during or after a workout.

Treadmills
Stationary Striding

Think of it! A temperature-controlled environment. No wet leaves. No icy patches. No potholes. No snarling dogs. Just you and your treadmill. Once the domain of serious runners and cardiovascular physicians, treadmills have caught the interest and imagination of recreational walkers. And why not! For anyone on a walk-a-day schedule, they offer the ultimate in convenience. And they may help you increase the effectiveness of your workout.

The electronic or motorized treadmill motivates you to maintain a certain pace, according to Patrick Netter, author of *High-Tech Fitness*. "If you stop walking, you fall down," he says. And if you want to challenge yourself to a more vigorous workout, you can simply increase the treadmill's elevation to simulate hills. With some models, you can program a warm-up and cool-down, or train at intervals that push you to your limit and then ease you back to a comfortable pace.

Set up your track in front of a TV or even a full-length mirror and the time will fly while you walk.

Choices, Choices, Choices

Prices for treadmills can range from around $200 to $5,000. Generally, the more you pay, the sturdier the construction. The pricey models also boast extras—automatic elevation and computer capabilities, such as calorie-counting and course-setting features. But what's right for you is based on a number of important considerations, and price is just one.

If you're considering purchasing a treadmill, here are a few tips.

Be sure to get a written warranty and buy from a specialty fitness equipment store. The salespeople are usually knowledgeable about the equipment they sell. Often the shop will send someone to install the treadmill for you. And, if you have a question or problem later, you'll have someone to call.

Pass up the nonmotorized versions. They are practically impossible for walkers to use effectively. The belt creates too much of a drag and you use all your energy pushing rather than walking.

Choose a motorized treadmill that's appropriate for your weight and walking speed. While the more economical versions are made of flimsier materials, many of them will probably stand up fine for a 150-pound female walker. A 200-plus-pound male will need sturdier stuff.

Make sure the belt is wide enough for you to walk comfortably. Test it in the store at a minimum of 4 miles per hour.

Look for at least ¾ horsepower and a DC motor. AC motors have to work through a system of pulleys and levers to change speeds. DC motors generally run more smoothly and have more accurate settings.

Walking Nowhere Fast

A treadmill is a relatively simple piece of equipment. But here are a few pointers to help you adjust safely to the new experience.

Start slowly! When getting on a treadmill, be sure to use the handrails or hand bar. Straddle the belt with both feet, then step on after it is moving. Begin at a very low speed and slowly adjust the machine to your pace.

Give it your full attention! Don't expect to watch your favorite TV program on your first "walk." Get used to the machine first.

Learn to be light-footed. A treadmill is for walking, not tramping. If you plod along, you may disrupt the evenness of the belt motion.

Don't jump off. Straddle the belt, hold onto the rails, and step off very carefully. If you've been on the treadmill for any amount of time, you may feel dizzy and unbalanced for a few moments when you get off. Just walk slowly around the room until you've adjusted your equilibrium.

Vacations

Walking Away from It All

Sound the retreat! With the work week behind and a glorious weekend ahead, pack your walking shoes and escape to a special corner of America. Here are five choice destinations, perfectly suited to one or two day's exploration on foot. (Don't have a full day? See the mini-walking vacations chapter, beginning on page 104, for how to get away when you only have a few hours.)

Mesa Verde National Park, Colorado

For a walking adventure that at once challenges your body and your imagination, head to the southwestern corner of Colorado. Here, atop a piñon-pined mesa that rises 8,500 feet above sea level, you'll discover wondrous ruins—thirteenth-century condominiums of sorts—wedged into hollows on the sides of sandstone cliffs. Who lived here and what became of them? We can only guess. Clues to the mystery of this vanished native American culture lie buried in the rocks.

The paths leading to the various cliff dwellings vary in difficulty: Some meander along gently sloping terraces; others follow steep terrain that walkers occasionally must traverse on ladders and stairs. Benches along the way offer welcomed rest stops to pause, meditate, and wonder. After all, if the high altitude or steep terrain doesn't take your breath away, the scenery surely will. Gnarled juniper and piñon pines line the route. And every bend in the trail offers spectacular vistas across craggy ravines.

Trip Tips

For more information, call the park at (303) 529-4475 or 529-4461, or write to Superintendent, Mesa Verde National Park, CO 81330. Hotel accommodations within the park are available from early May to late October at the Far View Lodge. For information and reservations, call (303) 529-4421, or write to Far View Lodge in Mesa Verde, P.O. Box 277, Mancos, CO 81328. Campsites are always available on a first-come, first-served basis at Morefield Campgrounds, just 4 miles inside the park. Contact the park superintendent for information. The park is open from mid-April to mid-October.

Corkscrew Swamp Sanctuary, Florida

"A million years from Miami."

That's about as good a description as any of Florida's Corkscrew Swamp Sanctuary. This centuries-old virgin cypress grove, with its towering, moss-draped trees, placid black water, and haunting bird cries, echos back to an era untouched by asphalt or high-rises.

Considering that the only other way you might penetrate this area is with hip boots and a machete, the swamp is amazingly accessible, even to wheelchairs. A wide, flat, railed boardwalk winds for almost 1½ miles through a lush tangle of thick-rooted trunks, hanging vines, hibiscus, lilies, huge ferns, tall grasses, and lakes so covered with water lettuce that they look like fields.

Expect to see lizards skittering on the boardwalk or an occasional turtle or black snake out in the swamplands. You're also likely to catch an alligator, or two or three, sunning themselves on the banks of the lakes. But birds—ibis, wood storks, egrets, hawks, owls, woodpeckers, and during spring and fall, many kinds of migrating songbirds—are what this place is all about.

People who come here tend to talk and walk quietly and to be still for long, long moments, listening and watching. In fact, if you're quiet enough, you may hear the wind whistling through the wings of a stork as it slowly pulls itself across the sky.

Trip Tips

Operated by the National Audubon Society, Corkscrew Swamp Sanctuary is located about 25 miles northeast of Naples, on the west side of Florida. For more information, call (813) 657-3771, or write to Corkscrew Swamp Sanctuary, Route 6, Box 1875-A, Sanctuary Road, Naples, FL 33964. For information about accommodations, write to Naples Chamber of Commerce, 1700 North Tamiami Trail, Naples, FL 33940, or call (813) 262-6141.

Boston's Freedom Trail, Massachusetts

There's no city tour like Boston's Freedom Trail. You don't need a guide (although the National Park Service does offer tours of 5 of the 16 sites on the trail). You don't even need a map. Just put your nose to the trail and follow the red brick or red-painted path. In just 2 to 3 hours, you can walk across two centuries of American history.

Even if you've walked this trail before, it's worth doing again. Of course, some things—like Paul Revere's house or Old North Church—don't change. But you might be surprised to see that the refurbished Quincy Market and Faneuil Hall now house an assortment of restaurants, shops and boutiques, exhibits, and food markets. And, of course, don't miss the people. Check out the Italian neighborhood in the North End, the "Old Boston" neighborhood on Beacon Hill, and the Irish community in Charlestown. Starting point: the Boston Common, a 48-acre green space in the heart of town.

Trip Tips

Freedom Trail maps are available at the Visitor Information Booths on the Boston Common and at Prudential Plaza. Cassette tapes that guide you along the trail with music, sound effects, and dramatic narrations are available for $9.95 at the visitors' booths and the Globe Corner Bookstore in Boston or by writing to Boston Walkabouts, 7A Fillmore Road, Salem, MA 01970.

For information about the National Park Service guided tour, call (617) 725-4006. For additional information on the Freedom Trail or accommodations, call the Greater Boston Convention and Visitors Bureau at (617) 536-4100, or write them at Prudential Plaza, Box 490, Boston, MA 02199.

Arizona—Sonora Desert Museum

Museums are great places to put miles on your shoes without realizing you're moving. And here's one with an extra bonus: It's a *living* museum! Breathe the warm, arid air. Bask in the deliciously golden light. And gaze in awe at the natural wonders nurtured in a desert landscape. A winding walk over a 15-acre spread will take you through cactus gardens, past desert songbirds, through the insect and reptile house, and by a mountain lion's "den" (where you can peer through a window and see the cats at play or asleep). The Arizona–Sonora Desert Museum is also home to prairie dogs, coyote, fox, mule deer, bighorn sheep, and other native desert creatures.

Here, the walking is easy. But the midday sun is unrelenting. So plan your walk for early morning or late afternoon and dress accordingly (hats and sunscreens are musts). A caution for photographers: Keep to the path. One step backward to frame a shot could result in a close encounter with a cactus spine.

Trip Tips

The museum is a scenic 14-mile drive from downtown Tucson through a forest of giant saguaro cacti. For information, call (602) 883-2702 (for a taped recording) or 883-1380. Or write the Arizona–Sonora Desert Museum, 2021 North Kinney Road, Tucson, AZ 85743. Visitors' guides are available through the Metropolitan Tucson Convention and Visitors Bureau. Call (602) 624-1817, or write the Bureau at 450 Paseo Redondo, Suite 110, Tucson, AZ 85701.

Mt. Tamalpais, California

Here's a 4½-mile challenge that's well worth the walk: the East Peak of Mt. Tamalpais, rising 2,571 feet above San Francisco Bay.

If it's a bright autumn afternoon, ocean fog may be fingering its way into the bay under the Golden Gate Bridge. The bay will be dotted with the white sails of pleasure boats. You'll see the beginnings of the Sacramento Delta, Mt. Diablo, the cities of Berkeley and Oakland, San Francisco's urban towers, and seemingly half of creation.

Walking trails up the mountain (on state parklands) begin at the Pantoll Ranger Station on Panoramic Highway in Mill Valley. A second trail leads to the western peak with a view of the Pacific coast and a third route winds 4 miles to the coast at Stinson Beach.

Trip Tips

For more information on the trails and campgrounds, call the California Department of Parks and Recreation at (415) 456-1286, or write them at 1455 East Francisco Boulevard, San Rafael, CA 94901. For information on accommodations, contact the Marin County Chamber of Commerce at (415) 472-7470, or write them at 30 North San Pedro Road, Suite 150, San Rafael, CA 94903. Mt. Tamalpais is also easily accessible from San Francisco.

Volksmarching

The People's Sport

Volksmarches, like Volkswagens, are an affordable import from Germany. In fact, they couldn't be any more affordable—if all you're looking for is a nice, well-marked course with water and rest stops and friendly walkers to chat with, they're *free*. Even if you go all out, you're not exactly parting with a bundle. A commemorative gift—like a pin, patch, or mug for completing the walk—might set you back anywhere from $4 to $6, depending on the merchandise. And if you're a registered member of the American Volkssport Association, you'll be charged a colossal $1.50 to have your event book stamped.

Volksmarching, which translates as "people's march" began in Germany around 1968. The International Volkssport Verband (IVV)—"people's sport union"—believes that everyone should be encouraged to exercise, regardless of whether they go home with a ribbon or a gold medal. Events for swimming, biking, walking, and cross-country skiing were designed to make everybody feel like a winner. Today, 15 countries have joined the IVV (mostly northern European), and Japan is considering joining—they would double the existing membership!

The American March

In 1978, the American Volkssport Association (AVA) was created in the United States. As of 1991, there are more than 600 clubs in 49 states and on military bases overseas. The number of yearly events has grown from 200 to over 1,900, involving more than two million participants.

Volksmarches usually happen on the weekend. A local club sets up a course that is open to the public for two days. Anyone can walk the course at no charge. Walkers are simply asked to register and to turn in their registration cards at the end of the walk so they can be counted. Courses open at 8:00 or 9:00 A.M. and walkers may begin any time before noon or 1:00; there are no mass starts. Events are held rain or shine, so Volksmarchers learn to come prepared for inclement weather.

Walkers who wish to receive an award for completing the course must pay a fee. (Advance registration saves you a $1 shipping and handling charge for the award.) AVA stamp books are sold at all officially sanctioned Volksmarches for $4. There are "event" books and "distance" books. Many Volksmarchers make it a hobby to travel all over the country and in Europe, collecting event stamps. Or you can chart your accumulated mileage. When you complete a book, you send it to AVA headquarters, where a file is created in your name. AVA sends you the special pin or commemorative patch for your accomplishment. There are books for 10, 30, or 50 events. And there are distance books for 500 kilometers (310 miles). You receive additional awards as you accumulate mileage books.

How the Course Is Run

Volksmarch courses are marked with signs or ribbons, and there are always water stops along the way. Participants walk at their own pace and can stop to rest or picnic if they like. Sometimes food and beverages are offered at the end of the trail—sausage and beer seem to be popular! And a sponsor may support the event, providing free goodies. Baby strollers are a common sight, and Volksmarches are often family affairs. The trails often wind along rivers or through historical sections. There is always a minimum

10-kilometer (6.2-mile) walk, and some events have a 20-K, too. (Or you can walk the 10-K twice for extra mileage in your stamp book.) Most people finish the course in about 2 hours, but there is no time limit.

Often, local AVA clubs create walks with a special theme. A club in St. Louis planned a walk through the city in memory of policemen who died in the line of duty. Proceeds from the event were donated for a special monument being built in Washington, D.C. In San Jacinto, Texas, the Houston Happy Hikers created a walk following the footsteps of General Sam Houston, who outsmarted the troops of Santa Anna and won independence for Texas in 1836.

The Volksmarch Persona

"People participate in Volksmarches to stay fit, to meet people, and to see things they might miss if they were driving through an area," says John Neely, assistant director of the AVA.

All kinds of people get involved in Volksmarching. You are as likely to meet someone who never finished high school on the trail as you are to meet someone with a Ph.D. About a third are four-year college grads. It's a solidly middle-class group, with an average age of 35, most of whom were introduced to the sport by a friend. They walk for the exercise, because they love the outdoors, and because the awards and the socializing are fun—in that order.

When asked if a Volksmarch is an event one might attend alone, Neely replied: "You will hardly ever see a face without a smile on it. I've met people and made friends on every walk I've ever been on. Within 5 or 10 minutes on the trail, someone will ask to walk along with you. Volksmarchers are superfriendly."

Neely ought to know. He's attended over 200 events, trekking over 2,500 kilometers (1,550 miles); about 50 percent of Volksmarchers attend more than ten events a year. Many of Neely's miles were put in overseas, during his Air Force career. He considers any Volksmarch within an 8-hour drive to be "local." (Maybe that comes from living in Texas, where AVA headquarters are located.) One of Neely's pet projects is to get AVA events on a computer bulletin board for easier access to the public.

Tracking Down Events

Most people find out about Volksmarches by subscribing to the bi-monthly AVA publication, *The Happy Wanderer,* for $12 a year. It lists all the events in the United States and Canada as well as the names of folks who qualify for awards. There *are* local chapters. They have great names like the Pennsylvania Baloney Stompers or the Trotting Texas Turtles. The predominant activity of local groups is socializing. Each club generally runs about one or two sanctioned events a year. Monthly meetings are held to organize volunteers, plan events, and have fun. (Some local clubs do plan regular walks for club members only.)

If you're planning a trip and you'd like to know if you can include a Volksmarch on your itinerary, you can call the AVA and they'll give you a computer readout over the phone. The number is (512) 659-2211. Or send a self-addressed, stamped envelope to AVA, 1001 Pat Booker Road, Suite 203, Universal City, TX 78148, and they'll be happy to send you a complete information packet, a list of events, or any information about finding or establishing a club in your area.

Walkathons

Fitness with an Altruistic Twist

They're fun. They're fashionable. They're fitness fund-raisers. Since the March of Dimes staged their first walkathon in San Antonio, Texas, in January of 1970, the idea of holding giant walking celebrations to raise money for local charities has mushroomed into big nonprofit business. In a recent March of Dimes event, 700,000 walkers in 14,000 communities raised over $53 million to help prevent birth defects. The Multiple Sclerosis (MS) Society began annual, across-the-country walks several years ago. A recent

Super Cities Walk raised over $15 million.

There are walks for the homeless, walks for AIDS, walks for peace. If you have a cause to tout, chances are you can find people willing to walk with you—and raise some money at the same time.

The Super Two

People who put on the March of Dimes (WalkAmerica) and Multiple Sclerosis Society (Super Cities Walk) have become walkathon experts. While their main purpose is to raise money for their respective causes, a top priority is to make the walks fun for walkers!

According to national WalkAmerica director Tony Chopper, walks are great fund-raisers for the same reason walking is a great exercise—they appeal to all ages, they can be held anywhere, and just about everybody can participate.

The walks—usually 15 to 20 kilometers—are planned with the walker's safety, convenience, and pleasure in mind. The routes are well-marked and well-patrolled. Checkpoints are set up with water, Port-O-Lets, entertainment, food, and beverages. Medical personnel are on hand to treat everything from heatstroke to blisters. For those who wear themselves out early, there are "victory vans" to carry them back to the starting point or on to a festival site for an *après* walk party. "We used to call them 'poop-out' vans, but we decided everybody who walks is a winner," says Chopper.

Have the walkathons been boosted by the fitness walking movement? "You bet," says Chopper. "Besides getting even more enthusiastic corporate walking teams, who use WalkAmerica as a fitness incentive to get in shape as well as support the community, we have walking clubs joining us and helping us organize the events. We've seen major increases in walkers since 1986, when walking began to be recognized as a valuable fitness activity."

Getting Ready

Chances are, if you're reading this book, you're thinking of starting to walk yourself into shape, or you're already walking regularly. The walkathons can provide you with a challenging goal and a built-in celebration to kick off a spring walking program. Plus, you have the double satisfaction of knowing you're walking not only for your own health but for the health of those you're fundraising for. You get to feel good twice!

Sounds great, right? And it will be, if you're prepared. A 15- or 20-kilometer walk is no small feat, even if you're already walking an hour a day. Chances are these 9- to 12-mile walks will take the average walker 3 to 5 hours to complete. To finish your walkathon with smiling eyes and dancing feet, here are some things to do, both before and after your walk. Suzanne Levine, D.P.M., a podiatrist and physical therapist at Mount Sinai Hospital in New York City, author *My Feet Are Killing Me* and *Walk It Off,* is spokesperson for the MS Super Cities Walks. She's treated lots of postwalk problems in New York City and believes most of her patients could have avoided their pains and problems. Here are her suggestions.

Assess your shoes. Most people are in love with their walking shoes. They seem familiar and cozy and comfortable. What people don't realize is that the cushioning materials in the shoe do wear out after awhile.

They lose some of their shock-absorbing quality. On a long, long walk, this can have a very tiring effect, not only on your feet but also on your knees and back. You'll be walking on very hard surfaces during most of the these walkathons. Check your shoes for wear and tear. If you can feel any burning on the ball of the foot or can feel pebbles through the bottom, it's probably time for a new pair. Buy them now, so they'll be familiar and comfortable by the walkathon.

Sabotage shinsplints. One of the most common complaints that arise from these long walks is painful shins. Sometimes people can barely walk on the day after a 20-K event. That's because the muscles in the shin are usually weaker than the calf muscles. As the calf muscles become overworked and tight, they pull on those shin muscles, causing pain and soreness down the front of the lower leg. If you really want to avoid shin pain, start now by doing this simple exercise: while sitting, press your foot up and down, as though you were working the accelerator of your car. Do this about 50 times, every day, for three to four weeks before the walk. If you're new to walking, start slowly, doing 10 or 20 repetitions and working up to 50. You can also do this while standing in line at the supermarket. Just lift up your toes toward your shins. Repeat 10 to 15 times, rest and repeat. Besides walking as often as possible, this is probably the single best way to prepare for a long walk.

Walk Day

There are a number of things you can do on the day of the walk to make sure you come through the experience problem-free.

The massage is the message. Tell your feet you're getting ready for a long walk. Sit down before you start, take off your shoes, and gently massage your feet all over. This is great for circulation and will help cut down on any cramping sensations and swelling.

Protect your toes. Black-and-blue toenails are another common complaint of long-distance walkers and runners. On a long walk, the shoe will tend to rub against the top of the nail, causing friction, which results in bleeding under the toenail. If you rub petroleum jelly over the nail, it will cut down on the friction. Sweat will not dissolve the petroleum jelly. Put some on your big and little toes to avoid blisters, too.

Powder those pups. Still have your shoes and socks off? Sprinkle them with powder or cornstarch to cut down on friction. Powder will help to keep your feet dry, cool, and blister-free.

Pack an extra pair. People with very sweaty feet, or those who just like to feel fresh, should carry an extra pair of socks in their fanny packs. Sit down at the halfway point, take off your shoes and socks, rub down your feet, apply more petroleum jelly and powder, and put on a clean, cool, fresh pair of socks. Your spirits will get a lift right along with your feet. Dr. Levine says she may be old-fashioned, but she still recommends white cotton socks. In her practice, she has found that many people are sensitive to synthetics, even though they may have greater wicking action. Cotton socks may get drenched. That's why it's good to carry an extra pair—or two!

If you have very smelly feet, you may want to take a small plastic bag to store your socks. After all, half the fun is having people to talk to! Don't let your socks scare them away.

Do drink the water. Even if you are not thirsty, take a glass of water at every checkpoint. Many people experience a feeling of light-headedness toward the end of the walks. That's sometimes because they sweat more than they think and their blood pressures lower. Drinking plenty of fluids will help to maintain your blood pressure and avoid that dizzy feeling.

Aprés Walking Advice

Congratulations! You've made it! You met the challenge, raised the money, walked the miles. Don't sit down yet! Make sure you cool down slowly. Don't throw yourself down on the grass. Walk around in a leisurely fashion. Do some gentle stretches. Then sit down. Take off your shoes and socks. Massage your feet. Don't stay still too long! You're bound to stiffen up. Go home and take a warm bath. If you can afford a full-body massage, or have a friend who'll trade the favor—go for it! You'll feel terrific!

If you're interested in joining the ranks of walkathoners in your town, call your local March of Dimes and/or Multiple Sclerosis Society offices. They'll send you registration forms and helpful hints for fund-raising and may even provide pre-walk clinics.

Walking Sticks
Support Yourself in Style

It took the wife of a rock star to make the walking stick newsworthy again. Back in the 1970s when Bianca Jagger, then the wife of Mick, started carrying one, few people had ever seen a woman with a walking stick—except perhaps in those Mae West movies set in the Gay 90s when, corseted and jeweled, the legendary actress swaggered across the screen carrying one with a sequined handle.

Society columnists and fashion reporters were agog at Bianca's innovation. And the walking stick, long in eclipse, was suddenly "in." The sloe-eyed Mrs. Jagger had given it a dash of panache, but actually the ground swell had already quietly begun. More and more Americans, male and female, were rediscovering the health benefits of walking, not to mention the sheer joy of it. And they were finding that carrying a walking stick added to their pleasure. Far from being simply a good-looking prop or fashion accessory, a stick improves your balance, adds spring to your step, and helps work out your arms and upper body as you walk.

A Stick in Time

Historically, dedicated walkers have always known the value of walking sticks—Moses and Socrates, Benjamin Franklin and Henry David Thoreau, Harry S. Truman and Winston Churchill. Walking with a stick comes as naturally as . . . walking. You find yourself falling into a natural rhythm as the stick coordinates with the motion of your legs.

Once upon a time, a walking stick really was a stick, a broken branch of suitable size that the walker simply picked up during the journey. But that was a very long time ago. By the time the stick had made it into the seventeenth century, craftsmen were already having a go with more exotic materials—ivory, ebony, malacca. Well-dressed men were coordinating their walking sticks with the colors of their waistcoats and the lace on their shirts. Their sticks were more than mere fashion accessories. They *needed* them to keep their balance on the high heels that were de rigueur for the high-born gentlemen of the period. In fact, the fashionable man or woman had a whole wardrobe of sticks.

And once you start collecting anything on a grand scale, you're almost certain to start looking for novelty. Napoleon had a stick with a music box attached. Certain ladies of his imperial court carried sticks with shafts that concealed elaborate fans. By the end of the nineteenth century, more than 500 novelty or gadget sticks had been patented here in the United States. Financier J. P. Morgan had one with a built-in battery-operated flashlight.

Of course, you don't need to get quite so elaborate when you decide to buy your first walking stick. What you *do* need is some basic information.

A Stick or a Cane?

How does a walking stick differ from a cane, which some walkers prefer? Actually, very little. A stick has a straight handle known in the trade as a bulb handle. Curve that handle and it becomes a cane. In trade jargon, a curved cane handle is known as a PW handle, shorthand for Prince of Wales and named in memory of Queen Victoria's portly, dandyish son (later King Edward VII).

But what if you want something a little longer, a little heftier? Carrying the evolution of the stick to its ultimate, when it's made to measure approximately 54 inches (shoulder high)—as compared to a 36-inch (hip high) stick for men and a 34-inch stick for women—it's called a hiking staff. Most staffs have a hand strap of leather or nylon webbing attached at the top and a spike tip at the bottom, making them a kind of third leg for a hiker picking his or her way across a trail packed with snow or ice or hopping, rock by rock, across a stream.

Staffs, as you might surmise, are more useful for strenuous hikes as opposed to city promenades. Anthropologist Margaret Mead, a diminutive woman, always carried a staff when she was on a research expedition, for example. She had a Y cut into the top of hers so she could insert her thumb there for added support.

Most of the hearty "2,000 Milers" who have covered the entire Appalachian Trail (Springer Mountain, Georgia, to Mount Katahdin, Maine) have carried hiking staffs. Not only are they a help when going up and down hills, but they serve as a potent dissuader for the hostile dogs hikers sometimes encounter along their routes.

What to Look For

Stan Novak, owner of one of the nation's largest walking stick companies, knows sticks. He has sold more sticks, canes, and staffs in the last 5 years then ever before in the 25 years he's been in business. He says that nowadays there are no particular rules, no particular etiquette or custom for using walking sticks or canes. "People buy whatever they happen to like." And some women like and buy walking sticks with the elaborately fashioned heads that have long been associated with men.

Certainly there are enough sticks and canes to suit every taste. Ash is the most popular wood because of its strength and relatively light weight. Ebony is even stronger but more expensive. Hiking staffs are crafted of ash, too, as well as hickory, oak, and chestnut. Especially popular are canes with handles that feature the likenesses of dogs, cats, horses, and ducks. Novak's New York store even has a stick with a tiny beaver intricately carved into the handle.

"People have finally gotten over the foolish idea that walking sticks and canes are only for invalids and the elderly," says Novak.

Even for the young and supremely fit, not a few orthopedic surgeons recommend carrying a stick as a way to stave off fatigue on a particularly long walk. Furthermore, a walking stick's strength, rigidity, and lightness make it a dandy prop for stretching and isometric exercises.

Waterfall Walks

Refresh Your Spirit

Waterfall walks can challenge your body and refresh your soul. Here are three walking trails that range from sedate to awesome.

Pennsylvania's Niagara

What is so romantic about tons of water dropping over a bunch of rocks?

Stand on a wooden suspension bridge, breathing in the moist, cool, mossy-smelling air and gazing into the crashing, sparkling, thrashing water and you, too, will fall in love with the power and magic of waterfalls.

One thousand, two hundred sixty-seven wooden steps lead to the Main Falls at Bushkill Falls, Bushkill, Pennsylvania.

The most spectacular of the eight waterfalls at Bushkill, Main Falls spills 100 feet into a deep, emerald pool. Rainbows flicker in and out of view, where water meets water and spray meets sunlight. Endless motion and sound are at once soothing and awe inspiring.

The backwoods adventurer might be put off, at first, by the

apparent commercialism of Bushkill. But once you get beyond the clutter of cars, souvenir shops, and the smell of homemade fudge (you can try it on the way back!), you'll be delighted with the tasteful preservation of natural beauty of what is known as the Niagara of Pennsylvania.

Bridges and walkways constructed of sturdy black-locust timber wind down the inner slopes of the Bushkill gorge, allowing you to view the falls from every possible angle. Some of the steps are quite steep, but benches are placed strategically for resting and catching your breath.

The falls crash and spray beside you, beneath you, behind you. Water rushes endlessly, seemingly out of nowhere and into infinity. It is a paradox that the constant motion creates a sense of stillness, that the energy of the stream evokes calmness. The atmosphere is hushed, almost reverent, as walkers pass, light-footed, on the boardwalks.

Tourists travel here from all over the country, and although many are unprepared for strenuous walking, the Bushkill trails are easily navigable for most people. You'll even find sightseers in heels and sandals making the rounds!

If you're a beginner, the walk around the Main Falls may be enough to exhaust you. For the more conditioned walker, there is a trail leading from the top of the Main Falls up through the woods to the Delaware Valley Lookout, for a spectacular view. You can wind your way down along Pond Run Creek to view the Bridal Veil Falls and Bridesmaid Falls. Then it's on to Little Bushkill Creek and the view of the Lower Gorge Falls. This trail returns you to your starting point, where you can either call it quits or continue to Laurel Glen and the Upper Canyon, a woodsy, relatively flat trail that ends with a deck overlooking Pennell Falls.

With plenty of stopping to o-o-h and a-a-h, this walk took our group of *Prevention* Walking Club staffers 3 hours to complete. By that time we were all pretty tuckered out. We saw all eight falls, and each one tempted us to sit awhile and soak up the view. Although you're not supposed to soak in the water, there are plenty of spots along the trail to rest and dip your feet in if you like.

Bushkill is open from April to mid-November. Located on route 209 about 2 hours from New York City, it's a great stop on the way to the Poconos. There is a charge for entering the trail area—adults: $3.50; senior citizens: $2.75; children under 12: $1; children under 6: free. For information call (717) 588-6682.

Honeymooners' Walk

It's hard to imagine growing up in the United States and not knowing about Niagara Falls, honeymoon capital of the world. Besides being one of this planet's major scenic attractions, Niagara sports one of the world's largest hydroelectric developments, with the ability to produce 2,400,000 kilowatts.

What many people do not know is that there are miles of trails surrounding this granddaddy of American/Canadian falls.

The Schoellkopf Museum Geological Society offers "The Walker's Guide to the Niagara Gorge" ($2), which describes these walks. Although the museum does give some guided group tours, the booklet was prepared to allow you to take these treks by yourself.

Eight walks are described, ranging in length from about 2 miles to 16 miles round-trip. Some of the paths are well-traveled and level; others are steep and somewhat treacherous, with a "hiking boots only" admonition from the museum guide.

The descent into the Niagara gorge at Devil's Hole includes a scramble over a rock slide, reminding you of the relative instability of gorge walls that tossed two hydroelectric power stations into the river in 1956. In general, the paths around the top of the gorge can be negotiated with little effort in ordinary footwear. Paths in the gorge are more rugged and require effort and caution.

The Schoellkopf Museum humorously reminds you that "what goes down into the gorge must come back up." That means under your own foot power, so don't exuberantly walk your way to an unexpected overnighter.

Maps and geological and historical information are included in the booklet, as are descriptions of flora and fauna. The walking, which is all on New York State parkland, is free.

For more information, write to the Schoellkopf Museum Geological Society, Niagara Reservation, Niagara Falls, NY 14303. Or call (716) 278-1780.

For the Fabulously Fit

Not for the frail or unsure of foot, the waterfall attractions of Yosemite National Park invite the experienced walker to explore exhilarating heights.

Yosemite Falls is one of the highest in the world. The trail rises 2,700 feet and is a 7.4-mile hike to the top and back. The park rangers call it strenuous and say it takes 6 to 8 hours to complete. If you'd be content to stand at the bottom of the falls, that's a short walk from the parking lot.

There are 11 other falls within the park. The most popular waterfall trail is the Mist Trail, which offers spectacular views of the Nevada and Vernal Falls.

From the Happy Isle Bridge, the Mist Trail ascends 400 feet in 0.8 mile to the Vernal Falls Bridge, where there is an excellent view of Vernal Falls. The climb is strenuous and slippery in spring and early summer, due to the continual waterfall spray. Two-tenths of a mile farther, the trail connects with the horse trail, which ascends by a series of switchbacks to the top of Nevada Falls.

There's no denying the rigors of this walk. Five or 10 minutes into the hike, you realize you are going to be drenched. You are really close to the falls; you feel like you're in them.

Very few people actually make it all the way to the top of Nevada Falls. When they do, they're soaked. There is a huge flat rock at the top. Everyone who makes it peels off layers of wet clothes and lies down on this rock to dry out and soak up the sun. And the view is incredibly beautiful.

The National Park Service will gladly answer your questions about Yosemite Falls. Write to Public Information Service, National Park Service, P.O. Box 577, Yosemite National Park, Yosemite, CA 95389.

Weight Loss

Shed Unwanted Pounds, Permanently!

You will never find a better way to lose weight than walking. The results may not be as fast as you'd like, but they will probably be far more permanent and pleasurable than any diet or weight-loss scheme you'll ever hear of or dream up. In fact, sticking with a regular walking program may be a more successful way to lose weight than most programs that combine dieting and exercise!

Sound impossible? In a study conducted at Baylor University in Waco, Texas, people who just dieted and people who combined walking and dieting lost weight quickly, but two years later, they had gained most or all of it back. People who just walked took longer to start shedding pounds (partly because they were building muscle), but two years later, they had maintained their weight loss and were still losing.

Why Walking Is Best

John Foreyt, Ph.D., the psychologist who conducted the study, feels that dieting simply puts too much psychological pressure on people. Eventually they break down and return to old habits. The interesting thing about the walkers, though, is that after a while, many of them spontaneously changed their diets. They began to eat healthier foods—less fats, fewer goodies, more fruits and vegetables—because they *felt* better. They lost their craving for fattening foods. And there are lots more reasons why walking is the best exercise to get thin.

Easing into Your Goals

As obesity experts point out, one of the most common pitfalls of starting an exercise program is trying to do too much too soon. "Many people have an all-or-nothing attitude about exercise," points out Scott Rigden, M.D., a Tempe, Arizona, bariatric physician (one who specializes in weight loss). But walking offers a wide range of acceptable paces, from a slow stroll, for starters, to a brisk arm-swinging stride later on.

Walking burns calories at any speed. Of course, brisker walking burns more. But if you can't (or don't want to) walk fast, you can simply spend more time on your walks to make up the difference. For example, if you weigh 150 pounds and cover 1 mile in 15 minutes (that's 4 miles per hour), you burn about 110 calories. But walk at a slower (3-miles-per-hour) pace, and you get the same calorie burn in just 1.1 mile. "This is truly a race that the tortoise wins, not the hare," says cardiologist and walking expert James M. Rippe, M.D., director of the Exercise Physiology Laboratory at the University of Massachusetts Medical Center in Worcester.

Powering Up Your Cells

You probably know that you continue to burn calories at an increased rate for some time after your walk is over. But you may not realize that this short "after-burn" can, in a sense, turn into a "continual burn." That's because regular walking signals the muscle cells to increase the size and number of mitochondria—the tiny structures inside the cells that help burn up calories—just as engines burn gasoline. So the more you walk, the more engines you build to burn increasing amounts of calories. Your fuel guzzling is faster, and it may go on for hours and hours. "We're talking about a Ferrari compared with a Volkswagen," says Peter D. Wood, Ph.D., a professor of medicine at Stanford University Center for Research and Disease Prevention at Palo Alto, California.

Once you become a walker, your body uses up more fat for energy. Why? Two reasons. First, walking increases the concentration of certain enzymes in your cells that are needed for fat metabolism. Doctors explain that exercising improves the body's ability to use body fat for fuel. Second, walkers employ the so-called slow-twitch, rather than fast-twitch, muscles. A bird that flies the Atlantic Ocean has slow-twitch muscles in its wings. Your legs have them, too. And guess what? The mitochondria in slow-twitch muscle fibers prefer fat. "Muscles designed to do long, continuous movements tend to be the fat-burning type of muscle," says Dr. Wood.

Getting Thinner All Over

You'd expect walking to trim and tone your legs. And it does. But the flab trimming may not stop there. A study done at the University of California found "a striking loss of fat over the arm in both walkers and cyclists after six months of regular exercise." Walking can take off fat anywhere—from jelly belly to thunder thighs—claims the study's chief investigator, Grant Gwinup, M.D.

When you diet without exercising, up to 30 percent of every

pound you lose may be muscle. And not just any old muscle. A study showed that even valuable heart muscle was lost when dieters did not exercise.

Get out and pound the pavement, however, and you lose lard and only lard. The pounds you drop are more likely to be pure pudge. Which leaves you with more muscle per square inch than when you started. Muscle looks better. It takes up less room, so your clothes feel looser. And muscle burns more calories than fat does, even when you're asleep.

You've heard it a million times: Exercise regularly and you'll slim down. Very true. But did you know that you'll also be able to eat up? Once they've reached goal weight, walkers can eat more than nonwalkers, yet stay trimmer. Think about that the next time you're tempted to skip your walk!

If you maintain a constant food intake without dieting, you'll lose weight slowly. (Walk 45 minutes a day, four times a week, and you could drop almost 18 pounds in a year.) Snip out a few hundred calories per day on top of that and the pounds will leave faster. Either way, you'll be much less hungry and better nourished than someone who cuts calories drastically.

Sidestepping the Blues

Many people put on extra pounds because they use food to deal with stress and tension. For these people, a bowl of ice cream takes the place of a tranquilizer. But while high-fat goodies travel straight to your hips and set up house there, a walk can take you way beyond the tension of the moment.

In a study done at the University of Massachusetts Center for Health and Fitness, researchers found that walking reduces anxiety no matter how casual or intense the workout. And this calming effect lasts for at least 2 hours after exercise.

Going Easy on the Joints

Even when you first start your weight-loss effort, you'll find that walking is ideal in many ways. Custom-made for folks with lots of excess poundage, walking is ever so gentle on the joints, even on the back, hips, knees, and ankles—prime trouble spots for overweight people.

And walking in shallow water is even gentler. "This really saves the lower joints and helps osteoarthritis," says Dr. Rigden. Water has a buoyant effect, yet offers resistance that helps tone muscles and burn fat.

Prescription for Weight Loss

When you're walking for weight loss, you're more interested in calories burned than in aerobic fitness, although ideally the two eventually go hand in hand. So, rather than working to maintain a fast pace, simply make sure you meet a goal of 3 to 5 miles a day. Even if you can only manage ½ mile to start, walking every day gets you into the habit.

To figure out how you're doing, here's a simple equation: If you walk at the leisurely pace of 3 miles per hour (1 mile every 20 minutes), you can burn about 300 calories in an hour. Do that every day, and you can lose 2 pounds per month with no change in your diet. Find a variety of ways to trim fat from your diet, and you'll lose even more. But don't think of the fat cutting as dieting. Think of it as healthy eating habits you're adopting for the rest of your life.

If you move at a brisker pace of 4 miles per hour, you'll burn 400 to 500 calories an hour. If the terrain is hilly or you walk faster, you burn even more than that. These are estimates, of course. The actual number of calories you expend varies according to the distance you walk, the terrain (hilly or flat), fluctuations in your pace, and your weight.

By comparison, jogging burns only about 20 percent more calories than brisk walking. But compare how you feel at the end of a 3-mile walk with how you feel when you jog that same distance. Jogging may take more out of you in terms of discomfort and exhaustion if you're overweight. Because there is less chance of injury and fatigue, even out-of-shape people can exercise longer and more frequently by walking. That translates into a greater number of calories burned.

If you're more than 20 pounds overweight and you've been inactive for awhile, make it a point to get good-quality walking shoes before you start a walking program. Look for good arch support and plenty of toe room. Good shoes are important for all walkers, but even more so for inactive people with a lot of weight to

(continued on page 214)

They Strode Their Way to Slimness

Robin Simon, of Whitefish, Montana, and Bob Grohne, of Decatur, Illinois, were both overweight and suffering from disabling illnesses when they each discovered the remarkable benefits of walking. Here, they tell how they took weight loss and health recovery in stride.

Robin's Story

"It didn't happen overnight. Years of stress-induced eating, after-work snacking, second helpings, and no exercise left me 55 pounds overweight.

"I wouldn't admit I was fat. I never looked in a full-length mirror. I liked to think of myself as being big-boned and pretended to disguise the fat behind oversized clothing I sewed for myself.

"After marriage, babies and baking became my favorite hobbies and I assured myself that I could lose weight if I really wanted to.

"The excruciating pain of a ruptured disk convinced me that perhaps now was the time. I was confined to bed for several months and faced back surgery. For the first time in my life, I took a serious look at myself and made up my mind to lose weight.

"I went on a diet and managed to lose 30 pounds before the operation. But I had another 20 to go after the surgery. My doctor suggested daily walking in order to recover fully. I literally had to learn to walk all over again.

"At first I could manage only ½ mile a day, but I soon worked up to 2 miles. The pounds melted off and in no time at all, I reached my goal.

"With less weight to carry around, I felt more energetic and self-confident. I began setting higher walking goals for myself. I now try to walk 25 miles a week. Sometimes I challenge myself to see how far or how fast I can go. Walking supplies me with a feeling of control over my body. I can tune in and experience my heart beating faster and my lungs working harder as I climb a hill or increase my speed. It's a great feeling.

"Walking helped me to discover a wealth of personal power to draw from. It took a major obstacle to get me to accept the challenge, but meeting the challenge was worth the countless benefits. I'm living proof that walking can help a person succeed in losing weight."

Bob's Story

"At 6 feet tall and 330 pounds, I qualified as 'gorilla' on most life insurance medical charts. Happiness was a warm bowl of potato chips and a good football game on the tube.

"Thirty years in heavy construction taught me how to drink three pots of coffee per day and then calm down on an equal number of packs of cigarettes. Other than setting the office wastebasket on fire now and then, no great damage seemed to have been done.

"Then a funny thing happened. After a nasty conference with the local business agent for the union, I went back to the office to calm down with another cup of coffee and the ever-present cigarette. The funny thing was not being able to find the end of the cigarette to light. My hand seemed to be missing, too.

Blank!

"I woke up in the intensive care unit with hoses going in and out, machines going 'huckey-puckey' and a group dressed in white gathered around my bed looking grim. I had had a simultaneous stroke and heart attack, which brought on blocked kidneys, a blood pressure reading of 280 over 220, and a loss of eyesight. I had some peripheral vision, but the rest was as though someone had popped a flashbulb at close range.

"On my sixth day of hospitalization, a beam of hope came skipping into the room. An old buddy of mine, flashing his Baptist minister's pass to the head nurse, parked his sweat suit next to my bed. 'First,' he said, 'get yourself out of here. Then try walking to get some of this blubber off you. We'll do it together.'

"Three years later, 80 pounds of that blubber has evaporated. My blood pressure has fallen back to a controllable range, so my eyesight is 20/20. There's no sign of heart problems, and my kidneys are doing their thing.

"In the beginning, I could barely walk one block before sitting down and puffing like a wounded water buffalo. With my friend's prodding, I worked up to a mile, then 2. By the end of the summer, we did a 14-mile stint together.

"The conquistadors may not have found the fountain of youth, but, had they kept walking, I think the net effect would have been the same. I have a body that renewed itself at age 55.

"Slimmer and more toned than ever before, I plan to continue walking to keep my body in shape."

lose. People carrying a lot of excess weight are more prone to over-use injuries, such as plantar fasciitis (a common cause of heel pain), and general circulation problems in the legs and feet.

If you're 50 or more pounds overweight, seek a doctor's advice before beginning any type of walking-for-weight-loss program. And once you get your program under way, see your doctor if you get chest pains during exercise or have chronic foot or leg problems.

Weights

The Pros and Cons

Ever wonder about those flashy guys with the hand weights? They stride briskly past you on the trail. Thin neon-colored weights match their shorts and headbands. They're usually sweating, often smiling, and actually look like they're enjoying themselves.

Why, you might ask, would anyone want to haul along extra weight on a walk? Actually, there are several good reasons to do so. (And a few reasons why you may not want to.)

As you become a conditioned walker, it may be increasingly difficult to walk fast enough to reach your target heart rate or to really feel as though you're getting a good aerobic workout. Or, when you do walk at speeds fast enough to make you breathe heavily, it's not fun anymore. And you certainly don't want to leave your favorite walking partner in the dust at the side of the road.

Even if you are not reaching your target rate, walking is still good for your heart health, your blood pressure, and your cholesterol levels. But to lose weight or gain a greater aerobic capacity, you really do need to exercise hard enough to get your heart pumping.

A Weighty Matter

If brisk walking just doesn't do it for you anymore, are weights a good option for you? Here's what the experts have to say.

Peter Hanson, M.D., director of cardiac rehabilitation at the University of Wisconsin, did a study a few years ago with 13 men recovering from heart attacks. Once they became conditioned walkers, they had a hard time reaching the training heart rate that had been set for them.

"We took simple backpacks and weighted them with 5-pound bags of sand or flour. The sand or flour tends to conform to the shape of the back and distribute the weight evenly," says Dr. Hanson. "We found that most people began to benefit with the addition of 10 to 15 pounds of added weight. When we took them up to 25 to 30 pounds, they were reaching their target rates."

The men in this study maintained a steady 3-mile-per-hour pace throughout the study.

Handy Little Items

At the University of Alabama, Joe Smith, Ed.D., associate professor in the health, physical education, and recreation department, studied the use of hand weights to increase cardiovascular output while walking.

"The main problem with hand weights is that people don't know how to use them," says Dr. Smith. "They let them hang at their sides. You have to swing your arm, pumping the weights in order to have any effect on your heart rate."

Pumping means raising each arm alternately from a straight-down position to either waist or shoulder level or to the top of the head. Dr. Smith advises starting slowly. "We had our people do the arm pumping without any weights at first. Then we gradually increased the weight." he says. "You can't carry much more than 3 pounds when walking if you're pumping them as you should."

Some experts think that carrying hand weights may do more harm than good because carrying weights tends to change the biomechanics of your walk. You hold your body differently and your gait may change; that may cause harm, they explain. Pumping weights may cause injury to your back, neck, or arms. (One avid walker we know used hand weights for a few miles to step up her weight-loss program and caused a flare-up of bursitis in her shoulder that took months to heal.)

Alternatives to Weights

Your safest bet may be learning to walk a little faster and getting comfortable with it, according to James M. Rippe, M.D., director of the University of Massachusetts Medical School's Exercise Physiology Laboratory. In a study he conducted with 343 men and women who were asked to walk as briskly as possible, two-thirds were able to reach their target heart rates. They averaged 14 to 15 minutes per mile.

Research suggests that it is the overall physical conditioning that results from regular walking, rather than cardiovascular conditioning, that is important. "If you are out there walking, you are having a very positive effect on your overall health," says Dr. Rippe. "Who knows, it may be more important for you to slow down and listen to what your walking partner is saying, particularly if it's your spouse!"

If you were thinking of walking with weights to give yourself bulging biceps, we think that perhaps the safest and more enjoyable thing to do is some kind of resistance training separate from your walks. If you're trying to burn more calories by increasing your heart rate, you might try adding a few hills to your workout. Or finding the time to walk farther.

If hand weights or weighted vests fascinate you or give walking the appropriate macho image you're looking for, then by all means, give them a try. Just remember to go slowly. Start out with ½-pound weights and build up very gradually. Pay attention to your posture and make sure the weights aren't dragging you down, making you lean forward or backward. You might consider the kind of weights that double as water bottles. If you get too tired on your walk, you can empty them, or take a refreshing drink! If you feel any soreness or tenderness in your back, neck, or arms that does not go away in a day or two or does not feel like natural muscle soreness, stop using the weights and see your doctor.

Words for Walking

A Universal Language

I t's been said that a good gauge of the importance of something in a given society is the number of different words used to describe it. In Arabic, for instance, there are reportedly dozens of different words for a camel's legs. In the Eskimo tongue, there are innumerable words for snow.

If that's true, then walking certainly must be counted among the most important activities of English-speaking people. We have, in all likelihood, more words for walking than any other activity, with the possible exceptions of sex and the process of losing one's mind.

While a foreigner used to getting around on a camel or in a kayak might look at you and say you're *walking*, a fellow American, Canadian, Briton, Australian, or New Zealander might well call what you're doing:

Ambling	Fitness walking
Rambling	Power walking
Perambulating	Speedwalking
Sauntering	Racewalking
Traipsing	Heel-and-toeing
Hiking or alpine hiking	Wogging
Trekking	Sashaying
Trudging	Bush walking
Tramping	Bushwhacking
Meandering	Strutting
Strolling	Tip-toeing
Marching	Lumbering
Parading	Toddling

While the meaning of many of these variations on pedestrianism are obvious, others are more obscure.

Bushwhacking vs. Bush Walking

Bush walking was the reason given in an Australian news-magazine for the visit to that country of one of our authors, Mark Bricklin. When he protested that he had no intention of walking through bushes, it was quickly explained that bush walking is the Australian term for what Americans call *hiking* and what the English generally refer to as *rambling*. "The bush" is what Aussies say instead of "the country."

Bushwhacking can be another confuser. It's definitely not waiting behind some rocks and shooting some guy who needs a shave, as in cowboy movies. Bushwhacking in walker's lingo means hiking off the designated trail, through the brambles and bushes (not to be confused with bush walking!). Bushwhacking sometimes looks like the shortest path between point A and point B, but it can get you thorns in your arms, burrs on your pants, poison ivy on your legs, yelled at by nature lovers, or lost.

The Tough Stuff

Alpine hiking is our term for what may be the most physically and spiritually satisfying of all forms of walking—traipsing up and down mountains, along designated trails. It's a different animal from just *hiking,* because the uphill (and especially the downhill, as you may have learned) will challenge your legs and stamina in a very different way.

Because such *trekking* often involves a trip lasting many hours, it also challenges your mental stamina. But assuming you've conditioned yourself thoroughly and know the terrain and weather to expect, alpine hiking can be a special joy. Any hill with an altitude gain of over 300 feet, by the way, qualifies as alpine. (Since we invented the term, we can choose the altitude!)

A Faster Pace

Wogging is a term coined some years ago to refer to forward motion that is half-walking, half-jogging. If the term hadn't been coined (by pediatrician Thomas W. Patrick, Jr., M.D.), we'd have a real gap in walking parlance, because wogging is exactly what is done by runners who enter a walking event and think they're race-walking. (If the event is a judged racewalking event, they'll be disqualified.) Not that there's anything *wrong* with wogging. In fact, some people who've experienced knee pains may do well to adopt the shuffle of wogging, as it reduces the impact of footfall considerably.

Others will find that normal walking at a relatively rapid pace—*fitness walking*—winds up feeling better than wogging. The impact pressure on the knees, hips, and lower back is even less. That saving grace of fitness walking can translate into longer, more frequent workouts. And that translates to more fat burned off in a given week.

Powering Up

If fitness walking simply means walking at a pace that feels like a bracing workout (and doing it regularly), there's nothing simple about defining its big brothers.

Power walking, despite its name, is a pretty mushy concept. Body-building immortal Steve Reeves used the term power walking to describe walking with weights. But many people use it to mean walking with great energy, though not exactly racewalking. So if someone invites you to go on a 5-mile power walk, you'd better find out *first* if they mean just swinging your arms or swinging a couple of 10-pound dumbbells, too. If they mean the latter, tell 'em to call Steve Reeves. (Walking with the weights strapped around your midsection, or carried in a vest or pack, is much safer. Even Steve'll tell you that.)

What then, is *speedwalking?* Basically it's a term we use to clearly imply the second meaning of power walking—walking at a very fast pace, but without great attention to "legal" racewalking form. When you're hustling from Terminal A, Gate 26, to Terminal C, Gate 28, after your plane arrived 30 minutes late, you're speed-walking. Actually, it's the same as fitness walking, but with consid-erable concentration on sheer speed.

Walking with Strict Rules

Racewalking is the only form of walking permitted in official competitions such as the Olympics. The rules are easy to express but not necessarily so easy to follow. To racewalk in such a way that you won't be disqualified in a sanctioned event, you must obey two mandates. First, one of your feet must always be on the ground, even if it's just your toe or heel (racewalking used to be called *heel-and-toe walking*). Runners are often in "full flight," with no foot contact at all. To detect even the briefest loss of contact, judges often get down on one knee—they're serious!

The other mandate is that as each leg passes under your torso, it must be precisely straight—actually "locked out" for an instant. This rule is to prohibit sneaky running in a race; in running, the knee is never locked. Actually, it isn't locked out in normal walking, either—there is always a certain bend at the knee. Which leads some people to wonder if this somewhat unnatural motion in racewalking doesn't promote leg injuries. The answer is that it only rarely does, unless there is an impediment of the joint, or you push yourself relentlessly.

The only shortcoming of technically correct racewalking is that you'll almost certainly need some coaching by a trained individual to do it. Short of that, you can always read a book on the subject, and just do the best you can. (See the racewalking chapter, beginning on page 145.)

Zoo Walks

A Walk on the Wild Side

W hom did you meet on your walk today? The mailman, maybe? A neighbor washing his car? Or a child on a tricycle? Les Cohen of Louisville, Kentucky, sneaks up on lions and tigers and trades whistles with exotic parrots. He's not on safari, exactly. He is a member of the Zoo Lopers Club at the Louisville Zoo.

Members of the Zoo Lopers Club enjoy the special privilege of walking in the zoo early in the morning, before it is open to the public. From 7:30 to 9:30 A.M., three days a week, they play Tarzan and Jane to the elephants and zebras. For their membership fee of $3 to $7, depending on zoo or other walking club affiliations, they receive maps that chart walking routes, giving mileage and designating uphill and downhill trails. With plenty of water fountains, benches for resting, and a first-aid cart with CPR-trained staff, what could be a safer or more congenial setting for walkers? No curbs, no noisy, smelly cars, no stray dogs or speeding bicycles to contend with. Just lush settings, unbroken trails and the adventure of watching zoo animals on their "off" hours.

"Sometimes the animals are a little shy in the morning, and they look up and run," says Cohen, a regular Loper. "I love the lion. We growl and purr at each other. The parrots whistle at me, and I whistle back. We keep it up until I'm out of earshot. It's really a different feeling when the zoo is closed to the public."

Richard Schnelle, a local pastor, takes an uphill course at the zoo on his way to work. A former mallwalker, he became bored with the indoor environment but finds the zoo always entertaining. There's the new baby elephant or the African gray parrots. He loves to watch the polar bears swimming, but he doesn't break his stride. "It's just 5 miles to work. The scenery and the safety are well worth the extra effort of driving there."

The zoo is open to walking club members from June 1 to October 31. You must be over 18 to join. It's not kids' sneak-preview time.

If you live near a zoo, you may want to contact the administration to see if they have a walking club. If not, maybe you could inspire them to start one!

MARK BRICKLIN'S 1-YEAR WALKING PROGRAM

From Beginner to Fitness Walker, Step-by-Step

Just about anyone can use fitness walking as a safe and sure road to improve their health, their shape, even their mind and nerves.

Unlike other sports that emphasize competition, fitness walking is dedicated purely to participation and enjoyment. The notion that we must go faster than someone else or constantly strive to break our own record, we leave in the locker room of history.

Walking, although we consider it a sport, is in some ways more like a basic element of life—like breathing, working, and eating—than a track-and-field event.

Prep Talk

Our first bit of advice, then, is to let go of any ideas you may have that it is necessary to propel your body at a certain rate of speed to attain the Big Benefits. It isn't.

Let go, too, of any desire to find a rigid program that prescribes how fast and how far you ought to walk. Such programs are holdovers from schoolboy coaching psychology. Based on bringing largely homogeneous groups of 16- or 18-year-olds into top competitive shape—so they can beat the other guys—that approach is dangerous for adults who come in all sizes, shapes, and ages. Your coach has to be you. No one else on earth knows better what feels good, and what feels scary, to *you*.

Expect Big Benefits

We do have one thing in common, though. We all benefit in much the same ways from walking. Regardless of how fast you walk, regardless of your age, you can expect walking to burn off fat, tone your muscles, relieve any low back pain, dissolve emotional tension, boost your HDL cholesterol (the kind that removes harmful cholesterol from your system), help control high blood pressure, fight bone-thinning osteoporosis, perk up your immune system, and more.

While you needn't go at any special speed to achieve these benefits, you *will* need one thing: *regularity.*

Regularity is, in fact, the very cornerstone of a successful fitness walking program.

While any walk is good, all the benefits mentioned above will not begin to kick in unless you walk at least three times a week. Five or six times a week is probably best. Personally, I aim to walk every day. Inevitably, bad weather or a killer schedule knocks a day off here and there, so I wind up walking an average of five days a week. That way, I don't feel frustrated when I can't walk: I just say, here's my off day.

Make Walking a Habit

Walking nearly every day does something else besides drive home the health effects. It makes walking a natural, habitual part of your life. You don't have to think about whether it's the right day to walk, whether you feel like walking, or anything else. You walk just like you brush your teeth or go to work. Get off your schedule, though, and the whole program can get wobbly real fast.

That's why we urge you to keep a walking diary. There is something satisfying about keeping a log of your walks. Every week, you add up your weekly total miles, and then the cumulative total since you began the program. It's like watching a stock you own go up, up, and up in value.

Another good way to encourage all-important regularity is to join a local walking club or the nationwide *Prevention* Walking Club. The latter, which is our group, is specifically designed to keep you motivated, free of injuries, and involved with special club activities. (Write to *Prevention* Walking Club, 33 East Minor Street, Emmaus, PA 18098).

Joining a club like ours is also a good way to tell yourself "Yes—I am a walker!" That sense of identification is like a little engine that gets you out of the house even on days when there are lots of handy excuses to skip your walk.

Check with Your Doctor

Before beginning any new exercise program, it's a good idea to get a medical checkup. If you're over 40, haven't been physically active in a while, have any chronic health problem, are taking medication, or simply need an excuse to get an overdue routine physical, seeing your doctor is especially advisable.

The purpose is not only to find problems. When beginning this program, it can be very educational to know your weight, blood pressure, and cholesterol, among other things. *Ask your physician for the specific numbers.* For cholesterol, request an analysis that will give you total cholesterol, LDL, and HDL cholesterol. Ask your doctor to explain the numbers to you. The ratio of the latter two (LDL is considered harmful if high, HDL beneficial) can be revealing. Six months or so from now, you might want to go for another checkup and see how these various numbers have changed.

There's still another reason for getting a medical consultation now. Besides saying yes or no to a walking program, your doctor can give you specific tips, based on your condition and possible problems (like asthma or angina), that will make your walking safer and more comfortable. And many walkers have told us that their doctor's enthusiastic endorsement of a walking program gave them added motivation.

A Shoe-In for a Good Start

Now it's time to get yourself shod. Look for shoes specifically designed for walking. Although some running shoes will do fine, many are too flimsy, being designed more for speed than comfort and support over the long haul. Wear a pair of athletic socks to the shoe store, and be prepared to try on *everything* until you find shoes that feel great.

User tests by *Walker's World* show that most walking shoes are somewhere between good and wonderful, but the key factor is how they feel on *your* feet. Some of us will feel good only in sturdy, generously soled shoes, while others delight in shoes that seem nearly weightless. Some brands seem to accommodate the narrow foot best; others, the wider foot.

Here's a special tip. When you go to the shoe store, purchase a pair of *cushioned socks,* put them on, and then try on your shoes. Although these socks cost about twice what a good pair of regular athletic socks go for, they will last much longer and be far more protective of your feet. If you decide you want them *after* you buy shoes, you may find that they make the shoes feel too tight.

The Sensuous Shoe

Now, here's the important part. Lace on the shoes and go striding throughout the shoe store or, with permission, out on the street or hard mall floor. Get moving! Keep moving! Pay attention to how they feel on your feet and how your legs, hips, and back feel as you take stride after stride, just as you would on a morning constitutional. Are they too stiff and cloppy? Do they let through too much street feel? Does your big toe jam against the front? Your little toe against the side? Does your heel slide up and down? Relace if you want to, and try again. Don't buy anything that doesn't feel like it was custom-made for your foot.

Eventually, you may want to buy a second pair, because heavy sweating or a walk in wet weather can put shoes out of commission for 48 hours or more (never force-dry your shoes).

Wear good-quality athletic socks, and turn them inside out so the toe seam doesn't press against your toes.

The rest of your gear, I'll pretty much leave up to you. All that's important is that it be loose and not make you too hot or cold.

Where and When

Now that you have your shoes, you must decide where and when you're going to walk.

As to where, a park is best. Failing that, look for part of your neighborhood that's as close to level as possible, where the sidewalks are not uneven and where it's safe to walk.

But what if you have nowhere to walk in your immediate neighborhood that is safe or reasonably level?

Ironically, that is most likely to be true if you live in the country. As an ex-country boy, I know that many country roads have no shoulders, lots of blind turns, and loose dogs. So—as I did—you may have to actually drive into town to find a safe walking area.

When is just as important. The all-important job is to choose a time when you can walk every day. A time when there won't be irresistible pressures to do something else.

You may have to "carve" that time out of your schedule, just to find it. Let family members know it's your walking time and that it's just as important to you as dinnertime, time to go to sleep, or time to work.

Now we're ready to walk.

Fitness Walking Progress Plan

Week 1

Day 1

Depending on your energy and physical condition, start with a walk that is comfortable for you. It may be anywhere from around the block to 2 miles. Do not go farther—even if you're in terrific shape. *Do less than you're able to.*

If possible, drive back over the course you walked and make a note of how long it was. This is not critical, because your body doesn't really care whether you walked 1.6 miles or from the drugstore to the Congregational Church. It'll feel the same, because it is the same. Still, for historical purposes, it's fun to know how far you walked the first day.

Whatever you do, though, don't try to walk farther than what feels comfortable. If you want to stop and rest for a minute, fine. The worst thing you could do is to walk too far the first time out. You're courting blisters, sore toes, leg fatigue, and maybe more by trying to see how far you can go.

When you come home, make an entry in your walking log of how many minutes you walked, and if you know it, the distance. Your walking log should be kept in a spiral notebook or other substantial tome, not just on a piece of paper. Hey, this is important stuff!

Day 2

How do you feel today? Is there any residual soreness? If there's just the slightest hint that you did something you're not accustomed to, that's okay. But if it's more than a hint—if it's a certified letter from your buttocks to your brain that you are guilty of muscle abuse—read that message carefully. You're doing too much!

Examine your feet carefully for blisters or unusual redness. Do you need a moleskin patch, thicker socks, maybe even a new pair of shoes?

If you're a bit sore, but there's nothing scary going on, try a walk that's a little shorter than yesterday's. Does the soreness subside as you continue walking? That's a good sign. It means the soreness is probably not serious. All athletes, even hikers, experience a little stiffness or very minor discomfort when beginning the next day's workout. After the blood begins to flow and your muscles warm up, it vanishes.

If the soreness doesn't dissipate in 10 minutes or so, however, what you have is an injury. It may be minor, but if you persist, it could become major. So head home, nice and slow, and see how you feel tomorrow.

If you took our advice, though, your first day's walk should have left you with nothing more bothersome than an itch to do more.

In that case, do more—but just a little. If you walked for 10 minutes yesterday, try 11 today. Twenty yesterday, 22 today. And don't walk any faster.

Make a log entry immediately after you finish your walk.

Day 3

Repeat yesterday's body scan. This is a ritual every fitness walker needs to do daily. Run your fingertips over your feet, exploring for anything unusual. Are your toenails nice and short? Good. Getting some toe problems? Maybe your shoes are either too short or too long. Either one can hurt. Ingrown toenail acting up? See your podiatrist immediately.

We walkers pamper our feet, and for good reason. A tiny spot of pain on the feet can make walking sheer misery, or downright impossible.

But what if your feet are just ever-so-slightly irritated or roughened by walking—either today or some other day in the future? Should you immediately apply some kind of bandage? If the spot isn't actually tender to the touch, you may be better off leaving it alone. What's happening is that your feet are going through a perfectly natural toughening-up process. While we don't want to wind up with a mass of calluses, it's good that your skin is adjusting to the pressures of walking—walking in the specific shoes that you wear. Over time, this gradual toughening will help protect you—unless you suddenly increase your mileage. Still, I think it's a good idea to carry a Band-Aid or two in your pocket at all times—just in case.

Now we're ready to walk again. *Today, walk the same distance as yesterday.*

But don't think you aren't making progress. You are! But it's invisible. The progress is happening in your muscles, your connective tissue, and (as we mentioned) even your skin. All parts of your body need time to adapt, so progress is occurring (and will continue to do so) even on days (or weeks and months) when your distance stays the same.

As always, make your log entry.

Day 4

On today's walk, learn to become conscious of your posture.

Your head and neck should be in a straight line with your spine. Basically, we're saying, don't hunch over. Many people habitually walk that way, especially when lost in thought. But walking with a stoop creates muscular tension in your neck and shoulders—

exactly where you don't need any more tension.

Your shoulders should be relaxed, your arms free to swing.

When walking, try to keep your gaze on a spot perhaps 25 yards in front of you. But do periodic eye sweeps of the ground just in front of you to make sure you won't trip.

As for today's distance, *do the same as you did yesterday*. If you feel you could easily do more, fine, but don't. Please!

Day 5

Are you experiencing any chafing on your inner thighs or armpits? If so, welcome to the petroleum jelly lifestyle. Buy a big jar, and apply (rub it in; don't just dab it on) before your daily walk.

Be conscious of your posture again today. You'll need to remind yourself over and over, probably—that's natural. If you walk by a reflective window on your way, check yourself in it. Do you look like someone walking in a funeral procession? Not good. Or do you look like someone walking into a county fair, full of anticipation and energy? Better!

If you feel good, walk just a little farther today. Anywhere from one more block to another quarter of a mile. No farther.

Day 6

If you don't have a digital watch, today would be a good day to buy one. They're convenient for timing your walks—even portions of them. They're also good for generating basic fitness data (if you've a mind for such matters).

On today's walk, try counting your strides per minute. Each time your right foot hits the ground counts as one stride. Most people will find that they're doing about 60 strides per minute (SPM). Take several measurements at different points in your walk. At this point in your walking program, your SPM should be nearly identical at every stage. If they slow down toward the end, your pace in the beginning is too fast.

Record your average SPM in your log.

Day 7

Off day. Let your body catch up with your fitness ambitions.

Week 2

Day 1

This morning, shortly after you awaken, take your pulse. Use your sweep-hand bedroom clock or your digital watch. To take your pulse, grasp your right wrist with your left hand. Place the first two fingers of your left hand on the inside of your right wrist, just about an inch from where your hand begins. You should clearly feel a pulse. If you don't, switch arms: maybe your left arm pulse is clearer. Measure the number of beats for 1 minute: that is your resting pulse, or heart rate. Write it down in your log. Take your morning pulse once a week, always at the same time.

Over time, your pulse may come down somewhat, which is generally considered a good sign of cardiac health. The walking you've done so far is not challenging enough to have lowered your pulse. But maybe your future walks will be. This is not a critical point. But it's fun to see quantitative changes in health . . . at least when they're improvements!

Today, try walking a little farther than you did last week. By "a little" I mean just that: anywhere from one to three blocks, or about 2 to 5 extra minutes.

Day 2

We haven't really talked about *when* you're walking. That can't be dictated by anyone except you. And it doesn't matter much at all when you walk, as long as it's safe and you can see where you're stepping. I am not a fan of nocturnal perambulation; neither do I recommend it. The three classic times are early in the morning, at lunchtime, or right after work. Where there's enough light, a stroll after dinner, perhaps with your spouse, can be very enjoyable.

Some people eventually find two shorter walks more convenient than one longish one. As long as one time period gives you a solid half hour of opportunity to walk, you're okay, at least for now. In another two weeks or so, you may find it necessary to open a second time period. While 30 minutes of walking a day will do you a lot of good, what we're aiming for is to comfortably settle into 45 minutes a day—maybe 60—four or five days a week.

Today, walk the same distance you did yesterday. Remember your posture!

Day 3

When walking today, check your feet from time to time. Try to get them to point straight ahead. Don't get upset if this proves difficult, though. Some people just naturally toe out. But if you can correct it, you may find your walking becomes less of an effort.

Today's distance: same as yesterday.

Day 4

Although we're encouraging you to walk with a proud, erect posture, we aren't saying to hold in your belly. Let your abdominal muscles relax. You can breathe much easier that way. Holding in your tummy isn't really going to make you any slimmer. It's the walking that'll do the trick. And the more comfortable you are, the more you'll walk.

Try adding another minute or two to your daily walk. Note your total time in your log.

Day 5

Do another foot check today, if you've been neglecting what should be a daily ritual. Although you may not be having any acute problems, ask yourself if you're experiencing any low-grade, mildly annoying problems, anywhere from toenails to ankles. Even if you had such problems before you began your walking program, we urge you to see a podiatrist. If your local foot medic hasn't been able to help you, consider a major clinic. There are new techniques today, sometimes offering surprisingly fast treatments.

There are two reasons for this foot fetish. First, a problem that's minor now could turn into more-than-minor as you pursue your walking program. Second, a small pain—sometimes without your even realizing it—may be causing you to adjust or accommodate your stride in such a way as to put unnatural pressure on another part of your foot, ankle, leg, hip, even your spine. Something as simple as a shoe insert can make a world of difference. In fact, I recommend trying such custom-made inserts before consenting to surgery, if they offer a possible answer. Talk to your podiatrist.

Today's distance should be the same as yesterday's.

Day 6

As we wind up the last active day of the second week of our walking program, you may be wondering why we've been progressing so slowly.

Actually, the most important thing we've done over the last two weeks is to establish the *habit* of walking. Without doing that, there will never be a program—just sporadic walks. And, if we went too far, even on one day, there's the possibility of pain or fatigue. And with it, two or three days of no walking at all. When that happens, the habit that you're trying to establish—a lifestyle, really—can be nipped in the bud.

But make no mistake. You're making more progress than you may think. Your leg muscles have become stronger and more supple. Your body has begun to store more carbohydrate fuel—called ATP, adenosinetriphosphate—in your leg muscles, so as to have a better energy supply close to the muscles that need it. Tiny new blood vessels may be beginning to appear in the same area, to bring a better supply of blood to the action zone. And, although the change may be as yet very small, it's likely that your leg and hip bones are beginning to add a bit more calcium and other materials to make themselves stronger. Your body already knows you're a walker!

Day 7

Your day of rest.

Week 3

You're now walking anywhere from 20 to 40 minutes a day in all likelihood. How long doesn't matter. How far doesn't matter. How fast doesn't matter.

As long as you feel stronger ... a bit lighter on your

feet . . . energized while walking, relaxed later . . . and free of pain, you're on the right track.

This week, try adding 2 to 3 minutes to your total weekly distance, in small daily increments. If this feels like too much, bag it. The increments, that is, not the walking. Cut back your distance, if that feels wise. Or even take an extra day off.

To make your feet feel good at night, try to prop them up on a stool or a chair. Take your shoes off and put a cushion under your heels. All of this improves circulation.

Week 4

Add a few more minutes to your walk this week, again in small daily doses. By the end of the first month, you ought to be walking about twice as far as you did that first day—assuming you have no health problems that might hinder progress.

You should not have added more distance than that. Although you may be walking without marked effort, those miles have a way of adding up. The concept of "the straw that broke the camel's back" holds true in fitness walking. Give the camel time to get stronger!

Take a look at your walking log at the end of this week. It's a great feeling to see that steady march of entries, isn't it?

Week 5

Have you been weighing yourself? It's unlikely that you'll notice much of a loss at this point unless you are 30 pounds or more overweight. But not to worry! What we're doing now is building a *foundation* for weight loss. That foundation consists of a body that can walk, without undue strain, from 45 to 60 minutes a day. Day after day. Week after week. When we arrive at that point—and we will in a few weeks—the really noticeable progress begins. Even then, you'll notice it more in your looser clothing and belts than on your scale. A few of those pounds of fat you're going to lose may be supplanted with more lean tissue in the large muscles of your lower body. No, your legs won't get bigger—but they will look better.

As for distance this week, hold at the level you achieved last week.

Week 6

Once again, stretch your walking time by another few minutes—anywhere from a cumulative total of 1 to 5 minutes by week's end.

Now I know that some people haven't been able to walk as often as I'm suggesting. And if you're only walking, say, three times a week, adjust your rate of increase to reflect your more modest schedule. The three-times-a-week walker will probably only be at twice his or her first-day time, while the five-or-six-day walker is more likely to end this week doing three times the original time or distance.

If, however, you're only walking once or twice a week, don't attempt to increase your walking time at all. The progressive nature of our fitness walking plan is built on regularity, not willpower.

Week 7

If you added less than 5 minutes to your walk last week, add a bit more this week. If you can manage it comfortably, make the two weeks' total increment equal 5 minutes. If you *did* add 5 minutes last week, hold at that level.

Is one of the reasons you're walking the hope of alleviating or preventing back pain? If so, you are hopefully already noticing an improvement in that area. But here's something else you can do; in fact, several things.

First, do the modified sit-up called the abdominal crunch. Put a pad of some kind on the floor, so your hips won't hurt, and lie down on your back. Lift your knees so your legs are completely bent. *Don't* put your feet under a bar; let them be free. Let your arms lie by your sides. Now lift your head and shoulders off the floor while exhaling. Don't come all the way up; just about 18 inches or so. Return and repeat for as many repetitions as feel comfortable. Do *not* do more than feel comfortable. If you do, you are setting yourself up for an attack of sore "abs" 24 to 48 hours later.

After a few daily sessions, try adding another set, allowing a minute breather after the first. After a week or two try a third. When they become too easy, fold your hands across your chest instead of leaving them at your side.

More quick back tips:

- Use a back support while sitting or driving.

- Don't move furniture. Hire some husky teenagers, or some professional movers. And don't lift large or awkward objects out of a car trunk.

Always lift things by squatting down and rising with a straight back. Never lift anything that can't be held closely against the body—a large basket loaded with wash, for instance. Make three trips with lighter loads.

- When it comes to walking, always try to relax, and walk erect. Fall into a rhythmic stride and hold it for a good half hour or more. Short walks through heavy pedestrian traffic are much less helpful to your back than a true fitness walk.

Week 8

This week, try adding a few more minutes to your walk *on alternate days only.* On the other days, keep to your original distance. This is a good way to slip-slide into progress when you're reaching the end of the initial conditioning phase. Maybe you only want to go for the longer distances twice this week. As always, listen to your body.

Speaking of listening to your body, do you know what your blood pressure is? You do if you took our advice and visited your physician before beginning this program.

If your blood pressure was on the high side, it's smart to have it checked periodically—either by your doctor or nurse or by using your own sphygmomanometer. Walking is a fine natural way to help bring mild hypertension under control. If you're losing weight, you should see even more of an improvement. Eat lots of fruits and vegetables, keep fat down (that helps more than you think!), and keep alcohol at a minimum—ideally one drink or less a day. Make sure you get enough calcium, too—1,000 to 1,200 milligrams a day, mostly from nonfat milk and yogurt. Take supplements, if necessary. And avoid spinach; it carries calcium out of your system. Finally, go easy on salt. And keep in touch with your doctor.

Week 9

You've now completed two whole months of walking, or close to it.

Most people don't have the perseverance to do that. In my experience, the average person sticks with a walking program two or three weeks. Then, somehow, the program falls into a psychological pothole. Sometimes it surfaces months later and the person tries again. Well, there's nothing wrong with that. Maybe that's *your* story. If so—congratulations on coming this far!

To keep your motivation up, we strongly suggest keeping that walking log. Think about walking, read about it. Read this book, and others, too. Don't permit casual events to interfere with your walking. Instead, build your daily schedule *around* your walking time—shopping, doctor appointments, whatever. Walking must be a highly prioritized part of your lifestyle if it is to survive the inevitable onslaught of business lunches, late nights at the office, visits by friends and relatives, taking the kids here and there, not to mention VCRs, CDs, HBO, and MTV

But you've done it *so* far—so you know you can keep it up. The rewards are more than worth the effort.

Begin your third month of walking in a car. Measure off a section of your course that's exactly 1 mile long. Preferably it should be a level stretch with a minimum of busy intersections. Whenever you want to see what your time for a mile is, you can check it on this course.

And while cruising, see if there are other streets or parks in your neighborhood or town that offer good walking turf. As your walks grow longer, you'll need new territory to conquer.

This week, continue to explore the short-walk, long-walk routine. Your longest shouldn't be more than 10 minutes longer than your shortest, though. How do you like this schedule? Do you notice any difference at all in how you feel? Write down any comments in your log.

Also this week, record your time for the 1-mile stretch. Don't walk it any more rapidly than you normally do.

Week 10

To help you decide if you should increase your walking distance this week, consider two questions.

First, do you feel no sense of strain, no huff-and-puff factor, while walking? Are you free of unusual aches or pains? Do you feel refreshed after your walk? If you answered yes to all these questions, you're okay so far.

Now ask yourself, do your legs feel unusually fatigued a half-day after your walk? I don't mean a mild sense of fatigue, or even a slight stiffness that quickly fades when you rise out of a chair. Those sensations are normal while your program is still in the growth phase. If the fatigue really is bothersome, then don't go for any more distance this week. Hold steady. Otherwise, you can try adding a few minutes (or ¼ mile) to your total daily distance, adding less than a minute each day.

Week 11

Is it okay to take a rest during your walks? After all, they're getting kind of long now! The answer is: absolutely. The rest shouldn't be longer than a minute or two, though. If you feel you need to rest more, do so, but cut back on distance tomorrow. Either that, or slow down.

Brief rest stops are especially good for shaking off mild cramping sensations in your feet or calves, or some other minor annoyance. Sometimes you will want to adjust your socks, replace your shoes, or tie your sweater around your waist as your body warms up.

Time yourself on the 1-mile stretch again this week. Do it several times. Times that are nearly identical are good—they mean you've established a comfortable pace.

If your daily walk is less than 45 minutes but you feel strong, try walking for a full 45 minutes at least once this week. On the other days, hold at the top distance you did last week. If you feel 45 minutes is too much for you to handle, don't try it yet. Just go with what feels right for you at this point.

Week 12

Along with shorter walks, try to take two 45-minute walks this week, assuming you can do the distance without distress. If you don't have more than half an hour to spend on walking at one time, try a ½-hour walk at one period, and a 20-minute walk later in the day—maybe at lunch.

If you feel that walking is taking up a lot of your time, you're right. But for most of us, it's still a lot less time than we spend watching television or videos.

One thing you can do is get a personal cassette player and play music, inspirational tapes, or spoken books while you walk. Or walk and talk with your spouse or friend.

Ultimately, though, the rewards you get from walking are paid for in the coin of time. With many other sports, it's time plus great effort. With diet control, it's eternal vigilance over your impulses. No matter what you do for yourself, there's a price. But don't get carried away with a feeling of sacrifice. After all, you're not *losing* that time. Your mind is free to think of whatever it wants to. Many of us come to regard our walk time as one of the day's highlights: a chance to relax, daydream, exercise, and get in touch with nature all at the same time.

Week 13

This week marks the windup of your third month of regular walking. Another important milestone!

Whatever the greatest distance you managed to cover *twice* last week, try to do *three times* this week. Keep the other walks 10 to 15 minutes shorter. This is actually a kind of test, but it's important not to try too hard to pass! What you want to know at this point is how far you can *comfortably* walk on a regular basis. More about that soon.

In the meantime, while walking this week, try taking two or three especially deep breaths once every minute or so. Relax your lower belly and get the feeling that the oxygen is getting all the way down to your navel. Your belly, not your chest, should swell out during these breaths.

Remember, two or three deep breaths, once a minute. Every day, on every walk.

You don't want to breathe this way *all* the time. But periodically, yes. It will relax and regenerate you. On all your future walks, you'll follow the same pattern.

Week 14

If your longer daily walks have not yet reached 45 minutes, continue with your established pattern. Every week, though, attempt to add just 1 minute to your time, or a block to your distance. Even this modest rate of increase, though, is in no way essential.

Remember, no matter what your maximum comfortable distance is, you are reaping benefits that will do *you* just as much good as the much longer and perhaps faster walks of a person who was in better shape than you to begin with.

So keep at it. And keep reminding yourself: *Easy* does it. Hard ruins it.

Now, if you are one of those who found that doing three 45-minute walks in one week was no ordeal and didn't leave you pooped, you may want to consider adding a new dimension to your daily walks: exploring what it feels like to walk just a tad faster. I said "explore," and that is the operative word, not "train," "pursue," or "buy six new sweatbands."

Remember that 1-mile stretch you measured? Today, note your time when you hit the beginning of the course. Then proceed to walk it at your usual comfortable speed. When you get within two or three blocks, or ¼ mile, from the end of the mile, pick up the pace—just a little. Do that by moving your legs a little faster—not by taking longer strides. Be sure to maintain a perfectly erect posture—don't hunch over.

At the end of the course, check your time. What we're looking for is a time for the mile that is just 5 to 10 seconds less than whatever time you first recorded for the mile.

If you took off 30 seconds, that's way too much. If you took off nothing at all, that's fine. The purpose of this playful bit of exploratory work was not to see if you *can* walk faster but how trying to walk faster *feels*.

Was it fun? No problem? If so, do the same tomorrow and the day after, trying to replicate the same clocking you got today. On the last two days of the week see if you can manage your speed for the mile so that you take off another couple of seconds—no more than 5.

If you've been following our advice to walk only at a normal, comfortable speed until this week, cutting these seconds off your time ought not to be very challenging. If your normal speed for the mile is say, 16 minutes, the new speed is just about 1 percent faster.

The remainder of the walk should be at your normal speed, for whatever distance you've become used to. Don't increase distance this week.

Week 15

People often ask if they should stretch before walking. Some are eager to do it, convinced that any worthwhile exercise needs to be proceeded with a bout of vigorous bending, twisting, and assorted odd postures.

Relax. Literally. Stretching before you walk may easily lead to needless injury. The purpose of stretching is to gradually elasticize muscles that are relatively contracted, or taut, so that exercise doesn't harm them. But there is no real stretch you can do that will not put more stress on your muscles than walking. Walking is itself the gentlest of stretches, and needs no special warm-up—least of all serious stretching of the hamstrings and calves. Nor is there any reason to stretch after walking.

Now, all that applies to normal, regular-speed walking. Once you begin to walk at a pace that is decidedly more rapid than normal, maybe you can benefit from a little stretching.

The very best way to get that stretch is by first walking at a normal speed for a good 15 minutes before shifting into a higher gear.

At the pace we want you to go during those brief bouts of slight acceleration, that should be all the warm-up you need.

Be sure, though, that the part of your walk when you may be stepping rapidly does not occur at the beginning of your daily course. It's best if the "measured mile" segment of your walk doesn't begin for at least a mile into the total distance. That way, you should be more than ready when you begin walking faster.

Should you, however, feel a certain cramping or constraining sensation in your shins, calves, or hamstrings during or after your short speed session, here are a few very gentle stretches you can try. Stop walking and do them just before you speed up, or maybe just after, if you feel the need. The whole routine should not take more than 1 minute.

First, do a few partial squats, nice and slow, with your heels planted firmly on the ground. Lower your body only about 1 foot or less.

Second, put one foot about 18 inches in front of the other, place your hands on your hips, and sink down on the outstretched leg a few inches, with your rear leg held perfectly straight. Hold for a few seconds, then shift your weight backward and bend the rear knee. Hold briefly and stand upright. Change so that your other leg is in front, and repeat.

Finally, if there is a curb handy, place the heel of one foot on the street just in front of the curb and the ball of your foot on the curb itself. With the leg held straight, bend forward—*very slowly and gently*—until the stretch feels pleasant, kind of like a good massage. Then bend the knee and experience a different kind of stretch. Then change legs.

Be very cautious and gentle when stretching. If it hurts, stop. If any pain lingers, forget about stretching for the time being. Normally, these moves will cause no problem, because your leg muscles have already been warmed up and stretched somewhat by normal walking.

This week, try to begin your stint of slightly fast walking a few blocks before the point where you started last week. Don't walk faster than you did before—the idea is to maintain that brisk speed for another few minutes.

You needn't do it every day, either. Two or three times is enough. On days when you do this, your total time for your measured mile may be 5 or 10 seconds less than it was last week. Go no faster!

Week 16

One day this week, perhaps a day following one that was a day of rest, try walking 10 to 15 minutes longer than your longest walk to date. Just one day. And do no fast walking that day. The other days, walk as usual, trying several sessions of "hurry-up" walking.

For all those who do not have the desire or wherewithal to walk *any* distance at a faster speed, concentrate more than ever on correct posture. Periodically, thrust your shoulders down. If you're surprised at how far down they go, you're walking with needless tension. Tell yourself: shoulders down, arms swinging free and easy.

Week 17

The exploration of slightly-faster-than-normal walking we've been doing the last two weeks has two purposes.

One is to inject an element of change. Change is important for keeping up your interest.

The other is to begin raising your heart rate by a small degree. Doing that—as long as it's sensible, gradual, and not stressful—increases your lung capacity, strengthens muscles, and burns a few more calories.

At one time, it was widely believed that to do your heart much good, you had to keep your pulse quite high through your entire workout. Today, there is some question as to just how important that is. It's quite possible that your heart will be just as happy with activity no more vigorous than regular walking, as long as it is done regularly.

But what is certain is that putting just a bit more effort into exercise *does* increase strength and stamina, and consume more calories. If these things are not important to you, and you feel no desire to walk faster just for the fun of it, then forget about it. Be content with taking your few deep breaths every minute.

Here's something else to keep in mind. If your weight is more than 10 or 15 pounds over what it should be, you are, in effect, walking with a burden. That in itself is providing all the extra challenge you need, especially if your overweight amounts to 25 pounds or more. It's doubly true if your walks cause you to breathe quite deeply, and you're working up a sweat walking at a "normal" pace.

For those ready and eager for a bit more, your assignment this week is to find a very gentle hill or upgrade—what I asked you to avoid before—and try walking on it. Plan your walk so that the hill begins approximately halfway through your course. Slow down as you walk it, because walking on a grade requires much more energy than walking on the level. If the hill is very gentle, try walking up it for the equivalent of about two blocks. If steeper, one block or less. In any case, if walking on a grade causes you any distress—such as a pounding heart, huffing, or dizziness—stop immediately. When you've walked the appropriate distance, either turn off to a side street or simply walk back down the hill. On this day, incidentally, don't do any "fast" walking at all. And only do your hill walk one day this week.

Note in your log how you felt during and after your first bout of easy hill walking.

Week 18

If that little hill felt good, do it twice more this week. If it seems easy, you can even increase your distance by another 50 yards or so. But *only* if it's easy.

When walking up hills at this stage of your program, your pulse ought not be very much higher—if at all—than when you're walking on the level. That's because you're purposely slowing down on the hill.

The real reason for caution, then—unless you're a heart patient—is to protect your muscles from possible strain until they've become accustomed to hills. You see, even someone who is a very fit and fast walker on the level will be using his or her muscles in a different way on hills, both going up and coming down. Only with repeated hill work—done at least twice a week—will your muscles and connective tissue feel comfortable on grades.

Week 19

Five months into your training program is a good time to take stock.

How is your resting pulse? A bit lower, perhaps? (Even a few less beats a minute is a significant sign of a training effect.) If not, don't worry. But if you should find that your resting pulse (taken at the same time in the morning as you took your pulse initially) is actually higher now, that could mean you're stressing yourself. Either that, or you stayed up too late last night, had too much to eat or drink, or have worries you didn't have before. Take your pulse every morning this week. If it remains higher, make adjustments in walking or lifestyle. Of course, if it's *much* higher, or erratic, check with your doctor right away.

It's also a good idea to recheck your weight, blood pressure, and cholesterol profile at this point. A medical recheck now is especially advised if you have any sort of chronic illness or you're taking medication. Changes in metabolism brought about by walking may make it advisable for your doctor to adjust the dosage of medication.

Check your shoes, too. Are your toes causing the fronts or sides of your shoes to bulge out? Maybe your shoes are too small. If you've lost weight, your shoes may now be too big, causing your feet to slide around and produce sore areas.

Check the bottoms of your shoes, too. Are the wear patterns on your two shoes quite different? Are you wearing through the tread? Is the heel area (called the heel cup) collapsing? Maybe you need a consultation with a knowledgeable purveyor of athletic footwear, a new pair of shoes, or even a trip to a sports-minded podiatrist.

Check your socks as well. Are they radically thinned out at toe or heel? Make shoeshine rags out of them, before they irritate your feet.

If your walks are still relatively easy, try shaving a few more seconds—I mean, *a few*—off your mile time.

Adjust the pace on your twice-a-week hill sessions so that you feel pleasantly challenged. Be careful not to hunch over, though. That only makes it more difficult to breathe.

Week 20

If you want to explore easy speed work a little more, fine. But don't do it by walking faster. Or by stretching your speed session for longer than ½ mile or 10 minutes. Rather, finish one speed session, walk at a normal pace for another 10 minutes, toss in one more 2- or 3-minute slightly speeded-up session, then return to your normal pace and head back home. During the next two weeks, that second session can be gradually lengthened until it's as long as your first. Together, they should eventually equal no more than 15 to 20 minutes out of a 45-minute walk. And that should come only a few weeks from now.

Week 21

Whether you're doing regular walking, or regular-plus-speed walking, there is no doubt that your walks are now of considerable length. Half an hour minimally, and hopefully, 45 minutes. Maybe even an hour if weight loss is a priority. Here are a few tips to help you over those long hauls.

■ Drink at least one tall glass of water about ½ hour before you head out. And empty your bladder before you leave.

■ On hot, sunny days, wear a hat that protects your head, eyes, and face from the sun.

■ Always carry a Band-Aid or two with you, in the event of an unexpected blister.

■ Carry some money to buy a drink or make a phone call.

■ On long walks, your legs can grow a tad weary, which may cause you to trip while stepping over a curb. Be extra careful to make sure your toe clears the concrete.

■ Likewise, look out for uneven sidewalks.

■ Remember that while pedestrians generally have the right of way, they are generally outweighed by automobiles.

■ Don't blunt the healthful effect of your long walk by impulsively eating junk food the minute you reenter your home. Take a long, slow drink of cool water, instead. If you're usually hungry when you get back, have something nutritious waiting. A bowl filled with ready-to-eat cereal, for instance. Instead of blunting the healthful effect of the walk, your food should accentuate and complement it.

Keep the overall distance of your walking program at the same level it was last week, with possible gradual extensions of the fast walking and gentle hill walking portions.

Week 22

During this week, continue trying for small increments in either distance or speed. The idea is to finish your walk feeling as though you've had a great workout and with plenty of pep to have a great day.

As this week ends, you will have completed about five months of systematic fitness walking. That in itself is a major accomplishment. With any luck, you've burned off considerable flab, strengthened and rejuvenated your body, and conditioned yourself to take walks that would leave most others pooped or downright hobbled.

You have now reached another major transition point.

If you wish, you can keep on with your walking program pretty much as it stands, remembering that regularity in walking tells the big story.

Or, if you wish, you may want to explore what we call advanced fitness walking. To decide if this is for you, ask yourself these questions.

- Am I able to walk 45 minutes at a stretch, at least several days a week, without feeling pain or fatigue?

- Am I able to walk short stretches at a faster-than-normal clip without feeling that I'm at my limit for exertion?

- Am I able to walk up hills at a moderate pace without distress or a pounding heart?

- Have I proven that I'm able to follow a fitness program without doing too much too soon?

If you answered all these questions in the affirmative, you are now ready for advanced fitness walking.

Advanced Fitness Walking

Prep Talk

Advanced fitness walking offers the opportunity to turn your daily spin into more of a workout. For those of you who are looking for it, you'll find here the means to pump your heart rate as high as you want it and embellish your T-shirt with world-class sweat stains. For those who currently don't feel the need for quite that much, advanced fitness walking can be used to just slightly boost your speed and heart rate, add a new element of challenge to your walks, and develop a new, more fluid style of walking.

It cannot be said that speedwalking—the term we use for the style of walking you'll be introduced to here—confers anything unique in the way of health. Fitness, yes; health per se, not really.

The walking program we described previously—building up to 30 to 45 minutes of walking five or six days a week—will provide most or all of what you need to gain the major health benefits of exercise. Especially when you occasionally give yourself short challenges on hills and quicker-than-usual striding.

On the other hand, it's possible that the pulse-lowering effect of regular speedwalking will someday be recognized as being independently valuable. Or that the greater lung capacity and "reserve" strength of the heart that can be developed with more vigorous exercise will also be recognized. Some people may find that speedwalking also produces better tone and freedom from pain in the hips or low back. But, since none of these things is known, our conclusion must be that the major reason for taking up advanced fitness walking is nothing more than the sheer fun of it.

Fun, of course, may turn out to be rather important in the overall scheme of health. Like companionship and love, fun perks us up both emotionally and physically. More specifically, though, having fun may be just what you need to keep your walking program alive and well. Maybe you'll find that with speedwalking.

Then there's the question of whether you're *ready* for advanced walking. If you progressed through our basic fitness walking program, and answered all the questions at the end of that section in the affirmative, you are ready for sure.

Are You *Really* Ready?

Some people may feel they're ready for advanced fitness walking solely on the basis of being quite fit from other sports; but not so fast!

First of all, fitness activity that doesn't involve long bouts of leg work will have virtually no effect on your ability to walk considerable distances at challenging speeds.

But even if you're a person who's been racking up the miles as a runner, you are not ready to simply jump into speedwalking.

Walking rapidly for more than a few blocks is a highly specific activity. No other activity—not even long, arduous hiking—will prepare you for it. The first day or two, you may feel pretty good speedwalking, but—you have to take my word for it—in short order you will be hobbled by smoldering shins, a groaning groin, and barbecued buttocks.

My advice to runners and other very fit nonwalkers is to go back to the previous section and follow the program outlined in accelerated fashion. Instead of taking five or six months, you may be able to get through it in six to eight weeks. Certainly, you must be able to pass the little "test" given on page 249 before you become involved with speedwalking.

Run It by Your Doctor

In any case, everyone should have a thorough medical evaluation before beginning this program. Tell the physician what your experience with walking has been until now: your routine and your performance. Explain that the new program will begin to take you gradually beyond that level. But it will not force—or even encourage—you to go any faster or farther than you feel like going.

Explain that to *yourself* while you're at it, and listen closely. Or rather, *watch* closely. Because the success strategy is best explained with a picture.

Picture yourself in a tunnel inside an Egyptian pyramid. You have just discovered an ancient cart loaded with gold jewelry and precious gemstones.

If you can manage to get that cart outside, its cargo is yours to keep. The only problem is that the wheels on the cart have grown fragile with the rust of centuries. If you push it too hard, those ancient wheels are just liable to shatter under the strain, and you will never get your treasure. So you don't push at all. What you do is *lean*. You lean against that cart until it begins to move ever so slowly. And you keep leaning. You don't get impatient and start shoving, no matter how slowly the cart moves, because time doesn't really matter. Only progress matters. If you get tired, you rest. Then you continue leaning, getting your precious cargo closer to the end of the tunnel.

That's how I want you to go after advanced fitness walking. You *lean* into it. You don't push. You take your time.

With that image ever in mind, let's begin our program. Besides your walking shoes, you'll need just one piece of equipment: a digital sports watch. Find out how to go from the time of day to the elapsed-time mode, because you're going to time yourself.

Week 1

Day 1

If you haven't already done so, lay out a walking course that, at a normal walking speed, will take you between 45 minutes and 1 hour to cover—probably 3 to 4 miles. If you have to do several loops around a given area to get the mileage, that's okay.

In your car, find a stretch of the course that's as flat as possible, and measure off exactly 1 mile. Note the landmarks. This stretch should be approximately in the middle of the course. At least, it shouldn't be any closer than a 15-minute walk from your starting point.

If your course is in a park closed to traffic, the "mile stretch" can simply be a part of the course that takes you 15 minutes to walk at a normal speed. That's the average speed good walkers take to travel a mile when just "rambling."

Now walk the whole course from beginning to end, at a perfectly normal, easy, "rambling" speed. Make a note of your time for the entire course, and also your time for the mile stretch. If you can't measure the mile, assume it's 15 minutes.

Make a note of these two times in your walking log. They are your *base times*.

Day 2

Repeat the same course. Only this time, walk the mile stretch slightly faster. As we mentioned before, do that by increasing the rapidity of your steps, not the length of your stride. Try to take off about 15 seconds, no more. Your time for the rest of the course should remain the same.

After your walk today, begin keeping a graphic record of your progress. Using something like a large yellow tablet, lay it out as we've shown in the illustration below. Notice that as your time goes down, the line goes up. That's psychology, not math.

The exact numbers you write on the left edge of your graph will depend on your base time. Begin with a number about 10 seconds slower than your base time.

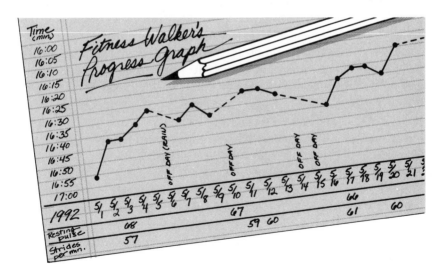

Day 3

This morning, take your resting pulse, as explained in the first part of the Fitness Walking Progress Plan on page 233. Note it in your log and also on the bottom of your graph, as shown in the illustration on page 253. Take your pulse several times a week from now on, always at the same time of day, and record it.

As you did yesterday, put your watch into elapsed-time mode when you begin the mile stretch. But this time, begin walking a little faster after about 5 minutes. Aim to take another 15 seconds or so off your base time for the mile.

If you can do that—without pain or strain—you're ready to proceed with the rest of the program. If not, continue as before until you can knock 30 seconds off your base time without great effort. Don't rush things, either. You've plenty of time!

Day 4

The kind of quick walking we've done until now has been variously called pep-stepping, powerwalking, pacewalking, and just plain hurry-up walking. Today we're going to begin something new. We call it speedwalking.

Speedwalking doesn't so much refer to walking at a certain speed as it does to a style of walking that increases whatever forward velocity you can comfortably manage.

Speedwalking has much in common with racewalking. Racewalking, however, has certain technical requirements that are not easy to learn without personal instruction. (The chapter on racewalking, beginning on page 145, will help you get started if you're interested.) Unlike racewalking, speedwalking does not insist that the leg passing under your body be perfectly straightened. Aside from that, there's little substantive difference between the two styles.

To get a quick overall picture of speedwalking, imagine walking with your arms pumping by your sides, your feet landing almost (but not quite) in a straight track, and your leg strides clicking away much more rapidly than normal. Instead of doing the usual 60 strides per minute (SPM) of rambling, the speedwalker may be doing 65, 70, 80, and—with many months of training—as many as 90 strides per minute. Posture is erect, though the whole body may be bent forward a few degrees, from the ankles upward. And because the steps are being placed in an unusually straight line, there may appear to be a certain amount of rhythmic action going on around the hips. All in all, a picture of concentration, grace, and fluid motion.

But . . . you can't actually learn it in one day, unless you're very talented. Some are; some aren't. In any case, how fast you pick up on the style does not dictate how well you'll eventually learn it, or how fast you can go (if you even care).

Here, we'll take it step-by-step, emphasizing correctness and safety over speed of learning.

Today, about 5 minutes into your 1-mile stretch, begin to pump your arms. Here's how.

First, relax your shoulders so your arms are as low as they can be. Then bend your arms at the elbow and form your hands into loose fists. As you walk, your arms should pump up and down very close to your sides. To get the "pump" going, thrust your elbows back, and let your arms rebound in a forward direction without any special effort on your part. Your hands should come up very close to your body, to sternum or breast level, no further. If they go higher, they will be carrying you up off the ground, instead of forward.

The mistake most people make is to raise their shoulders instead of relaxing them and to let their hands pump up too high.

Even if you begin doing it right, you must check yourself every half-minute or so to see if you're *still* doing it right. The tendency is to get careless, and the result is a subtraction of efficiency and grace in forward motion.

Okay, so we're walking with arms pumping now. You'll notice that without any effort on your part, you've fallen into a pattern where your left arm comes forward just as the right leg does. This balances you, just the same as spontaneous arm swinging when walking in a normal way.

Don't make an effort to walk especially fast. In fact, don't even time yourself today. Just get used to the feeling of walking with the help of your arms. But do one thing. Glance at your watch and count the number of strides you take per minute. Count one stride for every time your right foot hits the ground. Take several 1-minute readings. After your walk, record your SPM on your graph as shown in the illustration on page 253. Your number will probably be in the 56 to 64 range.

Day 5

About halfway into your 1-mile course, begin to pump your arms. But today, try picking up the pace a bit. Do whatever speed comes naturally. It should feel like a pleasant, interesting sort of effort that produces an enjoyable rush of energy and circulation. If there are any twinges, pains, or strains, a hammering heartbeat, dizziness—anything at all unusual, you're going much too fast. If symptoms persist, see a doctor. This advice goes for every day you walk.

Note your time for the mile and record it on your graph and in your log as well, along with a comment that today was your very first timed speedwalk.

Day 6

Along about this time, many people begin to experience a very annoying and sometimes painful "burning shin" sensation.

That is perfectly natural. Walking for a significant distance at a pace faster than you're used to puts a unique strain on the gastrocnemius muscles that cover your shin bones. You can't "walk through" this pain. It will only get worse. So slow down, or even rest for a minute. Continue walking at a slower speed. Soon, you will learn to walk at a speed that just barely *warms* your shins without setting them ablaze. And each day, your muscles will become more accustomed to the peculiar challenges of speedwalking. Usually, the problem recedes after four or five days, although it may hang on for a few weeks. There is nothing you can do to improve it except to continue walking at a pace that is quick enough to condition your shins but slow enough not to hobble you.

Today, if you can, repeat yesterday's performance. Your speed for the mile may be anywhere from 30 to 60 seconds less than base time. Walk the rest of your course at a comfortable, normal speed.

Day 7

Your day of rest.

Week 2

Day 1

Once again, speedwalk about half a mile. This time, think more about style. Specifically, notice if your feet are striking the ground heel-first. If the middle of your foot is clomping on the ground, adjust your gait. Your foot should land on the heel, roll forward, and come off so that you're pushing forward with your toes. There is nothing particularly difficult or odd about this. But some of us either land with too much shoe, or take off without bending the foot enough to "toe off."

Day 2

Increase the duration of your speedwalk by 1 minute. Don't try to increase pace today.

Check your posture every minute or so on today's walk. Your head should be straight with your spine; not thrust forward. Your upper body should not be bent forward at the hips. Some people like to *tilt* forward somewhat while speedwalking, though. Their body is still straight, but the entire length is leaning forward at a very slight angle, from the ankles up.

Day 3

Speedwalk the same distance as yesterday. But today, after your 15-minute warm-up walk (the regular walking that precedes the speedwalking) stop for a minute or two and try some very gentle stretching. For instructions on some easy, basic stretches for walkers, refer to page 244. While stretching can be much more elaborate than this, it's best to be conservative.

What I want you to notice today is whether or not the stretching made you feel better, or perhaps even walk faster. If it did, keep it up. If not, stretch anyway. If it made you feel *worse,* though, forget about stretching, for the time being anyway.

Day 4

Take an extra day off. You may need it to let your body rest and recuperate.

Day 5

Speedwalk the same distance as the day before yesterday. Refocus attention on your arm swing. Shoulders down. Thrust elbows back, and let your arms come forward almost under their own power, nearly grazing your body. Your hands should come no higher than the bottom of your breastbone.

Day 6

Extend the distance of your speedwalk by another minute, but don't increase your pace.

After showering, check your feet closely for abrasions or blisters. Blisters can be punctured with a sterile pin and drained. Don't tear away the skin covering them, though. If you have problems with corns, bunions, or anything else, see a podiatrist. A speedwalker cannot afford foot problems. The slightest irritation left untreated, or unprotected by moleskin, can ruin a day's walk and more. (See the footcare chapter, beginning on page 53.)

Day 7

Take the day off. Stroll, or even go for a hike if you want to, but don't do any serious fitness walking.

Week 3

Speedwalk a little more each day—maybe a minute more—until you can comfortably walk the length of your mile stretch in the new style. Don't push for more speed; instead, concentrate on good, fluid style. Keep checking your posture and arm swing. Tip: Your fists should pass your sides at the hip bone. If they're crossing closer to the rib cage, your arms are bent too acutely. Or you're hunching your shoulders up.

Getting your style right is extremely important at this stage. The habits you develop will be hard to change six months from now.

Clock your time only once this week. Again, don't try to shave off seconds. That makes it harder to develop a relaxed, efficient style.

People sometimes ask how they should breathe while walking. There is no special technique to follow; just breathe naturally. About once a minute, though, relax your belly and take several fast, deep breaths, exhaling forcefully.

Week 4

While walking the first day this week, measure your strides per minute four times at different points in your 1-mile speedwalk stretch. All four readings should be just about identical (assuming you're walking the same style the whole distance). If the SPM are more than two strides off toward the end of your speed session, you're probably walking too fast in the early stages.

The second day this week, attempt to increase your SPM by *one*. Yes, just one. You may be surprised at how much control you have over your speed. Doing this is a good exercise in body awareness, too. But don't push for more than the smallest increment in SPM during a given week or even month. Gaining just one SPM per month, is, in fact, a notable accomplishment.

The increase you strive for today should be just during the three or four measurement periods. The remainder of the 1-mile course should be taken at a slower pace.

If you find *any* increase in SPM difficult, forget about it for a week. Then try again. We're talking gentle persuasion here, not compulsion.

By the way, do not attempt to go faster by lengthening your stride in an unnatural way. That will quickly lead to groin pulls and other problems. Boosting SPM is the smart ticket for improving your speed.

Week 5

We've been talking, so far, only about the "speed" part of your walk. But let's not forget the rest of your 45-minute walk, done at normal speed. That's building fitness, too. It's also serving as both warm-up and cool-down for your speed session, which occurs in the middle portion of your walk. Although your arms should be swinging naturally, not pumping, during this part of your walk, your posture should be erect, your shoulders down, and your feet striking the ground heels first.

During this week, you can playfully experiment with counting your SPM to see how many measurements taken during speed work can match the higher (by one) SPM you achieved last week.

Week 6

The side stitch—an annoying, sharp pain in the side that occurs during prolonged heavy breathing—can affect speedwalkers just as it does runners.

In many cases, this problem—like burning shins—disappears after a short time. What's evidently involved is a muscle spasm produced by the diaphragm in response to a breathing rate you're unaccustomed to.

There are several ways to get past the side stitch. One is to take a number of deep rapid breaths and expel them forcefully and vocally, while relaxing and distending the lower abdomen. *Shout* that air out!

Failing that, you can jab a couple of fingers into the aching area while doing the shout-it-out routine. Sometimes that breaks the spasm.

You can also slow down. Or stop altogether for a minute or two, and begin walking again.

One of these techniques should work for you.

This week, continue playing with your SPM. Add another minute or two of walking at the higher SPM you established in week four.

Week 7

People looking for ever-greater calorie-burners and fitness-builders often ask about walking with weights.

If you are trying to develop a good speedwalking style, carrying weights is not a wonderful idea. They will constantly yank you forward and backward. They also put an unnatural strain on many body structures and tissues, posing an entirely unnecessary degree of risk.

If you want to develop your upper body, you're better off doing resistance training at home or in a gym, two or three times a week, to complement your walking.

This week, see if you can string together about eight or ten minutes of hitting the higher SPM rate you've been experimenting with.

Week 8

Attempt to end the week walking the whole 1-mile stretch at the higher SPM. Check your time and compare it to what you were doing the very first week. Chances are, you're about 40 to 60 seconds under that time now. And it's a good bet that you significantly improved your fitness without suffering anything worse than an occasional "hot shin" or side stitch.

Month 3

This month, we're going to zigzag our way into higher fitness. The technique is something like walking up a mountain on switchbacks or zigzags, instead of marching straight up.

During the first week of this third month, extend the distance of your speedwalk in short, daily increments. Maybe one hundred yards, or one block, a day. *Do not increase the pace you established last week. And never go too far.*

Here's a new definition of "too far" that may surprise you. "Too far" is not just the distance or speed that's so great that it causes you to sputter to a halt. "Too far" is also that distance that's the maximum you can do without hurting yourself.

What we're saying is, *always do less than you think you can.* Leave yourself a safety zone, a reserve for tomorrow's walk. Doing all you can muster the strength and willpower to do—day after day—is a prescription for strain, injury, even psychological burnout.

By doing less than you are able to do, you are laying the foundation for continued progress. You are following a system that will take you closer and closer to your maximum potential over a long period of time. But try "maxing out" every day and you will never get close to your greatest potential. Instead, your progress will be continually interrupted by recoveries from injury.

Now that you know what "too far" is, you're on your own this first week to stretch the distance of speedwalking. As we said, go for short daily increases—a minute or two a day.

The next week, forget about the distance you've added (which will likely be something like ¼ to ½ mile). Instead, go back to the original 1-mile stretch and attempt to walk it slightly faster. The first day, increase your speed only toward the end of the 1-mile course. Note your time. On succeeding days, slowly expand the distance you cover at the faster clip.

Remember, increase speed by taking more strides per minute—not by taking longer strides. Maintain good posture, relaxed shoulders, proper gait. Slow down if anything hurts.

The third week of this month, forget about your new faster pace, and go back to extending your slower speedwalk. Each day, try adding another block. If you're tired that day, don't try to force it. By the end of the week, you will probably be doing about 1½ to 1¾ mile of relatively easy speedwalking.

The last week of the month, go back to the mile course and continue exploring the world of SPM.

At this stage, by the way, you may have reached the point where it's no longer easy to improve your performance each and every day. But not to worry. Although the numbers don't look better, your body is nonetheless conditioning itself to the new demands you're making on it. So you *are* making progress! Push too hard, though, and that progress will halt. Easy does it.

A frequent question we get, which can be answered now, is "How come I'm not sweating?"

Yes, some people worry about that. They think that not visibly sweating is a sign that they're not getting a good workout. But that is not an accurate gauge. Look to your breathing and your sense of exertion—they are better indicators. Do your lungs feel like they're working? Do your muscles feel like they're working? If so, you're doing okay—especially at this stage of the game.

Generally, the more you train, the faster you will begin to sweat on any given day. That's nature's way of keeping you cool when it's learned that you're in the habit of heating up your body. But some people just don't sweat that much, even when they've been breathing fairly hard for 20 or 30 minutes. So as for sweat being an indicator of a good workout, our advice is, don't sweat it.

Month 4

This month, try alternating days of gradually extending your fast speedwalking and days spent extending your time of relatively easy walking.

Toward the end of the month, your SPM for the fast mile stretch should have climbed by one or two. Your overall time for the fast mile will probably have come down a few more seconds. And the distance that you speedwalk on your slower days will gradually increase to cover just about the remaining distance in your walk, assuming you began with a distance of 3 to 4 miles.

If you feel that you're pushing a little too much, by all means take an extra day off from speedwalking—even from regular walking. Often, not doing anything is the best thing you can do—at least on a given day.

And if you feel that you could do with a bit of a rest stop during a day's walk, go for it. Resting a minute or so won't detract from the benefits of your workout. In fact, it can help a lot, by recharging you and letting you continue. If you feel your posture and walking style falling apart, that's a sure sign you need just such a rest.

Month 5

Let's see where we are.

Each day you walk, you're covering a total distance that's

somewhere between 3 and 4 miles.

The first mile (or 15 minutes) is done now (and forever) at a comfortable rambling speed: your essential warm-up.

At the end of the warm-up, you may be doing some gentle stretching, if experience has shown you that it helps.

Then you commence using the speedwalk style, but not going fast. After a few minutes or so, you should be in your 1-mile "speed stretch" and this is where you nudge the accelerator. Nudge, not stomp. Your breathing becomes fast but not labored; you feel your heart beat go up but not hammering; you feel exhilarated, not on the brink of exhaustion.

After 10 to 15 minutes, you slow down, and concentrate on style instead of speed. Finally, a few blocks from home, you change over to a normal walking style, arms swinging instead of pumping.

You've learned by now that you can't increase your speed every single day. A few seconds a week is now a respectable degree of improvement. You've learned to become aware of any aches at the earliest point, before they become pains. You back off on your speed, even take a day or two off, when you sense a problem.

It's become second nature to you to check your style over and over as you walk. You're always relaxing your shoulders, relaxing your belly. Making sure your arms are close to your sides, your hands rising no further than the bottom of your breastbone. Checking your gait to see if your feet are landing almost in a straight line. And adjusting your posture to insure that you aren't hunching over.

A good idea is to have a friend observe you as you speedwalk. Standing off to one side, the friend checks your posture, the angle of your head to your body, and how high your hands travel in front of your body. He or she also checks to see if your head is level as you walk, or if it's bobbing up and down. If it's bobbing, you're probably raising your hands too high in front, or even thrusting them back too far. Are you hitting the ground heel-first? Good!

Ask the friend to give you feedback as you walk at various speeds. Then make adjustments and get more reports until you're looking good. Repeat the "good" style several times so you know what it feels like.

Ideally, your friend can make a home video of your walking style at different speeds. Be sure the camera is back far enough so that your feet are well within the frame. Then study the video and see where you need improvement. It's quite common to see what you *thought* was good style begin to break down at higher speeds.

Veteran racewalkers always emphasize that proper style is more important than sheer speed. Without good style, you'll never be able to reach your true potential as a walker.

This month, gradually let your fast speedwalk increase in distance, eating up the portion you were covering at a slower pace. Go for very small increments, maybe 50 yards every other day.

Once or twice a week, experiment with walking a small portion of the course—maybe 100 yards—at a faster SPM.

Month 6

By now, you may want to lengthen the entire course by a short distance—maybe ¼ to ½ mile. After all, you're covering it in less time now than you were five months ago. This is not "mandatory," but if you have the time and desire, try it.

Eventually, though, you will find that going beyond a certain distance becomes counterproductive. You'll feel whipped instead of invigorated. You'll want to take more and more "off" days. You may even find that your morning pulse reading is getting higher instead of lower. All these are strong signs that you're doing too much. That goes for everyone from the strictly amateur speedwalker to the world-class track athlete. Back off . . . and perk up!

In any event, continue the same pattern of nudging your SPM for short distances. But now, try to insure that your style is as clean and fluid as possible while walking at the faster pace. Speed shouldn't be attained at the expense of form.

This is a good time to review your general health. Another medical checkup may be in order. It will be especially valuable to know how your blood pressure, weight, total cholesterol, and HDL fraction of cholesterol are doing. If you were in "perfect health" before beginning your walking program, you may not see any dramatic improvements. But you can be pretty darn sure that your percentage of body fat has gone down, even if your weight hasn't. Further, it's been shown that regular exercise is highly beneficial to the heart even if there is no big change in the numbers on various medical tests.

For those who are especially interested in losing weight, remember that the total number of miles you walk is far more important than how fast you walk. If the effort of speedwalking is causing you to reduce the number of days you walk, you're not doing yourself any favors. Slow down, and put in more walking days.

As for nutrition and walking, you'll be best served by eating the same low-fat, high-fiber diet recommended for general health. Eat lots of grains, vegetables, beans, and fruit, along with fish and chicken. Learn how to cut down on excess fats by reading a good nutrition book or *Prevention* magazine. Good nutrition and your fitness walking program together make a powerful pair of health improvers.

Month 7

If you completed the five months of basic fitness walking before going on to the advanced program, this marks the beginning of your 12th month of fitness walking.

More important, it marks the beginning of your self-designed program for continued enjoyment and health benefits from walking.

Instead of telling you what to do this 12th month, we want you to decide for yourself what would be best.

Onward and Upward

The important thing is to follow the principles we've outlined here—if they've worked for you so far.

Always do a little less than you're able to do, on any given day. Remember to leave yourself some reserve to ensure continued progress.

Monitor yourself for smooth, rhythmic style. Good posture. Shoulders relaxed, arms traveling close to the body. Hands traveling only up to chest level—never to the neck. Feet landing heel-first, rolling forward, pushing off the toes.

Pay close attention to how your body feels. You should pay attention to this during your walk and during the rest of the day. What you're aiming for is a feeling of energy. A sense of lightness. A good night's sleep, and waking up fresh. What you're avoiding are strange aches, pains, or strains, and that wiped-out feeling.

Depending on many factors, you may or may not be able to reasonably expect to extend your walking distance or speed.

Our advice is not to make either of these a priority.

If you relentlessly pursue greater *speed,* you will eventually and inevitably collide with certain forces of nature that ensure human beings never confuse themselves with gazelle. If you're lucky, you will kind of bounce off that wall of natural resistance, chastened but not seriously injured. If not so lucky, you may never be able to speedwalk again without painful reminders of the collision.

If you relentlessly pursue greater *distance,* you will probably get bored silly before anything worse happens to you. Unless your spouse divorces you on grounds of airheadedness.

Notice we're saying *"relentlessly* pursue," without rest, self-mercy, or even common sense. Unfortunately, quite a few people who racewalk or run find themselves exhibiting just such behavior—often without realizing it.

What we suggest instead of making speed or distance a priority is to let these two flow naturally and easily from a program that prioritizes *regularity.*

If you feel you *need* to pump up your performance to keep your interest alive, that's exactly when and why to go for that small (but satisfying) improvement.

After you've walked for the first two weeks this month, and made your log and fitness graph entries, add up the total days and total miles you walked during that time.

Are these numbers notably lower than the previous two weeks' total? Either your program is too irregular or you're pressing too hard for speed, causing a sharp reduction in your overall mileage.

Are the numbers notably higher? Watch out. Some people may thrive on 90 minutes of walking a day, but after that, you're pressing your luck. Experienced hikers can do many hours a day without ill effect, but speedwalking close to your top speed for many miles puts far more stress on your system. Are your calves tender all the time? Do you feel like taking a nap after your postwalk shower? Do you have an unusual and insatiable craving for carbohydrates? All those could be signs of overtraining.

Do another review after your next two weeks of walking this month. Do the results look good? Do you *feel* good?

Finally, check your cumulative days of walking, total number of hours walked, and total distance walked since you began fitness walking a year ago.

Pin those numbers up in a prominent place where you can see them every day. In the weeks ahead, your pride in that accomplishment is going to help you. . . . Keep walking!

Index

Note: Page references in *italic* indicate illustrations.

A

Adrenaline, stress and, 169
Aging, 3–5
Air pollution, 120–21
Allergens, identification of, 6, 7
Allergies, 5–8
    antihistamines for, 6–7
    contact dermatitis, 58
    strategy for, 7–8
Alpine hiking, definition of,
    218
American Podiatric Medical
    Association Seal of Acceptance,
    165
American Volkssport Association,
    195, 196, 197
Anger, 171–72
Antihistamines, 6–7
Anxiety. *See* Stress
Aquatic exercise, 10, 180
Arizona–Sonora Desert Museum,
    192–93
Arthritis, 8–10
Automobile, walking vs., 172
Awards, 138–43

B

Back pain, 11–14
    patient profile, 11–13
    posture and, 13–14, 136–37,
    137
Bathroom facilities, 75
Beach walking, 181
Bees. *See* Yellow jackets
Behavior, type-A, 19
Blister kit, 16
Blisters, 14–16, 58
Blood pressure, high. *See* High blood
    pressure

Body fat
    cancer and, 22–23
    exercise and, 209–10
Body sculpting, 16–18
Bone health, nutrition and, 113
Bone strength, 9
Boots, for cold weather, 35
Boston's Freedom Trail, 192
Brain power, 18–20
Breast cancer, 21, 22
Bricklin, Mark, 1-year walking
    program of. *See* Walking program
Bunions, 59
Bushkill Falls, 204–5
Bush walking, definition of, 218
Bushwhacking, definition of, 218

C

Calcium, for bone health, 113
California
    Mt. Tamalpais, 193–94
    Yosemite Falls, 206–7
Calluses, 56
Calories, burned by walking, 208–9,
    211
Cancer, 20–25
    body fat and, 22–23
    breast, 21, 22
    colon, 21, 22–23
    immunity and, 23–24
    prevention of, 20, 21–22
Car, walking vs., 172
Cardiac rehabilitation, 79, 215
Chafing thighs, 74
Chest, stretching exercise for, 179
Children, 25–29
    orienteering for, 26–27
    scouting for, 26
    shoes for, 29

Children *(continued)*
  walking education for, 28–29
  as walking partners, 123
  weight loss in, 27–28
Cholesterol, 227
Clothing
  for summer walks, 181–82
  for winter walks, 34–36
Clubs, 30–31
  Prevention Walking Club,
    143–44
Coffee breaks, 31–32
Cold weather, 33–36
Colon cancer, 21, 22–23
Colorado, Mesa Verde National Park,
  190
Communication, in relationships,
  98–101
Compass, for orienteering,
  117–18
Confrontations, stressful, 171
Constipation, 23
Contact dermatitis, 58
Coolmax, 163
Corkscrew Swamp Sanctuary, 191
Corns, 55–56
Creativity, 76

D

Danger. *See* Safety
Delayed-onset muscle soreness,
  94–95
Dentist, visit to, 172
Depression, 18–19, 36–38
Dermatitis, 58
Diabetes, 38–41
  exercise and, 39
  foot care for, 40, 62–63
  weather and, 40
Diaries, 96–97, 226
Diet, wholesome. *See* Nutrition
Dieting, walking vs., for weight loss,
  208
DMS, 94–95
Dogs, 41–46
  angry, 72, 130
  exercise with, 41–42
  leash for, 43
  obedience training for, 42
  stray, 129–30
  volunteer, 44, 46

  walking, 42–44
  as walking partners, 122–23
Double-Lay-R socks, 163, 164

E

Easy Spirit's Performance Sock,
  163–64
Eating, from stress, 171, 210
Elderly
  bone health in, 113
  foot care for, 61–62
  mental ability of, 4
  sex and, 100
Emotional state, 18–19
Endorphins, 24
Endurance Walking Award, 140–41,
  143
Estrogen, 22
Evolution, 46–48

F

Fat (body)
  cancer and, 22–23
  exercise and, 209–10
Fat (dietary), 111–12
Feet. *See also* Foot care; Shoes; Socks
  blisters on, 14–16
  flat, 59
  size of, 158
  summer walking and, 181, 182
  types of, 160
Fitness walking
  advanced program, 250–67
  definition of, 219
Fitness Walking Award, 141
Flexibility, 173–79
Florida, Corkscrew Swamp
  Sanctuary, 191
Food. *See* Nutrition
Foot care, 53–66. *See also* Feet;
  Shoes; Socks
  baths, 65
  for blisters, 58
  for bunions, 59
  for calluses, 56
  checkups, 64
  for contact dermatitis, 58
  for corns, 55–56
  for diabetics, 40, 62–63
  for elderly, 61–62

exercises, 65–66
flat feet and, 59
for fungus, 56–57
for gout, 59–60
for heel pain, 91–92
for hiking, 89
podiatrist for, 54
surgery, 63–64
toenails and, 60–61
for warts, 57
Foot injury, shoe fit and, 159
Foot pain, shoe fit and, 155–56
Footwear. *See* Shoes
Forest, 166–67
Fund raising, 197–201
Fungus, feet and, 56–57

G

Glucocorticoids, 23
Glutei muscles, 178
Good deeds, 66–70
Gout, 59–60

H

Hands, swollen, 70–71
Hand weights, 214–16
Hat, for summer walks, 181
Hay fever, 5–6
Headaches, 76–78
Headphones, 108, 109
Healing walks, 166–68
Heart attack rehabilitation, 79, 215
Heart health, 78–82
    exercise and, 78–80
    mental stress and, 80–81
    nutrition and, 111–12
    prescription for, 81–82
    TPA and, 81
    weights and, 215
Heat, 179–82
Heel pain, 91–92
High blood pressure, 82–87
    borderline, 86–87
    exercise and, 82–86
    nutrition and, 112
Hiking, 87–89
    boots, 35, 89
Hill walking, 89–91. *See also* Terrain
    therapy
    avoiding fatigue from, 90–91
    knee pain and, 93–94

Hormones, cancer and, 22, 23
Humidity, 179–82
Hypertension. *See* High blood
    pressure

I

Immunity, 23–24
Injury, 91–95
Insects. *See* Yellow jackets
Interferon, 24
Interleukin-1, 24
Intermittent claudication, 95

J

Jogging, walking vs., 16, 211
Journals, 96–97, 226

K

Knee protection, 93–94

L

Life expectancy, 5
Love, 98–101
Lymphocytes, 23

M

Mallwalking, 101–4, 180
Maps
    for hiking, 88–89
    for orienteering, 117–18
Massachusetts, Boston's Freedom
    Trail, 192
Medical checkup, for walking
    program, 227
Meditation, 169–70
Mental ability, in elderly, 4
Mental performance, 20
Mental state, 18–19
Mesa Verde National Park, 190
Metabolism, 209
Migraine headache, 76–78
Mitochondria, 209
Monogamy, 47–48
Moonwalking, 106–7
Mt. Tamalpais, 193–94
Muscle loss, from dieting, 209–10

Muscles
    glutei, 178
    neck, 177
    psoas, 176
    quadratus lumborum, 174–75
    slow-twitch vs. fast-twitch, 209
    stretching, 173–79
Muscle soreness, delayed-onset,
    94–95
Music, 107–9

N

NaturalSport socks, 164
Neck, stretching exercise for,
    176–77, *177*
Neck pain, 136–37
New York, Niagara Falls, 206
Niagara Falls, 206
Nutrition, 110–14
    bone health and, 113
    dietary changes, 110–11
    heart health and, 111–12
    high blood pressure and, 112

O

Obesity. *See* Weight loss
Orienteering, 114–20
    for children, 26–27
    getting lost, 118, 119
    maps for, 117–18
    participation in, 115–16, 118–19
Overuse injury, 91–95
Overweight. *See* Weight loss
Ozone, 120–21

P

Pain
    back, 11–14, 136–37, *137*
    foot, shoe fit and, 155–56
    posture and, 135–37
    terrain therapy for, 184–86
Parking lots, 172–73
Parks, for hiking, 87–88
Partners, 121–25
    children, 123
    choice of, 122
    dogs, 122–23
    for safety, 128
    walking with, 124–25
    work colleagues, 123–24

Pedometers, 125–27
Pennsylvania, Bushkill Falls, 204–5
Personality, type-A, 19
Personal safety. *See* Safety
Photography, 131–34
    depth, 133
    framing, 133
    lighting, 132
    positioning, 132–33
Podiatrist, 54
Pollen, 5–6, 7, 8
Posture, 134–37
    improving, 134–35
    pain and, 13–14, 135–37
    pride and, 135
    proper walking form, *137*
    yoga exercises, 176, 178–79
Power walking, definition of, 219
Presidential Sports Award, 138–43
Prevention Walking Club, 143–44
Program for walking. *See* Walking
    program
Psoas muscles, 176

Q

Quadratus lumborum muscle,
    174–75

R

Rabies, 131
Raccoons, 131
Racewalking, 140, 145–46
    benefits of, 148–50
    Masters competition for, 150–51
    participant profiles, 149–50
    perfecting technique for, 147
    Presidential Award for, 141–42
    proper form for, 146–47, 220
    videos for, 148
Rainy-day walking, 151–53
Relationships, 98–101
Restroom facilities, 75
Rheumatoid arthritis, 9
Rockport Walking Sock, 164, 165
Running, walking vs., 16, 211

S

Safety, 127–31
    with dogs, 72, 129–30

partners for, 128
  with raccoons, 131
  strategies, 128–29
  weapons and, 129
Salt, in diet, 112
Scalene muscles, 177
Sex, elderly and, 100
Shinsplints, 74
  avoiding, 92–93
  from long walks, 199
Shoes, 154–61
  blisters and, 14
  characteristics of, 154–55
  for children, 29
  for cold weather, 35
  fit of, 155–59
  foot problems and, 56
  heel pain and, 92
  rain and, 152
  shape of, 159–61
  for walkathons, 199
  for walking program, 227–28
  for weight loss program, 211,
    214
  worn down, 160
Side stitches, 73
Skin blisters, 14–16, 58
Snacking, 31–32
Socks, 161–66
  APMA seal on, 165
  blisters and, 14
  for dry feet, 164–65
  fit of, 162
  high-tech features of, 163–64
  natural vs. synthetic, 163
  for walkathons, 200
  for walking program, 228
  wear and care of, 165–66
Sodium, in diet, 112
Speedwalking
  definition of, 219
  program for, 250–67
Spine, 13
Spiritual walks, 166–68
Splenii muscles, 177
Sticks. *See* Walking sticks
Storms, 71
Stress, 19, 168–73
  adrenaline and, 169
  cancer and, 24–25
  eating from, 171, 210
  heart health and, 80–81

  in relationships, 99
  walking to avoid, 171–73
  walking to relieve, 168–70
  Zen perspective on, 170–71
Stretching, 173–79
  for chest and arms, 179
  ear-to-knee stretch, 174–75, *175*
  for glutei, 178–79
  neck exercise, 176–77, *177*
  oriental squat, 178
  Sun Salutation postures, 176
Summer, 179–82
  beach walking, 181
  indoor walking in, 180
  staying cool in, 181–82
Sun Salutation postures, 176
Sunscreen, 75
Swollen hands, 70–71

T

Tension. *See* Stress
Terrain therapy, 182–87. *See also* Hill
    walking
  beginning, 183
  course for, 184, *185*
  patient profile, 184–86
  self-directed, 187
  supervision for, 186
Thighs, chafing, 74
Thor-Lo socks, 164, 165
Tissue plasminogen activator, 81
Toenails, 60–61
TPA, 81
Traction device, for back pain, 12
Trapezius muscle, 177
Treadmills, 187–89
  adjusting to, 189
  purchasing tips, 188–89
  for terrain therapy, 187
Trekking, definition of, 218
Type-A behavior, 19

V

Vacation
  foot blisters and, 15
  walking, 104–6, 173, 189–94
Vacations
  Arizona–Sonora Desert Museum,
    192–93
  Boston's Freedom Trail, 192

Vacations *(continued)*
  Corkscrew Swamp Sanctuary,
    Florida, 191
  Mesa Verde National Park,
    Colorado, 190
  Mt. Tamalpais, California,
    193–94
Views, 167–68
Vocabulary for walking, 217–20
Volksmarching, 194–97
  course for, 195–96
  events schedule for, 197
  in United States, 195

W

WalkAmerica, 198
Walkathons, 197–201
  avoiding problems in, 200
  cooling down after, 201
  preparation for, 198–99
  shinsplints from, 199
  shoes for, 199
  socks for, 200
Walkers, famous, 48–53
Walking awards, 138–43
Walking clubs, 30–31
  Prevention Walking Club,
    143–44
Walking form, proper, *137*
Walking log (journal), 96–97, 226
Walking program, 225–67
  advanced, 250–67
  benefits of, 226
  developing habit, 226–27
  medical checkup for, 227
  preliminary advice, 225
  progress plan for first 22 weeks,
    229–49
  shoes for, 227–28
  socks for, 228
  time and place for, 229
Walking sticks, 201–4
  canes vs., 202–3

choices of, 202–4
  history of, 202
Walking words, 217–20
Warts, 57
Water
  summer walks and, 182
  for walkathons, 200
Water exercise, 10, 180
Waterfall walks, 204–7
  Bushkill Falls, 204–5
  Niagara Falls, 206
  Yosemite Falls, 206–7
Weapons, 129
Weather
  cold, 33–36
  rain, 151–53
  storms, 71
  summer, 179–82
Weight loss, 17, 207–14
  calorie burning, 208–9, 211
  in children, 28
  patient profiles, 212–13
  prescription for, 211, 214
  walking vs. dieting for, 208
Weights, 214–16
Wogging, definition of, 218–19
Woods, 166–67
Words for walking, 217–20
Workplace, 123–24, 172

Y

Yellow jackets, 72–73
YMCA/YWCA
  for children, 27
  water exercise at, 10
Yoga exercises, 176, 178–79
Yosemite Falls, 206–7

Z

Zen, stress and, 170–71
Zoo walks, 220–21

───── Special Offer ─────
Membership in PREVENTION WALKING CLUB
Regularly $9.97—Yours with This Coupon for $6.97!

The PREVENTION WALKING CLUB will help you get started on a fun and effective walking program—and help you stick with it! As a member, you'll receive an inspiring bimonthly newsletter, an awards certificate to highlight your walking achievements, discounts on Walkers' Festival registration, and more. **Plus you'll also receive a free copy of the Walker's Daily Log.**

- -

Yes! Please enroll me in the PREVENTION WALKING CLUB and send me the Walker's Daily Log free to get me started. Enclosed is $6.97 (check or money order) for my annual membership.

41014

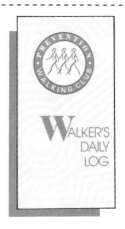

Name
_____

Address   Apt.#
_____

City   State   Zip

Canada: $12.97 CDN Funds plus 7% GST. Foreign: U.S. $14.97 prepaid.

Clip (or photocopy) and mail to PREVENTION WALKING CLUB, Rodale Press, Inc., 33 E. Minor Street, Emmaus, PA 18098.